Black Regions of the Imagination

D1473931

BLACK REGIONS
OF THE IMAGINATION

African American Writers
between the Nation and the World

EVE E. DUNBAR

Temple University Press
PHILADELPHIA

Temple University Press
Philadelphia, Pennsylvania 19122
www.temple.edu/tempress

Copyright © 2013 by Temple University
All rights reserved

Published 2013

LIBRARY OF CONGRESS CATALOGING-IN-PUBLICATION DATA

Dunbar, Eve
  Black regions of the imagination : African American writers between the
nation and the world / Eve Dunbar.
    p. cm.
  Includes bibliographical references and index.
  ISBN 978-1-4399-0942-3 (hardback : alk. paper)
  ISBN 978-1-4399-0943-0 (paper : alk. paper)
  ISBN 978-1-4399-0944-7 (e-book)
    1. American literature—20th century—History and criticism. 2. American
literature—African American authors. 3. Ethnology in literature. I. Title.
PS153.N5D85 2012
810.9'896073—dc23

                                                                    2012015152

♾ The paper used in this publication meets the requirements of the
American National Standard for Information Sciences—Permanence
of Paper for Printed Library Materials, ANSI Z39.48-1992

Printed in the United States of America

2 4 6 8 9 7 5 3 1

THE
AMERICAN
LITERATURES
INITIATIVE
A book in the American Literatures Initiative (ALI), a
collaborative publishing project of NYU Press, Fordham
University Press, Rutgers University Press, Temple University
Press, and the University of Virginia Press. The Initiative is
supported by The Andrew W. Mellon Foundation. For more
information, please visit www.americanliteratures.org.

For Clover Dunbar

CONTENTS

PREFACE

After making the nearly eight-hour flight from New York's Kennedy Airport to Paris's Charles de Gaulle International Airport, I was plagued by the sneaking suspicion that everyone in Paris spoke English, but none of them would do so with me. My suspicions were fueled by the myth that French people will speak English only once an American stumbles over a few French phrases: "*Bon-jore. Como tah-lay vu? Par-lay vu inglays?* I don't speak French" (said with sheepish grin). This myth casts the French as a perverse group of people who measure their national superiority by the yardstick of American linguistic ineptitude.

Walking through Charles de Gaulle, there were moments when I was convinced it was true. Every sign in the airport had subscript in English directing one toward various methods for travel away from Charles de Gaulle: they wanted to give me just enough English to hang myself because once I made it out of the airport, only God knew how I would navigate Paris proper.

Signs or no signs, for me, as I am sure it is for many Americans of a particular class background, there was something entirely overwhelming and frightening about leaving the United States and finding myself in a country where I did not speak the language. I know that admitting this is tantamount to admitting one is illiterate in a room full of literature teachers. I suppose my identity as an American academic is supposed to lift me above the masses of provincial Americans and deliver me into the bosom of the cosmopolitan elite. But for better or worse, I became a generic American in France. This is not a profound observation, I know. But on this particular trip to Paris, the relationship between internationalism and nationalism was at the forefront of my thoughts.

I was in Paris to deliver a paper at the International Richard Wright Centennial Conference, which was hosted by the American University of Paris. This conference was one of many centennial events held during 2008 to commemorate that fact that in 1908 Richard Wright had been born on a plantation near Natchez, Mississippi. Richard Wright was born less than half a century after the Thirteenth Amendment's ratification ended U.S. slavery, and in some ways his life stands as testament to the United States' ability to reinvent itself. In less than fifty years, the former prison house of black human chattel counted among its citizens one of the most prominent writers of the twentieth century. This writer also happened to be the grandson of black American slaves. American exceptionalism encourages us to look on the facts of Wright's life and stand astounded that it took only two generations to "turn" a slave into a great American writer.

Yet buying into the narrative of American exceptionalism requires that we blind ourselves to the harsh realities of black life in the United States from postemancipation and into the twentieth century: Jim Crow, urban poverty, racism, underemployment, high infant mortality, and so on. Richard Wright, unable to reconcile his sense of his own humanity with the historical reality of state-sanctioned inequality under which most blacks lived during the early twentieth century, spent his life critiquing the myth of American racial progress and arguing that it was the very notion of American exceptionalism that retarded such progress.

Wright honed an artistic vision of America as a nation imperiled by its refusal to admit black humanity. His responsibility, he felt as an artist, was to represent the negative realities that were generated by such a national incapacity. In his critically acclaimed novel *Native Son* (1940), Wright centralized his protagonist's social retaliation on the realization that Bigger Thomas's human potential would be forever denied by white power structures. *Native Son* is his graphically violent imagining of how black inhumanity is created by U.S. racism and racial inequity. Bigger's fear, flight, and fate are dictated by the destructive American racial landscape of which he is a product. In responding to one critic's negative review of the violence in *Native Son*, Wright retorted,

> If there had been *one* person in the Dalton household who viewed Bigger Thomas as a human being, the crime would have been solved in half an hour.
>
> Did not Bigger himself know that it was the denial of his personality that enabled him to escape detection so long? The one piece of incriminating evidence which would have solved the "murder mystery" was Bigger's humanity, and the Daltons, Britten, and the newspaper men could not see or admit the living clue of Bigger's humanity under their very eyes![1]

For Wright, more destructive than Bigger's murders is the racist nation that makes such deeds inevitable. Bigger murders because he is black and poor; and he nearly gets away with it because he is black, poor, and not human in the eyes of white people.

As James Baldwin would point out on numerous occasions, Wright's literary rendering of black inhumanity was disingenuous due to Wright's own unwillingness to accept the reality of black humanity. Trapped within the framework of protesting the beliefs and actions of the nation's racial majority, Wright may have found little solace in representing the African American capacity to manage, live, and even flourish within the confines of a racist America. And why would he? From the Three-Fifths Compromise of 1787, which codified slaves into a human-property hybrid worth three-fifths of a human life, to the Jim Crow laws, America had historically neither fostered nor accepted black humanity. As Wright stated in his posthumously published autobiographical novel, *American Hunger*, as the grandson of slaves, he was never able to be human in the United States: "What had I got of out living in the south?" he writes. "What had I got out of living in America? I paced the floor, knowing that all I possessed were words and dim knowledge that my country had shown me no examples of how to live a human life."[2] It was this quest for humanity, to live a life in which he felt fully human, that drove Wright first from the American South, then from Chicago, and then from New York to Paris.

It is rather common knowledge that Paris was the space in which Wright felt most free to explore and embrace his humanity. Still, he never fully learned French during the time he lived in France. If language is tied to national belonging, as many of the American ideological Right would have us believe, then Wright's failure to fully embrace the language of the country that "freed" him speaks to his deep failure to take root there. From 1947 to his untimely death in 1960, Richard Wright lived outside the confines of the United States and wrote fiction, essays, travel narratives, and thousands of haiku. His years of self-exile were years of experimentation in literary form and an opening up of the content of his literary production to the world. Confined neither by the geography of the United States nor narratives of the American racial landscape, throughout the 1950s Wright produced texts with topics as far-ranging as the decolonization of the Third World, Spanish fascism, and middle-class black life in Mississippi and Chicago; he produced this array of writings in order to expand his world beyond the family plantation in Natchez.

And one hundred years after Wright's birth, on a train heading into Paris to attend a conference meant to celebrate the international turn in his work, I was haunted by his birthplace: Mississippi, USA. And even though Wright wrote—screamed to the world—"I am a rootless man!" it was always hard for him to shake the United States.

The United States, both the concept and the place, was hard for me to shake, as well. Because even in France, especially in France, I kept sight of the self that was created when my grandmother gave me my family's story, one of the few keepsakes that has been passed down over generations: I must always remember that I am the great-great-great-granddaughter of a black woman who was owned, who toiled on a South Carolina farm for the man who fathered but never recognized her children. The mundane trauma of that keepsake stays with me and was reflected back at me through the windows of every Parisian storefront I passed. That keepsake is partially what motivates me to read, analyze, and write about the works of other American descendants of slaves who walked, thought, and wrote abroad.

So while I was officially in Paris to consider the significance of America, Paris, and elsewhere in the writing of one America's most important native sons and daughters, Wright's writing is just one of many things that compels me to examine African Americans in the world. These two concepts, "African American" and "the world," are at odds sometimes, but examining how various writers have lived and written works of art that bridge this spatial and imaginative chasm prompts me to ask and attempt to answer a variety of questions in this book. How have African Americans written about their travels around the world or their relationships with other blacks around the world, their nation, and, most important, themselves? How do African American writers attempt to tell the stories of their travels in a way that fortifies their souls? Is self-fortification possible in the face of a predominantly white readership that expects to "know" something about black people from reading black-authored texts? These are some of the questions that motivate this study, questions that I imagine haunted the African American traveler-writers who populate this book.

ACKNOWLEDGMENTS

I owe much to the people and institutions that generously helped and supported me through the writing of this book. I am sure that I will forget some integral person, so please forgive me in advance and know that I am truly grateful to all who played a part. First, I would like to thank my colleagues in the English Department and Africana Studies Program at Vassar College for providing me with the intellectual support and space I needed to imagine, write, and finish this book. While many people at Vassar have shown me kindness, Peter Antelyes, Light Carruyo, Lisa Gail Collins, Robert DeMaria, Amitava Kumar, and Linta Varghese read my work at various stages, providing crucial critiques and generous affirmations. For this and more I am forever indebted to them all.

I am also appreciative to the English Department at Rutgers University–New Brunswick for providing me with fellowship support to develop this work. I am especially grateful to Cheryl Wall, one of the kindest and most generous scholars I have ever met, for her unwavering support and faith in the viability of my ideas. I am lucky to know her. I also thank Cheryl for introducing me to Andrea Williams, whose intellectual insights have

XVI / ACKNOWLEDGMENTS

made this work stronger and whose work ethic has been both my aspiration and inspiration. Thanks also to Brian Norman and Piper Kendrix Williams for their early support of my writing on Richard Wright.

I wish to thank Carlos Alamo, Mona Ali, Lisa Brawley, Kimberly Brown, Mary Coleman, Andy Davison, Sarita Gregory, Luke Harris, Bill Hoynes, Barbara Harlow, Keith Harris, Hua Hsu, Luis Inoa, Mia Mask, Molly McGlennen, Monica Miller, Quincy Mills, Hiram Perez, Lee Rumbarger, Mark Whalen, and Jennifer Williams, whose friendship and collegiality has fortified me for years. And thanks to Debra Bucher, Natalie Frank, Rachel Friedman, and Sophia Harvey for lending their ears as I spoke into existence this book's end.

Getting the words on the pages of this book would have been impossible without the help of Jennifer Bagneris, Amanda Zeligs, and Michelle Rosolie, all of whom served as my research assistants during their time at Vassar College. Their many hours in the library and at the copy machine made this project easier for me to write. And without Kathryn Chetkovich as my sounding board I might still be unable to articulate my project's center. Likewise, thank you to Jennifer French for copyediting an early draft of this book; her attentiveness to my words led me to a more refined prose.

I want to thank the editorial and production staff at the Temple University Press for making this book possible. A special thanks to Janet Francendese for her generous support, guidance, encouragement, and willingness take on my project. I am also grateful to the two anonymous readers who evaluated the manuscript for their constructive comments and kind consideration of my ideas.

And much appreciation goes to the Dunbar family for never accepting an incomplete from me—tough love is the family's hallmark and it has propelled me forward for years. "Thank you" is too weak a sentiment for what I owe my late mother, Clover Dunbar, and my late grandmother, Ellen Dunbar. Without them my life has no possibility. This book is my homage to them, a meager attempt to give thanks for the body and mind they have created in me. I will always value their lives as working-class black women, who were as sharp as any cosmopolitan thinker without ever having left home.

Finally, my deepest gratitude goes to Kiese Laymon for being here from the beginning to the end. My ideas and life are better from having known you. Thank you!

Earlier versions of Chapter 2 were published as two separate articles, "Black is a Region: Segregation and Literary Regionalism in Richard Wright's *The Color Curtain*," *African American Review* 42.1 (Spring 2008): 109–19 (reprinted in *Representing Segregation: Toward an Aesthetic of Living Jim Crow, and Other Forms of Racial Division*, Brian Norman and Piper Williams, eds., SUNY Press, 2010. 185–200), and "The Multiple Frames for a Dynamic Diaspora in Richard Wright's Black Power," *Papers on Language and Literature* 44.4 (Fall 2008): 354–64.

Introduction

Perhaps only someone who is outside the States realizes that it is impossible to get out.

JAMES BALDWIN[1]

On August 25, 1970, anthropologist Margaret Mead and writer James Baldwin met for the first time to have three recorded conversations, totaling more than seven hours of tape that, once transcribed, would compose the book *A Rap on Race* (1971). The Mead and Baldwin book is an amazing account documenting the meeting of two of the twentieth century's most paradigmatic thinkers and cultural creators discussing the meaning of "race" in the United States and in the world. Yet it seems most important to say that *A Rap on Race* is also a documentation of miscommunication, oversimplification, and overstatement.

In fact, a 1971 *New York Times* reviewer suggests that the book might have been better left unpublished: "Wisdom and baloney are as blither is to blather. . . . We're all capable of it, but only some of us ever bother to publish it."[2] It is a slight understatement to say that the *Times* reviewer found very little of substance in the transcribed conversations. It is also rather telling that all David Leeming could muster up about the book in his nearly four-hundred-page Baldwin biography was to say, "A book by James Baldwin and Margaret Mead was bound to become a best seller."[3]

Despite of what might be perceived as a failure of content perhaps resulting from the cult of personality surrounding Baldwin and Mead at the time, I believe it is no small accident that these two thinkers would "rap on race" and that the nation might listen. More than a gimmick, Baldwin and Mead's conversation speaks to the longstanding conversation between black American writing and ethnographic writing. And much like *A Rap on Race*, the connection between black writers and ethnography is neither uncomplicated nor seamless. Sometimes the two—the racialized writer and the disciplinary form often used to create and account for "exotic others"—are inevitably at odds, rendering entirely different stories out of the same materials. For instance, in *A Rap on Race* Mead expresses that she is perplexed by Baldwin's theory of the American experience, which he tells her he believes is specifically informed by a racial history only available to people born and living in the United States. Mead attempts to remedy her perplexity by suggesting to Baldwin that he should consider the condition of black Americans in relation to that of white South Africans (under apartheid) because both groups, according to her, make citizenship claims on countries in which they hold minority status. Although this was an interesting way for Mead to frame solidarity, Baldwin replies that such a comparison is "rather hideous" and that white South Africans might be better compared to white southerners in the United States due to what he perceives as their shared investment in white superiority and racial inequity.[4]

Mead's "hideous" comparisons aside, the juxtaposition of an anthropologist and a black writer seems to affirm the presumption that it is the job of black writers to report on their race/culture to a mainstream/white audience. Even if there is this presumption that black writers report, I would like to suggest that Mead and Baldwin's exchanges help to illuminate the intervention that black American writers might make into the "hybrid activity" whose principal function has been "orientation"[5] and whose historical impulse has been an attempt to make cultural generalizations. Baldwin may be on the stage to report on black culture and to represent black people, but that does not mean he is confined to a particular script or mode of representation. His is an intervention that simultaneously relies on his proximity to and distance from black culture and American culture in order to tell the story of American racial realities.

But Mead and Baldwin's recorded conversations were not as novel as one might be inclined to believe. Since the early part of the twentieth century, well-known black writers such as Zora Neale Hurston, W. E. B. Du Bois, James Weldon Johnson, and Sterling Brown[6] were making use of ethnographic techniques in the creation of both fiction and traditional ethnographies that portrayed and analyzed black life and culture. As Daphne Lamothe notes, the manipulation of the ethnographic encounter allowed many early twentieth-century black writers to enact a "paradoxical Black modernist gaze that look[ed] at Black culture and look[ed] back at the dominant culture."[7]

One of the most well-known early twentieth-century articulations of the black relationship to dominant/white American culture is encapsulated in W. E. B. Du Bois's notion of *double consciousness* and his employment of the veil metaphor. Du Bois begins *The Souls of Black Folk* (1903) by describing the black and white worlds as separated by a "veil" that he spends the rest of the text "stepping within," "seeing beyond," and "raising" in an attempt to help his readers understand his claims for black American citizenship: "Leaving, then, the world of the white man, I have stepped within the Veil, raising it that you may view faintly its deeper recesses,—the meaning of its religion, the passion of its human sorrow, and the struggle of its greater souls. . . . And, finally, need I add that I who speak here am bone of the bone and flesh of the flesh of them that live within the Veil?"[8] Du Bois's revelation to his reader that he is kin to the folks who live "within the Veil" in his "Forethought" to *Souls*, then, functions as an opening anecdote of sorts, not unlike the opening conventions that came to mark some of the most canonical ethnographies of the early twentieth century.[9]

The classical ethnography uses the convention of the "arrival narrative" to introduce the objective "Western" ethnographer who, due to his or her close affiliations with the culture/peoples being studied, via participant-observation[10] and time in "the field," has the capacity to reveal an assortment of material cultural evidence to the reader. In the case of Du Bois and other black writers of the period, however, writing about black American racial identity and the black racial experience is highly distinct from recounting one's time in "the field." As opposed to a revelation about New Guinea, Samoa, "the African bush," or even an Indian reservation in the American Southwest, in some deep sense there is no escape from "the region of blackness" out of which these African Americans write and into which they allow their readers to peer. Yet for these early African American (re)presenters of black culture, the ethnographic encounter becomes a recognizable and marketable trope and a method for them to begin the process of examining and explaining various sites and types of black cultural production. Of the many techniques employed in the creation of classical ethnography, throughout this book I explore how black writers use as tropes "going into the field" or either acting themselves or creating characters who act as "participant-observers." I argue that these troped techniques produce various modes of analyzing black culture within a variety of texts.

James Baldwin, much like Du Bois and other black writers who both came before and followed him, might be said to occupy the peculiar position of being black and narrating the topic of race and the black cultural experience to the nation: that is, he occupied the role of native ethnographer,[11] tasked with representing the American racial experience and writing about that meaning for what was surely a multiracial, but predominantly white, reading audience. More generally, what characterizes the role of ethnography within the production of African American letters, then, is the burden placed on black writers to act as cultural translators.

Of course, African American letters exceeds the boundaries of the genre of ethnography. I am, after all, not arguing that black fiction be read as ethnography, nor am I suggesting that ethnography be read as fiction. I would, in fact, discourage reading all black American fiction as ethnography due to the attending assumptions in authenticity implied by the genre, but I do think it is valuable to think about how black writers may combine techniques of fiction and ethnography to confound black objectification. And building off the work of Daphne Lamothe, who argues that New Negro writers used ethnographic writing as a strategy "to self-reflexively assume the roles of translators and explicators of African American and African Diasporic folk cultures to Western audience,"[12] I would like to suggest that ethnographic writing continued to be a useful tool for black writers both to effect change and to issue critiques of American race relations, while also seemingly adhering to a convention of cultural translation that would be easily embraced by a mainstream reading audience.

Thus, in *Black Regions of the Imagination* I focus on the formally unnamed literary period situated between the Harlem Renaissance and the Black Arts Movement (1930–1970)[13] to explore how four well-traveled, canonical mid-twentieth-century African American writers—Zora Neale Hurston, Richard Wright, James Baldwin, and Chester Himes—attempted to negotiate their roles as black cultural translators. Staying true to these four writers' biographies, which entail fairly extensive episodes of international travel and long periods of living outside the United States, I examine how these writers follow a previous generation of black American writers who made use of ethnographic techniques. I argue that these mid-twentieth-century writers used ethnography or ethnography-inspired writing[14] for a variety of reasons: to document versions of black life that they variously believed to be in danger of assimilation, to deconstruct racist constructions of African American inhumanity, to pay tribute to black cultural exceptionalism in the face of American racism, and to destabilize expectations regarding the scale and content of African American letters.

I also argue that these writers' own mobility prevented them from completely internalizing the previous generation's relationship to ethnographic methods. Writing amid landmark shifts in American race relations brought on by the Civil Rights Movement and the decolonization of Asian and African countries during the 1950s and 1960s that were to change even the way classical anthropology was practiced,[15] Hurston, Wright, Baldwin, and Himes represent characters practicing (or sometimes themselves practiced) particular ethnographic techniques of participant-observation in a way that might allow for an expressed critique of the American cultural practice of racism. More importantly, these writers' use of participant-observation shifted during their own careers and over the decades in which they wrote to enact a more knowingly critical relationship to the translation of black culture via black-authored literary writing. The chapters that constitute *Black Regions of the Imagination* tell the story of a growing critique of black cultural translation and a movement away from representing or practicing traditional "literary participant-observation." From Hurston's more straightforward ethnographic writings to Himes's creation and killing off of fictional detectives who behave like urban ethnographers in Harlem, I argue that these authors move from an unquestioning use of these techniques to a critical engagement with them.

En route to exploring the ethnographic impulse and critique inherent in these writers' works, one must also acknowledge that a geographical component comes into focus when one remembers that classical ethnography has always employed a site of "fieldwork." So in addition to thinking about how the stylistic lens of ethnographic technique may have shaped these writers' works, *Black Regions of the Imagination* also considers the role of geographical location and the representation of national belonging. What might be most provocative about these writers, then, is their sense of how the stakes involved in being an African American artist and an American citizen are played out when one moves out of and back into the United States. To this end, in *Black Regions of the Imagination* I attempt to articulate how these writers simultaneously represented an African American particularism born out of American racial segregation while also making clear the possibilities that arise when African Americans think more dynamically about both their metaphorical and literal positions in the world. In imagining this project, I am particularly drawn to Robert Reid-Pharr's sense that black people under segregation and in the midst of desegregation were "engaged in a constant process of choosing blackness, choosing a relationship to American history that privileges critique without insisting upon the destruction of either state or society."[16] This is no less true of the writers discussed in this book, all of whom create texts in which the negotiation of black American identity is central and must be seen as a critique of the U.S. racial dilemma that drove them from the country variously.

Engaging the conflicts that result when terms such as *African American, nationalism, black diaspora,* and *internationalism* are juxtaposed, I suggest that mid-twentieth-century artists such as Richard Wright, Zora Neale Hurston, James Baldwin, and Chester Himes consistently represent black Americans within both national and international settings, thereby creating a third narrative space, which I refer to as *the region. The region* is a way to make sense of the antinational narrative concerns of these black writers as they set about both documenting and reimagining a set of "homegrown" experiences within a more worldly[17] framework. One sees in the primary texts of this study the constant coupling of national and international settings and concerns: Hurston cannot write about the American South without mentioning Bahamian fire dancers in *Mules and Men,* and Wright cannot visit Indonesia without commenting on the hair-care proclivities of African American women in *The Color Curtain.* This coupling becomes a method for disallowing the privileging of either the national or the international as these writers seek, in various ways, to acknowledge the particularity of the African American experience while also endeavoring to escape the parochialism dictated by mid-twentieth-century American racial segregation. Unlike other antinationalist paradigms used to theorize black internationalism—namely, black diasporic or cosmopolitan thought, which themselves require the moving away from a national experience of race—I contend that the region becomes a way for us to think through the work done by black writers, particularly the four canonical African American writers of this text, as they stayed tied to America and worked abroad. It is best to think of the dichotomies that I variously call on in this project—national/international, America/the world, home/abroad, home/"the field"—as always existing in contrapuntal relationships that allow us to "think through and interpret together experiences that are discrepant, each with its particular agenda and pace of development, its own internal formations, its internal coherence and system of external relationships, all of them co-existing and interacting" with the others.[18]

Thus, the Baldwin quote that serves as the epigraph to my introduction hits on a theme he repeated in a variety of ways throughout his career: it is only through leaving the United States that one realizes how impossible it is to leave. For Baldwin the statement implies that national removal and national belonging are somehow linked—that for him, a black man, they are mutually constitutive. For *Black Regions of the Imagination*, Baldwin's quote is indicative of the sort of simultaneity of "inside/outside the nation" or "national/international" that I hope to explore in Hurston's ethnographies, Wright's travel writing, Baldwin's fiction, and Himes's detective novels. As I said earlier, key to understanding these works is the embrace of each writer's ability to bring his or her nationally constructed understanding of the black American experience into conversation with his or her life and experiences outside the United States. In other words, I argue that each writer variously aims to elucidate the ways in which U.S.-based African American narratives might be coextensive rather than antithetical to more international or global narratives.

A central concern I have in this book is fostering an understanding of place and its relationship to African American identity in the world. If *place* is the ground in which all narratives must take root, *place* in the context of this study has to move between being both literally and metaphorically understood.

That is to say, because black American citizens have such a troubled history in the nation as a place, the writers in *Black Regions of the Imagination* often describe themselves as physically fleeing the nation. Thus, my interest in their writing is in representing a new sense of the place that the United States holds in each author's mind, even when they reside and represent outside of the nation. This dual understanding of race and national belonging allows them to resist what Paul Gilroy has described as the "easy claims of African-American exceptionalism,"[19] without losing sight of the truly particular ways in which being African American continued to carry significance in their writing.

But to evoke Paul Gilroy is inevitably to summon black diasporic discourse. With this evocation I must make note that this book differs in various ways from many other narratives that focus on black international writers and writings. Most distinctively, I have elected not to use the black diaspora as the central paradigm for thinking through black internationalism. I have opted not to do this for a number of reasons. While I am deeply invested in examining the ways in which some of the writers in this study engage in what we have come to recognize as the practice of diaspora,[20] I do not believe diaspora is the only viable way to describe or analyze black international narratives. In fact, I argue that in the writings of Zora Neale Hurston the presumption of a black diaspora is rejected in favor of an American national belonging. Thus, the black diaspora as the single organizing framework for this book would not allow me to explore how the writers of this project embrace a variety of ways of belonging, be it nationalism, cosmopolitanism, Third World solidarity, et cetera.

Additionally, for me, black diaspora discourse often fails to account for intersections between "the local" and questions of gender in substantive ways. Because of scholarly emphasis on narratives of travel, dispersal, movement, and general removal from the "domestic" space, diaspora discourse is susceptible to the masculinization of its language and theorization.[21] A more fruitful mode of inquiry into black diaspora is one that does not "conflate the *politics* of travel and *actual* travel," because it helps us to retain both the domestic and the traveling subject.[22] This is my aim in this study.

Yet, even as I resist the black diaspora as the single theoretical paradigm for organizing and analyzing international black cultural production, I still consider *Black Regions of the Imagination* a study in representations of belonging. I am interested in the compelling narrative of the creative and personal engagements these black writers had with ideas of democracy and U.S. nationalism. I follow their respective ways of expressing an artistic commitment to the African American political quest for civil rights as a dynamic project that exceeded the boundaries of U.S. national belonging. To avoid the trap of signaling black "racial progress" by replacing U.S. nationalism with a type of black cultural nationalism, and thereby still privileging nationalism as the most important model of belonging, my project considers what it might mean to have an antinationalist mode of black articulation. This does not mean that I cede the language, scope, and significance of the nation-state as an organizing framework in the mid-twentieth-century world (neither American nor black cultural nationalism are off the table for this project); rather, in choosing to consider black a region, I engage a type of antinationalism that allows for the fullness of world organizing imagined within the artistic work of Hurston, Wright, Baldwin, and Himes. Also, considering black a "region" allows me to escape the binary of nationalism versus internationalism (or, as is often the case in black studies, nationalism versus diaspora) that traditionally frames black international narratives.

The antinational stance I intend to imply by moving toward *the region* and away from the black diaspora is not without its own problems. Regions tend to conjure up the pejorative sense of marginality or a lesser status in relation to the national, a meaning that can be especially dangerous when associated with African American life and cultural production. Regions traditionally refer to geographical places. And in the context of the United States, the region is often situated as the marginal and temporal "other" of the nation. That is to say, regions, and most notably the "American South," are characterized and self-constructed as the nation's "static but organic" foil: backward, romanticized, and racist.[23] The vexed history of African American political and social valuation in the United States has historically marked its cultural production as marginal to the center. This is especially complicated when we consider that African American musical and fashion styles (African American "cool") have been employed at various moments throughout the twentieth century to further the American imperial project.[24] From the top down, the relationship of the nation to blackness and black people has often appeared to be one of ownership, not equality. The American imperial project notwithstanding, regions have often been imagined synonymously to territories, which is to say, the phrase "black regions" may imply for some readers that black people occupy a relationally minor status within the United States.

Such an understanding of region's scale when compared to that of the nation fails to capture the powerful counternarratives that might be created out of regional spaces by writers who have embraced the extranational mode of representation that I am proposing by employing a concept such as *the region*. This extranational mode of representation is marked by a deep engagement with both the national and international questions of race and genre; it retains a sense of nationalism without losing sight of the world outside the nation-state. In the case of the black writers of this project, the extranational mode of representation requires that they stay attentive to their positions as black writers shaped by the U.S. racial policy of segregation, even when they move outside the U.S. racial landscape. Their personal and creative worlds speak to the friction that is caused at the intersection between national belonging/rejection and internationalism.

I would like to stress that *imagination* is the operative word for understanding how the writers in *Black Regions of the Imagination* attempted to negotiate issues of national and international "belonging." Unlike much nationalist writing, which seeks to create distinct boundaries between "the nation" and the rest of "the world"—and for the purposes of this book I would underscore the way in which ethnography undergirds nationalism—the narratives of this study resist such boundary keeping. Each chapter of the book is framed by its featured writer's desire to resist.

In chapter 1, I focus on Zora Neale Hurston's writings. I begin with her in part because she serves as a literary bridge between the Harlem Renaissance writers and the mid-twentieth-century black writers who inhabit the later chapers of this project. Also, the writing of Hurston, as the only trained ethnographer, provides a formal lens for understanding the ethnographic techniques employed by her later contemporaries. This chapter examines Hurston's ethnographies *Mules and Men* (1935) and *Tell My Horse* (1938) and argues for an understanding of black American citizenship as created through the coupling of both international and national representations of blackness. In reading her U.S.-based ethnography, *Mules and Men*, against her Caribbean-based ethnography, *Tell My Horse*, I contend that Hurston's constitution of a modern black American citizenship within a rural context becomes visible only through the primitivizing of the black Caribbean.

In chapter 2, I examine Richard Wright's travel narratives *Black Power* (1954) and *The Color Curtain* (1956). Whereas I argue in chapter 1 that Hurston used ethnographic writing to create a rural, black American identity within the United States, I argue that Wright employs ethnography's participant-observation technique in an attempt to distance African Americans from the United States. Unlike Hurston, who remained an American nationalist, Wright tried to transition from a national to a global perspective once he moved to France. This attempt was never entirely successful for multiple reasons. Not only did the publishing world refuse to embrace Wright's globally focused books, but Wright was unable to create a non-U.S.-based narrative that did not make use of an American racial narrative. For instance, in the first part of the chapter I focus on *The Color Curtain*, a text in which, even when Wright was writing about his participation in a 1955 Indonesian conference on nonalignment, he found himself drawn to critiquing black American conference attendees. The second part of the chapter focuses on *Black Power* to explore how Wright's writing about his travels to the Gold Coast (present-day Ghana) complicated his sense of his position as participant-observer as he tried to reconcile his blackness and his American citizenship in the face of black African culture. I finally conclude that the ties that continued to bind Wright troubled him, yet he found it nearly impossible to write about the world without writing about African Americans.

In contrast to Wright's attempts to use ethnographic techniques to create distance between himself and the nation, in chapter 3, I argue that Baldwin manipulates the "arrival narrative" that is so common to traditional ethnography in order to deny and complicate knowledge of the (black) "other" in a desegregating nation. Using romance and both heterosexual and queer sex as metaphors, Baldwin denies the easy racial knowledge claims that seemed to run rampant in the United States during the mid-twentieth century. Unwilling to allow an ethnographic figure to conduct a productive inquiry into "the other," Baldwin uses the interracial romance between *Another Country* protagonists Ida Scott and Vivaldo Moore in order to expose the true self-work that a white man / white nation must do before racial, sexual, and gender knowledge and equality can be achieved.

In chapter 4, I examine how Chester Himes, writing from Paris, attempted to create an alternative black identity by re-creating the black American ghetto from abroad. This chapter, which focuses on Himes's novels *A Rage in Harlem* (1957), *The Real Cool Killers* (1959), and *Blind Man with a Pistol* (1969), argues that Himes created a black space (Harlem) that was so hyperbolized that it would be unrecognizable to white readers. I pay close attention to Himes's use of his protagonists, a set of black detectives who, I argue, function as participant-observers by virtue of spending the entire detective series translating the motivations of black criminals to a white police force. Much like Baldwin, Himes is critical of participant-observation's capacity to produce any sort of realistic representation of black life, but unlike Baldwin, Himes disrupts this technique by rendering his detectives increasingly inept throughout the detective series. With my concluding discussion of Himes, I usher my readers into the moment just before the Black Arts Movement and the rise of black militant thought and artistic production. The very act of black cultural translation is fated for Himes, and the death of the participant-observer is foundational to understanding Himes's detective series as a whole.

Finally, in the conclusion, I mark the shift between the mid-century writers and the Black Arts Movement. Using Himes's final, posthumously published novel, *Plan B*, I examine how the Black Power Movement influenced but ultimately rendered outdated a certain relationship to black cultural translation and internationalism practiced by writers of the previous generation. In the end, I hope to mark influence and progression of black literary production and generational concerns.

I hope my refusal to cede the language of nationalism, my resistance to diaspora as a single framing paradigm, and my insistence on exploring parochialism/particularism in relation to black American cultural production will not result in my being taken as a proponent of American exceptionalism or national exaltation. My aim, ultimately, is not to make an argument for the exceptionalism of black American cultural production at the expense of other members of the black diaspora; it is, instead, to explore the ways in which midcentury black American writers negotiated, translated, and circulated to the broader world their identities, which were constituted by a variety of particular formative experiences born out of the nation's history of slavery and segregation. I would like to add that possible critiques of my attention to the particularities that shape African American cultural production must themselves consider the presuppositions that have to be made about black American cultural production's "authenticity." In other words, in order to offer up a critique of any study of black American particularity, one must assume that black American identity remains untouched by immigrant populations (both black, white, and "other") and that black cultural producers fail to absorb and be moved by the significance of mainstream and worldwide events that are transmitted through media outlets, or that they otherwise remain untouched by various international influences. Particularity does not necessarily imply isolation. For example, in Imani Perry's discussion of hip hop, she contends that hip hop is distinctly black American music, "and yet it is certainly 'impure.'"[25] Although it is a musical form influenced by Caribbean and Latino music trends, "one must remain aware of its location."[26] What Perry's work illustrates, then, is the tension between those scholars who see black cultural production as dynamic and those scholars who see it simply as parochial. I would go further to say that those scholars who critique others who focus on black American cultural production as inherently arguing for the purity and primacy of black Americanness fail to comprehend the varied and dynamic ways in which black American cultural production is shaped by a global world, even as it remains located in the United States in particular ways.

Finally, *Black Regions of the Imagination* follows the quest of Hurston, Wright, Baldwin, and Himes as they attempted to imagine black writing capable of fostering new ways of representing black American life. Their imaginations were not without complexity and contradiction. This inevitably means that the paradoxes of Hurston's, Wright's, Baldwin's, and Himes's writings are ones worth watching as they travel.

1 / Becoming American through Ethnographic Writing: Zora Neale Hurston and the Performance of Ethnography

Almost nobody else could stop the average Harlemite on Lenox Avenue and measure his head with a strange-looking, anthropological device and not get bawled out for the attempt, except Zora, who used to stop anyone whose head looked interesting, and measure it.

LANGSTON HUGHES[1]

In 1954, Zora Neale Hurston admitted to her friend William Bradford Huie that she was gripped by the desire to puke when she read the works of writers such as Richard Wright because she felt they pandered to the white desire for black pathology and inferiority.[2] Although she may have been a bit hyperbolic in her description of her reaction, Hurston's visceral aversion was not an isolated example of textual tension between Wright and Hurston. Back in 1937, Wright had reviewed and panned *Their Eyes Were Watching God* because he felt that Hurston merely replicated "facile sensuality that ha[d] dogged Negro expression since the days of Phillis Wheatley." As the Hurston-Wright debate goes, Wright believed Hurston to be a minstrelist of sorts, and while he allowed that Hurston could write, he was unable to see anything in her art beyond the pathos of rural black life that he found politically unproductive.[3] At the center of these two writers' differences was Wright's inability to appreciate black "folk," an appreciation that was the bedrock of Hurston's disciplinary investment in documenting, analyzing, and creating black folk culture that marks the content of her oeuvre.

Ironically, by the time Wright got around to panning Hurston, she had already weathered the rise and fall of what we have come to call the Harlem Renaissance, as well as established herself as one of the foremost authorities on black folklore within the American academy. Still, I begin with the Hurston-Wright debate not merely to enter where critics often do when writing of both Wright and Hurston but to highlight the notion of contestation that was central to Hurston's cultural production. Whether it was Lucy, her romantic rival in *Mules and Men*; Richard Wright and Langston Hughes at various moments in her writing career; or one of her overly critical and competing mentors—Franz Boas, Charlotte Osgood Mason, and Alain Locke—Zora Neale Hurston was frequently engaged in a discursive throw-down within and over her writing. Contestation, I suggest, fuels her writing in such a way as to allow the competing concerns of race, gender, and nationalism that run through her works to coexist without ever becoming fully cohesive. This lack of cohesion is sometimes frustrating, but it ultimately allows us to read Hurston's work in dynamic ways that challenge a variety of status quo assumptions regarding race, gender, nationalism, art, and science in the early- to mid-twentieth century.

More directly, I would like to suggest that Hurston's emphasis on nonnorthern black life, which Wright hated, produces multiple effects: first, it goes against the cultural climate of the moment in which she created, which insisted that black modernity and progress was commensurate with migration to northern metropolises; second, Hurston's work in the rural South and Caribbean requires that we think differently about how we constitute the relationship between "black modernity" and "black folk"; and, finally, because of the first two effects, we can see Hurston's attention to a revised but affirmed possibility for black national belonging that is carried out through the ethnographic form. More specifically, I suggest that it is through texts such as *Mules and Men* (1935) and *Tell My Horse* (1938) that we can begin to trace Hurston's theory of "black folk" and American national belonging. These two works, read in tandem, articulate Hurston's sense that black folk culture is always in the process of becoming, that black American folks are modern subjects, and that the aim of black cultural production should be to produce a representation of black American rurality that could resist long-held notions that northward urban migration was indeed the only method capable of producing black modern subjectivity.

Zora Neale Hurston serves as the starting point of this larger study for a variety of reasons, primarily because her life of literary production bridges the Harlem Renaissance and the mid-twentieth-century black writers who inhabit this project. She serves to begin the study secondly because as an African American female ethnographer during this period, Hurston's relationship to the "realism" expected of ethnography offers an initial insight to understanding why other mid-twentieth-century writers might have similarly taken up the tools offered by ethnography both to represent and to resist representing to a mainstream public particular aspects of African American culture. In this sense, Hurston's personal and publishing history offers a model for reading the anxieties and intentions of some of the most critically acclaimed black writers of the mid-twentieth century. Not quite Hurston's contemporaries, writers such as Wright, Himes, and Baldwin continued to explore, expose, and exile themselves in the hope that distance would bring them clarity on African American life in the United States and the world. Couple with these intentions and anxieties the act of "going into the field," and one can begin to see how ethnography might offer black writers some amount of distance needed to carry out a variety of critiques, from the personal to the national and international.

Focusing on the writings of Zora Neale Hurston, then, this chapter explores how she employs ethnography to orchestrate the difficult task of offering a public articulation of African American identity and artistic production in the midst of twentieth-century U.S. global expansion and a growing sense of black modernity, which would eventually help enable the integration of black Americans into a recognized public sphere as equal subjects to whites within the United States. Daphne Lamothe has argued that during the Harlem Renaissance black writers such as Zora Neale Hurston used ethnographic writing as a strategy "for representing their cultural identity and combating racist preconceptions at the same time that they maintained a firm grasp of themselves as culture-workers and creative individuals."[4] Ethnography served as a powerful tool in both inventing and documenting black culture for Hurston and various other black writers of the "New Negro" era. The invention of this identity-concept, reified in Alain Locke's edited collection also entitled *The New Negro* (1925), relied on the notion that one of the ways one could account for modern black life was by virtue of its distance from premodern black life. In Locke's introduction to *The New Negro*, he contended that the migration of African Americans from the rural South to northern cities was a flight "from medieval America to modern."[5] In linking the movement of blacks away from the rural South to northern cities, Locke imagines black rurality as temporally and developmentally distant from black modernity (read: black urbanity).

With the articulation of the primacy of black folk culture's significance to the modern black experience, Hurston's ethnographic monographs bear the hallmark of black modernism in that they toggle between what Houston Baker has described as the "mastery of form" and the "deformation of master."[6] These two relationships of mastery allow for both the mimicry of black minstrelsy that Wright accused Hurston of fostering within her novel and the deception that abounds within the employment of a minstrel's mask. Much like the narrator of Paul Laurence Dunbar's famous poem "We Wear the Masks," Hurston's works are filled with as much "guile" and as many "cries" as they are with "grins" and smiles. Reading more deeply, one understands that the larger projects of *Mules* and *Tell My Horse* are to do the work of deconstructing stereotypical understandings of black American life. It is especially important to understand Hurston's writing as situated between mastery and deformation because ethnography has a history of being an "instrument of imperialist containment."[7] Her formal training in the discipline of anthropology rendered her relationship to the discipline vexed, at the very least, and it is this conflict that provides the foundation for understanding the relationship between her work and modernity.

In this way, Hurston's writings provide a very clear sense of the way ethnography might be employed to expose racist U.S. society's relationship to black people and black cultural production through an exploration of the "fictive" nature of the discipline. As early as *Mules and Men*, Hurston was committed to a critical application of ethnographic methods to the study of black culture that was meant to complicate the notions of black primitivism and modernity as they relate to rural black folk. For instance, in *Mules*, the way Hurston describes the hoodoo tradition in New Orleans, a practice that she describes as starting "way back before everything," may seem out of line with the argument I offer regarding Hurston's devotion to reconstructing notions of black folks and primitivism. Yet Hurston complicates readings of hoodoo that seek to locate it in a preindustrial and prehistorical time by juxtaposing the "timeless" hoodoo practice with descriptions of female practitioners "reading cards and doing mail order business in names and insinuations of well known factors in conjure" and by alluding to the fact that the majority of hoodoo "doctors" buy their materials from supply houses.[8] In both instances, the geographical and temporal isolation presumed constitutive to black primitivism is refuted by the reality of interstate commerce implied by such resources as mail-order catalogues. And while Hurston suggests that these women's activities are not worth putting on paper because they engage in the commercialization of hoodoo practices, she does include them, illustrating the reality of the adaptability of hoodoo to a capitalist economic system. She thereby infuses the system and its practitioners with the dual responsibility of representing both prehistory and the modern black entrepreneurial class. This duality functions as a bridge of sorts between "Old Negro" and "New Negro" discourse that flourished at the moment Hurston was producing.

In exploring the ways in which Hurston's ethnography gives us insights into her figuration of the importance of black rural modernity and how it might be achieved, I make a number of moves within this chapter. First, I use Hurston's known biography and personal correspondence to further establish how she articulated her vexed relationship to the discipline of anthropology. I go on to suggest that out of this relationship Hurston wrestled to create a new understanding of black rurality that was able to coexist with the increasingly urban-dwelling African American experience brought about by the Great Migration of the early twentieth century. Second, I explore how Hurston narrates the ethnographic collection process as an exercise in performance. Rather than simply focusing on performances as a site of culture, which is a stance that a trained anthropologist might take, I argue that Hurston turned her gaze back onto the process of ethnographic collection to suggest that it is itself a form of performance. Again to quote Baker, Hurston's sense of ethnography as performance allows her to exercise the "mastery of form" and "deformation of mastery" as she represents herself out in the field. And in the last portion of the chapter, I turn directly to Hurston's ethnographies, *Mules and Men* and *Go Tell My Horse*, in order to explore the repercussions of her development of a theory of ethnography suited for describing black rural modernity. As the chapter closes, I suggest that although Hurston disavows the notion of black American primitivism in her ethnographic writing, she is only able to do so through primitivizing non-American blacks.

A Vexed History

A student of the pioneer of modern American anthropology, Franz Boas, Huston was the product of a social science education mixed with a soulful commitment to the power and beauty of black folk culture. Like many other black writers of the Harlem Renaissance, Hurston's creative career was shaped by a patronage system that required her to secure the financial capital that could allow her the freedom to make research and writing her life's focus.

In 1927, Hurston's chief financial patron, Charlotte Osgood Mason, provided the fiscal support necessary for her second trip into the field to collect ethnographic material.[9] Although Mason, herself an amateur anthropologist in her youth, was a great backer of black cultural production and cultural analysis—it is estimated that Mason contributed between $50,000 and $75,000 to black artists during the Renaissance, with over $15,000 of that sum going to support Hurston over five years[10]— she valued black primitivism above all else. Mason was known to invite black artists and intellectuals to her home with the expectation that they would perform the most "authentic" rendition of blackness they could muster. A lackluster performance risked not only Mason's critique that one was living insincerely but also the potential end of her financial support as retribution for such insincerity. Severing ties with Mason would have been a great monetary loss to Hurston's career, which would have translated into a great cultural loss for black studies. Luckily, much like protagonist Isie Watts in her short story "Drenched in Light," Hurston relished performance, but more than that, she understood the monetary value that came from performing before a white audience. Hurston recalls a childhood marked by white onlookers who paid her to "'speak pieces' and sing" and "dance the parse-me-la," which seemed odd to her because she wanted to perform and "needed bribing to stop."[11] Hurston's life and fiction, whose separation is often hard to distinguish, are reminders of the complicated intersection between racial exoticism and black autonomy. More pointedly, however, as Houston Baker notes, "it is, first and foremost, the mastery of the minstrel mask by blacks that constitutes a primary move in Afro-American discursive modernism."[12] As Hurston's relationships with her white mentors and benefactors prove, she was a master of the mask.

Yet the greatest price of Mason's patronage was her placement of Hurston under a strict contractual agreement that stipulated the content and form Hurston's fieldwork could take. Mason supplied Huston with the financial capital to continue collecting folklore in Florida and Louisiana, work that she had begun during her senior year at Barnard, yet Mason and Hurston's contract stated that Hurston was not to publish without Mason's permission any materials collected while under contract. She additionally stipulated that Hurston was forbidden from using collected materials to produce creative art for commercial purposes. In a March 1928 letter to Hurston's friend and fellow Renaissance writer Langston Hughes, Huston notes that she was pulling out of the folk opera they planned to write because of her contract with Mason but was sending him materials that he might continue to use: "I have the street scene still & 2 others in my mind—if you want them you can use them for yourself and its O.K. by me. Godmother asked me not to publish and as I am making money I hope you can use them."[13] In effect, Hurston's bar from commercial use of her research required her to find various other ways to make creative use of the materials she collected. The game of cat-and-mouse that she played with Mason—hiding her creative intentions and collecting folklore that became the foundation of her most famous works of literature[14]—must be seen as Hurston's ongoing struggle to contest the expectations and stipulations that a white audience might enact on black cultural production, even when black artists appeared to be willingly submissive.

Indeed, Hurston's ultimately tumultuous personal and intellectual relationship with Mason might be seen as an extension of the uproar that shaped her relationship to the discipline of anthropology itself. Throughout her career, Hurston found the objective methodological distance required by the discipline to be at odds with both her personality and her creative interests. In fact, Hurston found this distance, from the use of scientific language to the prescribed methods of objectivity, to be detrimental even to her ability to collect black folklore. In her autobiography, she admits that her first six months in the field were disappointing and diminished any confidence that she had in becoming a serious professional anthropologist. Hurston suggests that the "glamour" of Barnard and the professional-sounding language she had adopted, which she refers to as "Barnardese," prompted her informants to deny her the very access she had expected by being merely a black ethnographer: "The men and women who had whole treasures of material just seeping through their pores, looked at me and shook their heads. No, they had never heard of anything like that around there. Maybe it was over in the next county. Why didn't I try over there?"[15] Hurston is denied access to the very community to which Boas said she would have direct access, because she was working within the wrong social and linguistic register.

In response to the distance maintained by the southern black communities Hurston visited in the field, which were merely responding to the objective distance required of anthropology, Hurston was forced to develop her own relationship to both the people and the discipline. This ultimately took the form of Hurston's going "undercover" and taking on the identity of a bootlegger's girlfriend who was on the lam. This newly fabricated identity gained Hurston access to the black folk culture she had been sent to collect in the American South. Moreover, Hurston's theatrics, which were performed in the name of scientific collection, introduce key concepts that will be taken up in greater depth later in this chapter: ethnography as performance and performance as critical to the creation of ethnography.

Yet, much like the stipulations that Mason required of Hurston, Boas's early requirement was that she frequently check in with him before she offered analysis of the materials she had spent months in the field collecting. Boas's guidance of Hurston's work in the field exposes how personal and professional divides were nearly impossible to maintain under a patronage system. For instance, during her initial 1927 (non-Mason-funded) trip into the field, Hurston sent a letter to Boas that captures this conflation of the personal and the professional that was to mark Hurston's career as ethnographer. In this most annoyed letter, it appears as if Hurston has applied for a car loan while collecting data in Florida because, as she says, "it is terribly hard to get about down here."[16] However, because she lists Boas on the contract, he is informed of her plans, and she is forced to explain not only her desires but also her post-fieldwork financial plans. She implores him not to worry because "someone is telling [her] that this is the way cars are sold if not bought for cash." The letter then abruptly transitions to Hurston's acknowledgment that Boas will find enclosed the materials she had been collecting in the field. She tells him, "It is fortunate that it is being collected, now, for a great many people say, 'I used to know some of that old stuff, but I done forgot it all.' You see, the negro is not living his lore to the extent of the Indian. He is not on a reservation, being kept pure. His negroness is being rubbed off by close contact with white culture."[17] The juxtaposition of this very personal financial matter and her professional requirements combine to make her analysis regarding the importance of her trip an interesting entry point for us to begin thinking about the stability of black authenticity as it is both represented and (more importantly) read into Hurston's work within a growing sense of black modernity. The Hurston-Boas interaction illustrates how Hurston's personal financial situation requires a certain amount of discursive ventriloquism in order to ensure her ability to comfortably carry on with her research. Hurston is not a free agent in the field, a reality that allows us to ponder the importance of black pandering and how such pandering attempted to articulate its own relationship to the modern world and modes of modernity.

Because American ethnography during the early twentieth century was, among other things, invested in the project of legitimizing American nationalism, it was taken for granted that as an object of study, "America" and "Americans" had no need of anthropological study. Neither a culture in need of analysis nor one on the verge of extinction through cultural assimilation, mainstream American culture remained well into the twentieth century an unexplored topic of study. Instead, new immigrants, Native Americans, and black people occupied the majority of U.S.-based ethnography during the early twentieth century. The foundations of American anthropology call attention to the fiction of nationhood and nationalism as it is carved out through the study of the cultures of nationals who are perceived and treated as "noncitizens." The construction of the role of American minorities and ethnic immigrants in the discipline might have been what prompted Hurston to follow her personal revelation with a reminder of the importance of the work she had been sent south to do. In short, to justify what Boas might have mistakenly considered an unjustified personal indiscretion, Hurston ventriloquizes the rhetoric of Boas's school of liberal anthropology, reminding him of her unique utility to his larger disciplinary goals.[18] In this way, I am encouraging a reading of Hurston's compliance with the essentializing rhetoric that undergirded notions of black primitivism as strategic. Yes, compliance would result in her having to create narratives of blackness that were circumscribed by the conditions that white money and scholarly support required, but circumscription merely helps us to detect the limits and borders of genius. Though the parameters of her work were managed and contained by the consumptive practices of mainstream America, Hurston found a variety of ways to further a study of black cultural production. It is no coincidence, then, that Hurston rationalizes her need for the modern convenience of a vehicle by prompting Boas with a reminder of what might be lost if she were unable to get to her rural sites of analysis in a timely manner.

The increasing urbanization of black Americans during the early twentieth century notwithstanding, such a facile understanding of black folk culture's fragility ceased to be in line with Hurston's own vision as articulated in *Mules and Men*. In fact, as early as 1928, Hurston declared, "Negro folk-lore is *still* in the making a new kind is crowding out the old."[19] Hurston's assessment regarding black folk culture is illuminating, if not revolutionary, simply for the fact that it undermines the impetus of both Boas's and Mason's interest in sending her down South to collect black folklore. For Hurston, black folklore was not dead or dying, in need of a disciplinary intervention to document its final swan song. Instead, she saw that black culture was constantly developing and re-creating itself at multiple geographical sites, proving itself just as alive as the people who created it. It was an expression and affirmation of the particular experiences of the black people from whom the collected sayings, songs, dances, and so on emanated. Hurston had to develop a way of writing about black culture that was as vibrant, contradictory, and complicated as the people and the material she collected from them. The question, then, becomes, how does one write about black folks in such a way as to capture the ongoing human drama? For Hurston, the answer rested in integrating performance and play into her representation of black folk production.

The drama of black culture's transition from "dead" to dynamic is at the center of Hurston's work and this analysis. Many critics have documented Hurston's interest in bringing to the stage black folk culture as a means to "halt all" the "spurious efforts"[20] of contemporaneous white playwrights, whom she perceived as having an ill conception of how to represent "real" black culture. Take, for instance, Eugene O'Neill, who is credited with creating the theatrical atmosphere that allowed African American stage representations to move away from black minstrelsy toward human characterizing. One sees growth in black characterization in O'Neill plays as one moves from *The Dreamy Kid* (1918), *The Emperor Jones* (1920), and *All God's Chillun Got Wings* (1924) to his characterization of Joe Mott in *The Iceman Cometh* (1939). In this sense, O'Neill's career was marked by a slow coming to realization of how to represent black humanity. Yet, Hurston, like much of the black press, remained unconvinced that a white writer could create black characters who were not performing some version of blackface.

In April 1928, Hurston wrote to Hughes regarding her plans to bring something authentic to the stage: "Did I tell you before I left about the new, the real Negro art theatre I plan? Well I shall, or rather *we* shall act out the folk tales, however short, with the abrupt angularity and naiveté of the primitive 'bama nigger."[21] Hurston made use of satirical "self-reflexive code" in her reference to the "primitive 'bama nigger" in order to signify

her commitment to representing the lives of black folk. As Elin
Diamond notes, "'primitive 'bama nigger[s]' were the cherished
informants of her anthropological research, the working-class
black Southerners who, not without irony themselves, taught
her folktales, songs, dances and root magic, and allowed themselves to be 'salvaged' in her books, essays and plays."[22] Composed of a set of terms that were already highly mediated and
managed, Hurston's employment of "primitive" and "nigger"
signifies both the playful exuberance between black intellectuals
and a mode to distinguish her interest in differentiating the lives
of the working-class and rural poor from the racial uplift narratives that other members of the black intellectual bourgeoisie
would have felt a more appropriate tool with which to counter
the essentialism of white racism. This distinction is important
as we consider the grand narrative of black literary production
during the early part of the century. While Hurston may be
accused of placing too much emphasis on the lives of rural black
America, the cultural moment in which she wrote was filled
with the debates that often pitted notions of bourgeois, urban
propriety and progress against working-class, rural impropriety and underdevelopment. And if we consider Houston Baker's
provocative assessment that the quintessential Harlem Renaissance text, *The New Negro*, functioned to remove "the Afro-
American decisively from 'country districts' of the South and
cast a black mass movement . . . as a sign of an irreversible shift
from the medieval to the modern,"[23] then we can begin to see
more clearly what Hurston was writing against. It would be a
gross oversimplification to say that Hurston merely fed the white
racist establishment a form of black minstrelsy it loved best,
although such an argument can and has been made by many
critics.[24] Instead, it may be more fruitful to consider how Hurston's "'bama nigger" might function as a trope that allowed her
to say as much about race, power, mobility, and black modernity
as the traditional racial uplift narrative did. Moreover, this trope
allowed her to push back against black urbanity as the ultimate
sign of racial progress and black modernity.

In light of the fact that Hurston dedicated her career to studying and representing "the folk," there is a well-established scholarly conversation regarding the effect of her discursive emphasis
on rural black communities. Critiques put forth by scholars such
as Hazel Carby, J. Martin Favor, Madhu Dubey, Robin Kelley,
and Kenneth Warren suggest that we consider the motivations
for any author's reliance on "the folk" and how this might create crises in representation that point to the U.S. mainstream's
historical preference for a monolithic, geographically contained,
and historically inaccurate version of black life. Favor contends
that "Hurston helped to solidify a notion of [black] racial authenticity in southern rural geographies" that puts her work in line
with a long and problematic tradition of African American literary representations of black authenticity as hailing exclusively
from the American South.[25] Likewise, Hazel Carby has argued
that Hurston's work makes a political statement through its
emphasis on only those forms of black cultural production that
emanated from rural, black Americans.[26] Carby reminds us that
during the 1920s and 1930s, amid the growing black migration
away from the rural South to the more urban North, Hurston's
emphasis on rural black culture as the site of "true" black cultural production resulted in the "discursive displacement of
contemporary social crises."[27] Hurston's emphasis on rural black
life, according to Carby, failed to register the social realities that
encouraged and drove blacks from the American South to the
North, namely, racial violence and labor inequity of the rural
South and increased employment opportunities of the urban
North.[28] Ultimately, Carby critiques Hurston's cultural vision as
a nostalgic, prelapsarian fiction meant to remedy contemporary
social conflicts by creating narrative parodies of her own childhood.[29] One should note that Carby's intervention is as much a
critique of the state of the academy's impulse to racially dehis-
toricize racial politics and African American experience in the
1980s and 1990s as it is about the racial realities in the 1930s.

Yet I believe that if one reduces Hurston's work to nostalgia,
to a disavowal of social reality in favor of a reimagining of her

own childhood, then one misses the very representational voids into which her fictional and ethnographic writing attempted to speak. So while it might be argued that "Hurston wanted to preserve the concept of Negroness, to negotiate and rewrite its cultural meanings, and, finally, to reclaim an aesthetically purified version of blackness,"[30] I would suggest that Hurston's writing illustrates the impossibility of such black "purification," even as it appears to reach out for essentializing notions of blackness. As Robin Kelley reminds us, locating authentic blackness within "the folk" require that one be vigilant to preserve the understanding that it is a "socially constructed categor[y] that [has] something to do with the reproduction of race, class, and gender hierarchies and the policing of the boundaries of modernism."[31] A critical reader, creator, and self-described member of "the Folk" (as Hurston was) would inevitably understand not only the mediated nature of the category's construction but also that this category might be employed with the aim of breaking the bonds of social inequality usually ascribed to those who reside within the category. Describing Hurston's work simply as an attempt to inscribe an ahistorical blackness misses the very possibility that abounds in Hurston's work, especially her ethnography.

Thus, rather than arguing that Hurston was more deeply invested in promoting a singular sense of what constituted "authentic" black life in her literary and ethnographic work, it must be seen as competing within a cultural marketplace where claims on black propriety were in constant circulation and negotiation; and within this marketplace, Hurston created a space for what I call *black rural modernity*. Between white cultural consumers and black artists, as well as among black artists, there was a crisis of representation brewing, and this crisis shaped the way in which these varied parties consumed and created black culture. The politics of representation require that we engage, even if briefly, a more "meta" analysis of the issues that bound Hurston to a literary world in which we make central the various contests regarding who constituted "black folk," who got to represent them, and to what ends such representations were made. Understanding these contests is central to understanding the overarching importance of her work to black cultural production throughout the twentieth century. Although this distinction fails to remedy the issues that arise when cultural production is framed within the confines of "authentic blackness," it does encourage an acknowledgment of Hurston's work as part of an ongoing dialogue regarding the discourse of blackness, where its meaning and significance within the U.S. context is always in flux.

I make this distinction not to offer a revisionist's reading of the racial essentialism that many may see running through Hurston's work. Indeed it is difficult to argue that Hurston failed to police the boundaries of what constitutes "authentic blackness" when she did such things as critique black concert performers for performing spirituals in "a white manner" rather than a "Negro" one.[32] Instead, I am most interested in the various techniques that Hurston employed in order to offer a counternarrative to mainstream notions regarding black primitivism in the midst of growing U.S. and black modernization and internationalism. What many critics see as a form of racial essentialism resulting from Hurston's decision to narrate the stories of rural black Americans is better understood as one of the tools that Hurston uses to dispel racist notions of black social impropriety and ahistoricity.

She assigns a continued value to a place and group of people that risk either being despised for their lack of progress or valued only as artifacts of a premodern black American identity and, thus, proof of the "progress" of urban black Americans. This is especially important when one considers that the racial uplift narrative was a competing creative form employed in the circumvention of white-supremacist ideology of black inferiority. Relying on a culture and class-based parody of white bourgeois propriety, as early as post-Reconstruction, black writers engaged in creating uplift narratives that might prove "blacks were as capable as whites of expressing fine thoughts and feelings."[33] Rather than relying on parody, Hurston met black impropriety

at its perceived source: the working-class, black inhabitant of the
rural American South. Hurston's involvement in the ill-fated[34] literary magazine
Fire!! A Quarterly Devoted to the Younger Negro Artists (1926) is
an early example of her refusal to engage the imaginative constraints of middle-class propriety favored by many New Negro
writers and intellectuals. Hurston, along with Langston Hughes,
Wallace Thurman, and four other young black writers, sought
to create in *Fire!!* a cutting-edge literary magazine that would
"burn up a lot of the old, dead conventional Negro-white ideas
of the past."[35] Though short-lived, the issue contained some of
the most unconventional black narratives of the period: a play
that highlights colorism within the black community, a short
story in which a young man inadvertently becomes a young
woman's first "trick," one of the first explicitly gay narratives as
told through the decadent ramblings of a black bohemian, and
everything in between. Besides allowing Hurston and her peers
to showcase their own writing, *Fire!!* allowed them to be impolite,[36] to resist the racial landscape that required black artists of
the period to fall in line with an older generation of black writers
and intellectuals who, as the *Fire!!* group perceived, supported a
more assimilationist vision of black cultural inclusion.

As these young black writers had intended, *Fire!!* was panned
by the black establishment. Alain Locke critiqued the publication's sexual excess as follows: "But if Negro life is to provide a
healthy antidote to Puritanism, and to become one of the effec-
tive instruments of sound artistic progress, its flesh values must
more and more be expressed in clean, original, primitive but
fundamental terms of the senses and not, as too often in this
particular issue of *Fire*, in hectic imitation of the 'naughty nine-
ties' and effete echoes of contemporary decadence."[37] With an
emphasis on *cleanliness*, Locke allowed the possibility that writers might create art with the power to give the world a healthy
dose of black sexuality, as long as it was within the confines
of heteronormative sensuality that would uplift black sexuality from the shackles of sexual perversity/pathology created

and maintained by white-supremacist American culture. It is unclear what an anti-Puritan black sexuality would look like, but it is clear that it would not be gay or sell itself for money. Hurston and her cohort wrote against the cleanliness of racial uplift narratives in the hope that they might offer a less constrained vision of black identity and artistry.

From Hurston's inclusion as a founding editor of and contributor to *Fire!!*, she created a career out of attempting to show the white and black reading world a version of black life that was in many ways at odds with the period. Hurston's unique vision of black life is more fully drawn out by a comparison between her work and that of fellow New Negro artist Jean Toomer. Much like Hurston's work, *Cane* is marked by Toomer's refusal to take up the hallmarks of black middle-class propriety. Yet Hurston differs from Toomer in her particular demand that the rural black South and its inhabitants be understood not only as the contemporaries of more northern metropolitan blacks but as modern subjects in their own right. Toomer, who might also be thought of as having made an ethnographic foray into the southern "field" during the early part of the twentieth century, provides a foil for Hurston in both the intention and outcome of their works. If Hurston went to the field and found modern life alive within the "Black Belt," then Toomer went into the field and found himself surrounded by the alien landscape of Sparta, Georgia, that was incompatible with the sense of his own modernity. Toomer wrote of his Georgia experience that shaped *Cane*, "With negroes also the trend was towards the small town and then towards the city—an industry and commerce and machines. The folk-spirit was walking in to die on the modern desert. The spirit was so beautiful. Its death was so tragic. Just this seemed to sum life for me. And this was the feeling I put into *Cane*." He goes on to state more explicitly that *Cane* was a "swan-song," "a song of end."[38] Toomer's *Cane*, then, documents a group of people and way of life on the edge of extinction due to industrialization and modernity.[39]

So whereas Toomer was shocked into modernity by his encounter with the "dying" southern black culture, Hurston's encounter encouraged her to litter *Mules and Men* with signs and symbols of the possibility that black rural life and modernity might coexist within the same time, place, and people. More than merely making rural black life the object of an alternative modernity, Hurston resists the tendency of the period to insist that black progress and modernity were always enacted in that teleological movement to northern urban centers. This important rhetorical move on Hurston's part forces us to redirect our attentions southward. In the process of this geographical shift, we can begin to see a narrative of black modernity that resists the disavowal of black, southern, rural identity. And while the language taken up by Hurston concerning the importance of resisting this disavowal often took the form of "authentic blackness," the stakes of her intellectual resistance to the geographical importance of the northern metropolis are greater than her ill-articulated statements about what might constitute "authentic blackness." Hurston's works illustrate that modernity, blackness, and rurality were compatible and meant that one could find them resting within the bodies, stories, and performances of rural African Americans.

Performing Ethnography and Creating Black Rural Modernity

As Cheryl Wall has noted, Hurston's work anticipates much of modern anthropology's turn to performance.[40] The performance of stories became the method for demonstrating African American modernity in Hurston's ethnographic writing. In a July 1928 letter to Langston Hughes, Hurston notes that she has been holding storytelling contests in every town she visits during her fieldwork in order to facilitate her collecting.[41] Using Hughes's poetry as a model for poetic performance, Hurston encourages her black subjects to share their artistic creations. These contests serve as sites of contestation, performance, and black folk culture. Hurston's emphasis on this intersection allows us to see that black folk culture ceases to be simply an object of study—although it was still that—and grows into an ever-expanding community performance for her. Hurston notes that the black folks who worked the phosphate mines and turpentine mills were able to take the Hughes poetry, which she generally read to begin her collection contests, and to use both themes and lines from the poetry in their everyday lives. The Florida communities Hurston found herself in were quoting Hughes's *Fine Clothes to the Jew*, which not only speaks to the connectivity between folk art and high art (a hierarchical distinction that Hughes worked against in his blues poetry) but also supports Hurston's sense that folk culture was neither stagnant nor rote. "Negro folklore is not a thing of the past," Hurston writes. "It is still in the making. Its great variety shows the adaptability of the black man: nothing is too old or too new, domestic or foreign, high or low, for his use."[42] Her argument is one of black cultural adaptation and counters the notion that African American cultural production is either nonexistent or derivative. And in this line, we can see Hurston's sense that the imagination of African Americans is constrained neither by time, national borders, nor genre. The lack of national constraint is most interesting to me and is something I take up later in this chapter.

But Hurston is not the single authoritative voice on the adaptability and utility of black folk culture. She allows her informants not only to understand but also to provide analysis regarding the state of black folk culture:

"Aw shucks," exclaimed George Thomas doubtfully. "Zora don't you come here and tell de biggest lie first thing. Who you reckon want to read all them old-time tales bout Brer Rabbit and Brer Bear?"

"Plenty of people, George. They are a lot more valuable than you might think. We want to set them down before it's too late."

"Too late for what?"

"Before everybody forgets all of 'em."

"No danger of that. That's all some people is good for— set 'round and lie and murder groceries."[43]

In the dialogued scene from *Mules and Men*, Hurston speaks in the voice of the "traditional" anthropologist, nearly repeating the words that she used in her letter to Boas explaining why she needed a car to conduct her collecting, but Hurston allows her "informant" to provide analysis that contradicts her own. Besides undermining authority of the traditional ethnographer, this transposition exposes the reality of black folk culture's adaptability and speaks to the real function of the form: to create community. As George intimates, as long as there are black communities, there will be an impetus for members to keep telling and adapting the stories. The codification of those stories through their collection, then, becomes secondary to the function that they serve within the community. This shift in emphasis away from the collection of content to the occasion prompting the sharing of folk tales shifts the content of ethnography from a form of cultural imperialism to one of potential subversion of white cultural superiority embedded in the discipline of anthropology. To be more specific, *Mules and Men* mixes form, genre, and temporality in a narrative of the role of performance in producing black modern subjectivity within the genre of ethnographic writing.

As famed anthropologist Victor Turner notes, "performance is often a critique direct or veiled, of the social life it grows out of, and evaluation (with lively possibilities of rejection) of the way society handles history."[44] While Turner's use of symbolic analysis[45] in anthropology was not a recognized mode of analysis when Hurston was an anthropology student or a practicing anthropologist, his description of the critical possibilities that performance offers societies fits well into my reading of the work that Hurston embarked on in writing a text such as *Mules and Men*. Moreover, because Turner's emphasis is on the way in which cultural performance may illuminate social power relations, his work allows us to consider how Hurston may have been engaging with cultural performance, even before Turner introduced the dramaturgical phase to anthropology, to offer a critique of mainstream ways of knowing and representing blackness in the world. It is in Hurston's U.S.-based ethnography,

Mules and Men, then, that we see a clear articulation of the way performance both stages and offers the opportunity to articulate black modern subjectivity within the setting of the rural American South.

Hurston uses staging in the representation of her process of collecting black cultural production in the rural South to disrupt method, form, and genre; she ends up producing an ethnographic text in which residual evidence of black multiplicity and modernity in nonurban locations is evident. Using performance as both an activity and a literary trope in her writing, tapping into the discipline of anthropology, and committing to reimagining the role of both ethnography and ethnographer, Hurston creates documents of black folk culture that seek to resist black exoticization and marginalization that often marked the consumption of black cultural production during the early part of the twentieth century.

But one must begin to consider if it is possible to embrace potentially damaging notions of authentic blackness in order to deconstruct them. Moreover, analysis of Hurston's ethnographic work forces one to explore whether this embrace can be carried out without caricaturing the black people whose humanity she wishes to expose. These concerns might have been what motivated Hurston to combine in various renditions of her work ethnography, performance, and creative writing. As Cheryl Wall has argued of Hurston's ethnographic writing,

> The cultural relativity of anthropology freed Hurston
> from the need to defend her subjects' alleged inferiority.
> She could discard behavioral explanations drawn from
> racial mythology. Eatonville blacks were neither exotic nor
> primitive; they had simply selected different characteris-
> tics from what Ruth Benedict, another pioneering anthro-
> pologist trained by Boas, called the "great arc of human
> potentialities."[46]

I would take Wall's observation a bit further and argue that rather than just discarding the imagery of primitivism, Hurston chose to walk into the sites, sounds, and stories of the "primitive" to encourage readers to reconsider what it meant to be both "modern" and "primitive."

When Zora Neale Hurston published *Mules and Men* in 1935,[47] she had already spent eight years with the material, conducting the majority of her collecting between 1927 and 1930 and revising the book for publication between 1930 and 1932. With *Mules and Men*, Hurston was able not only to earn the support of her academic mentor, Franz Boas, but to shift the nature of ethnographic writing for her own benefit. Serving as the reader's gatekeeper and Hurston's anthropological authenticator, Boas notes in his preface to Hurston's text that the merit of her study rests in the fact that her race is the same as those whom she is studying:

> It is the great merit of Miss Hurston's work that she entered into the homely life of the southern Negro as one of them and was fully accepted as such by the companions of her childhood. Thus she has been able to penetrate through the affected demeanor by which the Negro excludes the White observer effectively from participating in his true inner life. . . . Added to all this is the charm of a lovable personality and of a revealing style which makes Miss Hurston's work an unusual contribution to our knowledge of the true inner life of the Negro.[48]

Critics have made much of Boas's emphasis on Hurston's race as key to her ability to penetrate the culture of black Americans. In his preface, Boas also presumes that what Hurston has procured for the field of anthropology with a text such as *Mules and Men* is insight into the collective psyche of a race: and then a reproduction of that psyche in prose. Boas is concerned with Hurston's ability to uncover some sort of "inner truth" about black humanity that had heretofore been inaccessible to the "traditional" (read: white) anthropologist.

However, Hurston makes no such truth claims. She begins *Mules and Men* noting that her ability to collect black folklore was like being thrown back into the "crib of negroism" that she had been born into. For Hurston, anthropology merely offered her the methods for distancing herself from the materials so that she could "see" and "read" them. Before becoming a professional, Hurston believed herself too close and the subject matter too intimate, like a "tight chemise," for her to see the inherent value in the stories of her culture. In fact, in her introduction to *Mules and Men*, Hurston solidifies Boas's sense that her collection is a superior addition to anthropology because earlier black folklore collections compiled by white men were inevitably handicapped by the fact that "the Negro, in spite of his open-faced laughter, his seeming acquiescence, is particularly evasive."[49] So while many have read this as Hurston's embrace of the disciplinary distance necessary for the collection of culture, Hurston's decision to frame *Mules* with the story of her return to her childhood home of Eatonville creates not merely distance but a stage for her to perform on, as well as a place for other black people in the study to become actors rather than merely "informants." Hurston embraces the performance of black evasiveness in order to produce rather than to uncover "truths."

In addition to performance allowing Hurston's "informants" to become characters and actors within her text, Hurston's ethnographic work occasions new ways to think about the role of the ethnographer. It is particularly innovative the way Hurston writes herself into these ethnographic texts as a character, but I believe the true innovation of the text rests in her capacity to present ethnographic collection as a performance, thereby calling the objectivity of the discipline into question. As Robert Hemenway notes, Hurston takes on the role of emcee in order to craft her only recognized ethnography, *Mules and Men*. The position of emcee allows Hurston to adopt a narrative stance that makes the reader a witness to "a midwife participating in the birth of the body of folklore."[50] Hemenway is mixing metaphors here: he describes Hurston's narrative persona as simultaneously performing the work of emceeing and midwifery. More than that, however, if emceeing is historically male work and midwifery historically female work, then Hemenway's metaphor is internally contradictory with regard to its understanding of Hurston's performance work. But it is a mixed metaphor that is useful because it encourages us to imagine mixed methods as a means for intervening and innovating, which is exactly how Hurston's ethnographic writing was able to achieve a varied and sometimes contradictory set of objectives. Guiding the readers between, for instance, the conversations that mostly rural black men have while sitting on porches and the hoodoo ceremonies performed by powerful priestesses, Hurston works to create continuities where we might presume there are none. This is not to say that Hurston eliminates gender, regional, and national differences, contradictions that I will shortly explore more deeply, but that she understands that the role of the emcee is to create a space for all the performers to present what they have to offer, while also engaging in the performance herself. *Mules and Men* becomes a stage that makes readers privy to black folk culture but also highlights the process by which Hurston births some of the first black-collected, black American folklore. Thus, more than *Mules and Men*'s content, its presentation style makes the ethnography a text that requires us the explore how gender, form, and content play both against and with one another. *Mules and Men* ultimately offers us the tools with which we can begin to understand *Tell My Horse* (1938), her underappreciated experimental ethnography.[51]

Being an emcee exposes the performative nature of culture but also implicates the production of ethnographic occasions and texts as performances in their own right. This is to say, Hurston's representation of ethnographic collection centralizes performance's integral relationship to scientific objectivity. To understand Hurston as a master of ceremony is to look at the way she presents herself in the textual representation of her fieldwork as a purposeful attempt to break the façade of objectivity that underlies the production of ethnographies. Hurston begins *Mules* by framing herself in relationship to the "stage" that will house much of the early collecting she does when she arrives in her childhood home: "As I crossed the Maitland-Eatonville Township line I could see a group on the store porch. I was delighted. The town had not changed. Same love of talk and song."⁵² As we watch Hurston approach her collection site, we are given access to both the personal excitement she feels in going home and the underlying sense that Hurston knows she is entering a performance space (the store porch) in which she will both document and participate. In this instance, an emcee, taking center stage, calls attention to the ethnographic performance shared between the subjects and producers of ethnography. I wish to capture the sense of scientific detachment that a discipline such as anthropology attempts to cultivate, while also suggesting that this detachment rests on the extensive cultural mediation inherent in framing ethnographic occasions that the ethnographer documents.

The paradox between ethnography and performance captivates many contemporary critics of Hurston, encouraging them to be attentive to the ways in which Hurston was aware of the mediation of ethnography and was invested, due to racial politics of the period, in disrupting the disciplinary methods even as she employed them. This distinction is very different, then, from the work of many contemporary anthropologists, such as Victor Turner, who turn to performances (both religious rituals and less sacred performances) as sites of investigation. I am suggesting that instead of merely investigating folk tales told on the storefront porch or hoodoo rituals enacted in the dead of the night, Hurston exposes the ways in which the act of collecting is a performance in and of itself; it is a ritual and, as such, deserving of its own analysis and/or deconstruction. Thus, her role as emcee, as textual performer and facilitator, encourages revision and reconsideration of the core principles regarding how one analyzes and represents cultures under investigation,⁵³ especially as they relate to race, gender, and even expressions of nationalism.

Hurston's calling to the reader's attention the conditions of ethnographic production is further illuminated by the reality that Hurston eventually stages some of the black folk culture about which she had written to Langston Hughes. Hurston spent her life steadfast in her interest in but variously success-ful at staging theatrical "concert" performances and black folk dramas. Her most successful staging came in the form of a 1932 concert by the title *The Great Day*, which was billed as "A Pro-gram of Original Negro Folklore." The concert traces the day in the life of a railroad work camp in Florida and culminates in a Bahamian fire dance. Staging work and leisure, Hurston is able to capture the duality of black life that existed in rural America in the early part of the twentieth century. More than that, *The Great Day* provides a cross-section of black diasporic life within this traditional rural American setting. Representing the interconnected lives of an international black community, or the black diaspora it might be called today, on American soil is a topic Hurston explores more extensively in her 1937 novel *Their Eyes Were Watching God*. Additionally, as I talk about later in this chapter, Hurston's relationship to the black diaspora is always mediated by her privileging of black Americanness. Besides highlighting the lives of a segment of the population on the verge of being representationally overwhelmed by "New Negro" discourse, Hurston's commitment to notions of *timeli-ness* as opposed to *timelessness* with regard to black folks, as well as her inclusion of black diasporic subjects in her representations of the rural South, undermines dichotomies of black urban/rural, cosmopolitan/local that traditionally mark critiques of black folk culture. Rather than break clean the divides between "Old" and "New" Negroes, rural and urban blacks, or parochial and cosmopolitan black subjects, Hurston's stage work intro-duces the reality that such dichotomies can exist at the same time without rendering one less important than another.

The distinction I make between the terms *timeliness* and *timelessness* works against the grain of much of Hurston criti-cism that regards Hurston's commitment to black folk culture with suspicion, at the very least.[54] Hurston's work resists the temporal stagnation[55] inherent in the notion that the folk retain

and live within a preindustrial landscape.[56] This distinction, as
I argued earlier, is what allows Hurston to imagine and represent black modernity in the midst of presumed primitivism of
the American South. Her notion that texts, black people, and
black art are always "in the making" provides a sharp contrast
to the underlying assumptions made by the dichotomous but
stagnant ways of describing black cultural production of the
period as versions of either the "New Negro" or the "primitive."
Hurston often found her work sandwiched between the two.
Marking two possibilities—"The New Negro," with its narrative
of black progress and arrival, and the "primitive," a narrative
of decline—leaves little room for the process of "becoming" in
black cultural production that Hurston was developing in her
ethnographic work. In both cases, the black cultural producer is
unable to develop a dynamic world representation.

Laboring for Black Modernity

Predating the postmodern crisis of ethnographic authority,[57]
Hurston's ethnographies are at their center explorations into the
distinct practices that constitute black culture in that interim
between the "New" and "Old" Negro. This is not to say that
Hurston is interested in a monolithic vision of black culture, but
she does seem to imagine one that is diasporic and exceeds the
particularity that national boundaries create and imply. I would
like to be clear, however, that her interest in the black diaspora
is only as this might be mediated by black Americanness. While
the *Great Day* performance makes use of Bahamian fire danc-
ing, it insists on illustrating how this dance and culture can be
integrated into the cultural experiences that take place in rural
black America. In this sense, the working-class subjectivity that
Hurston values above all others is that which is expressed and
experienced on U.S. soil, even if it is diasporic in content.

I would argue that *Mules and Men*, as Hurston's American ethnography, has three overarching concerns: illustrating that black
folk culture is always in the process of becoming, representing

black folks as modern subjects, and, finally, combining these two aims to produce a representation of black American rurality that resists the long-held notion that northward urban migration is the only method capable of producing black modernity. In fact, the first official folk tale Hurston collects when she returns to Eatonville is done so on her way to a party in the neighboring town.[58] What is particularly interesting about the folk story, which concerns a slave's outwitting his master, is not its content but rather that it is told in transit. Hurston's friend James tells the story in order to entice her to use her car to ferry him and his cohort to the adjacent town's party. James and Hurston engage in a barter that exposes James's understanding that the value of black folk stories is tied to modern luxuries, in this case a car, that enhances one's leisure-time experiences. Hurston's text provides an embedded commentary on black folk's nuanced sense that the relationship between folk culture and modernity is one in which the former might be manipulated to secure the latter. This is important because it creates a commodity relationship that is the hallmark of modern capitalism, which flies in the face of anthropological notions of "authenticity" and "timelessness" of black folk culture and rural black folks.

In addition to documenting the Eatonville residents' understanding of the way black folk culture might be exchanged for modern conveniences, Hurston makes clear that the social value of black folk tales and folk practices such as hoodoo do not rest simply in arbitrage. For instance, Hurston joins a group of men on their way to work at a timber mill, in order to collect stories because, she is told, "they lied a plenty while they worked."[59] During the late nineteenth and early twentieth century, much of Florida's economy rested on the lumber extraction of virgin pines and cypress trees, a process that was facilitated by the railroad. The working-class men and women of Hurston's ethnography are part of the U.S. economic expansion and modernization that often goes unnoticed in traditional readings of a black folklore collection such as Hurston's *Mules*. I believe the oversight is facilitated by the fact that the majority of the stories that Hurston documents while she spends time with these saw-mill and turpentine camp workers reference a set of plantation characters and narratives that appear out of date and step with the literary representations of "New Negroness." If upon first impression these highly allegorical stories seem retrograde, I suggest that the importance of these stories to the text, and to the sawmill workers, is twofold.

First, these plantation tales create an embedded critique of the contemporary labor system in which the majority of Hurston's "informants" find themselves. That is to say, while slavery is no longer a viable system of labor exploitation, Hurston's informants use folklore to expose the ways in which their working lives mirror those of "slave-master" scenarios. For instance, when the group of workers that Hurston joins in order to collect is delayed due to unknown circumstances, the men comment on their work delay by telling a story about slavery:

> "Looka here, folkses," Jim Presley exclaimed. "Wese a half hour behind schedule and no swamp boss and no log train here yet. What yo' all reckon is the matter sho' 'nough?"
>
> "Must be something terrible when white folks get slow about putting us to work."
>
> "Yeah," says Good Black. "You know back in slavery Ole Mass was out in de field sort of lookin' things over, when a shower of rain came up. The field hands was glad it rained so they could knock off for a while. So one slave named John says:
>
> 'More rain, more rest.'
>
> Ole Mass says, 'What's dat you say?'
>
> John says, 'More rain, more grass.'
>
> There goes the big whistle. We ought to be in the woods almost."
>
> The big whistle blew as the saw-mill boomed and shrilled and pretty soon the log-train came racking along. No flats for logs behind the little engine. The foreman dropped off the tender as the train stopped.[60]

This exchange between Presley and Good Black is not simplistic enough to make the argument that work conditions under slavery and postemancipation are synonymous; the men offer no direct equation. Instead, the easy transition from their contemporary moment to "back in slavery" points out the utility of those stories for the men in understanding coping mechanisms and tricks for living as a black American worker. But more interesting is the lack of transitioning language to accompany the move to a story about slavery and then back to the present lives of Hurston's informants. While the movement back is introduced by the phrase "back in slavery," the movement forward in time is abrupt and lacks any demarcation in time. There is no language available to document this transition. I suggest that Hurston notes this in order to highlight the way time fails to account for the lingering resonances of slavery in the black American worker's life. Since the "texture of freedom is laden with the vestiges of slavery,"[61] not only do these men see the value in folklore for coping with their present lives, but Hurston additionally denies the easy severing of a connection from work under slavery to black work postemancipation. This seamlessness has embedded in it, then, the very sort of social-racial critique that Hazel Carby suggests is lacking.[62]

Secondly, the result of linking these temporally discrete moments resists the easy dismissal of rural black folks as preindustrial subjects; as Hurston slyly suggests, the slave system and slaves, by association, were foundational to the creation of American modernity. In line with Paul Gilroy's contention that the intellectual history of modernity must move beyond the inclusion of black commentaries and critiques of the modern to an analysis of how black people and black culture have constructed and reconstructed notions of the modern,[63] Hurston's text makes apparent that black labors from the antebellum well into the twentieth century have ushered the U.S. economy and infrastructure into the modern world. For instance, the men exchange insults as they wait for a train carrying timber. Again the proximity among their bodies, their exchange of folklore, and the objects/signs of modernity illuminate Hurston's argument regarding black rurality.

The Miracle of the Stove: Making Black American Modernity from Afar

If *Mules and Men* represented Hurston's attempt to emcee the performance of black American rural modernity, then *Tell My Horse* was the continuation of that project on "alien soil." And while it might be a continuation of the project of modernity that Hurston undertook in *Mules and Men*, critics since *Tell My Horse*'s original 1938 publication have been fairly negative. An early reviewer characterized the book as a "curious mixture of remembrances, travelogue, sensationalism, and anthropology," noting that the "remembrances are vivid, the travelogue tedious, the sensationalism reminiscent of Seabrook, and the anthropology a mélange of misinterpretation and exceedingly good folklore."[64] What becomes obvious from this review is that as early as 1938, Hurston's text struck a contradictory cord with readers. Moreover, her biographer, Robert Hemenway, argues that *Tell My Horse* is her "poorest book, chiefly because of its form."[65] Documenting her research in Jamaica and Haiti, with particular emphasis on Haitian voodoo practices, the book has long been dismissed because of its noncompliance with the disciplinary expectations required of professional ethnographic writing. For instance, the text is multigenred, consisting of journalism, political commentary, and travelogue; Hurston vacillates between subjective and objective voice, a technique that worked in *Mules* but is not sustainable in *Tell My Horse* because of her lack of connection to the materials about which she writes; she explores her two locations, Jamaica and Haiti, without offering any comparative or cohesive analysis for their connection; she displays an unmistakable amount of U.S. nationalism and ethnocentricism, especially surrounding her political analysis of post-U.S.-occupied Haiti (1915–1934); and she ultimately fails to offer any final assessments of Haiti through cultural extraction and analysis.[66] Deborah Gordon assesses the seeming generic incoherence of *Tell My Horse* to argue that the text continues the innovative ethnographic work Hurston began in *Mules* by capturing and displaying the "conflicting visions that fieldwork involved."[67] In other words, *Tell My Horse*, bypassing the professional expectations of ethnographic writing, is a text that necessarily opens up the field for exploring issues of race, nationalism, and gender. Lomothe asserts that the generic fissures and unevenness that mark *Tell My Horse* might be best read as "narrative dissonances," which Lomathe suggests are created by the fact that "she was doubly marginalized as an African American and a woman," making her performance of ethnographer "a delicate and fraught operation."[68] These narrative dissonances and the opening up of the genre become especially important in light of Hurston's subjectivity as an African American woman doing international work because they introduce the notion of performance and staging that was so important to her capacity to render black American rural modernity.

Like many contemporary scholars regarding Hurston's *Tell My Horse*, I believe the text resists definitive readings that either condemn or praise Hurston's representation of black Caribbean culture. For instance, Ifeoma Nwankwo contends that Hurston's ability to create a black (diasporic) folk community through the use of techniques that allow her to shift between ethnographic insider and outsider in her U.S. research becomes increasing unstable as she moves away from the United States. I would go a step further to suggest that this instability is so much eroded that by the time Hurston reaches Haiti, the ease with which she deconstructs hierarchies, such as race and genre, is often superseded by her desire to maintain a national hierarchy that places the United States at the helm of international ethics, morals, and power. Maintaining insider status becomes less important to Hurston the longer she stays in Haiti. As Nwankwo concludes, "The work of Zora Neale Hurston, while pioneering within the context of the U.S. black (women's) intellectual thought, also provides an example of the shades of the ethnocentrism that have continued to haunt transnational engagements between black people."[69] Hurston's U.S. nationalism overwhelms her willingness to fully participate in the equalizing of national identities. Ultimately, I believe *Tell My Horse* resists the label of traditional black diasporic writing because of its failure to fully participate in a system of black global community. And while this is a meaningful critique for a text that has the potential to be diasporic, its lack of diasporic community building is central to understanding Hurston's larger cultural work with ethnography.

Hurston's insistence on American nationalism is entrenched by the fact that she assumes her most "traditional" anthropologist persona while collecting in Jamaica and Haiti. It is this embrace of the "anthropological persona" that allowed her to begin to craft a narrative of difference that would ultimately distinguish her, and by association, African Americans generally from the black Caribbean people she analyzes. In contrast to her entrance to Eatonville in *Mules and Men*, which she frames not only as a "delightful" homecoming but with the voices and faces of people,[70] Hurston enters the Caribbean (via Jamaica) through an interface with the landscape. Working within a primitivist version of ethnography, Hurston's entry into Jamaican culture through its landscape does the uneasy work of tying the people she introduces to the unchanging landscape of the island. She additionally narrates that her interest in the island is due to its ability to estrange her from her own reality: "What with the music and the *barbaric ritual*, I became interested and took up around the place."[71] So if hoodoo in the United States was far from the "laughable" "ritualistic orgies of Broadway and popular fiction,"[72] then Hurston's embrace and representation of voodoo practices within the Caribbean as "barbaric rituals" signifies an evaluative shift in her relationship to the materials she collects and analyzes in Jamaica and Haiti.

This evaluative shift does not end with her description of the rituals she encounters. In addition to assigning a value judgment on voodoo in the Caribbean, Hurston also describes Jamaicans as exhibiting backward racial politics because she believes they are a group of people for whom blackness is always denied in favor of whiteness: "Everywhere else a person is white or black by birth, but it is so arranged in Jamaica that a person may be black by birth but white by proclamation. That is, he gets himself declared legally white."[73] This is a complicated statement and further illustrates my argument regarding Hurston's resistance to the easy truth claims on which most academic disciplines rest. On one level, it points to Hurston's inability to understand the Caribbean's less rigid racial system, which differs from the U.S. "one-drop" practice in which individuals with any amount of black "blood" are classified as black. On another level, however, it speaks to her commitment to the elevation of black people and culture as a form of resistance to white supremacy. So when Hurston contends that "a new day is in sight for Jamaica" and that "the black people of Jamaica are beginning to respect themselves,"[74] she is offering a narrative of racial progress for the Caribbean, again via Jamaica. Yet this narrative of racial progress is not without its evaluative impulse, which implies that U.S.-based blacks have achieved a superior level of racial consciousness. Thus, more than merely a critique of Jamaican racial politics, Hurston's evaluation does the work of establishing U.S.-based racial politics as the model for the rest of the black diaspora. Americans come into being as truly modern subjects when compared to their non-U.S., premodern counterparts in *Tell My Horse.*

Hurston's discursive impulse to imply that Jamaican and Haitian blacks cannot be entrusted with ownership and/or proper valuation of their folk culture is especially telling in light of Sibylle Fischer's assessment of the role that black Haiti has played in construction of the Western world's discourse on modernity. Fischer argues that Haiti's revolution and, by extension, black modernity in the New World have been denied by the West since the Enlightenment because the idea of black revolutionaries— as revolution, freedom, and liberty are constructed by Western Enlightenment discourse—poses too large an ethical and philosophical threat to Western superiority. Fischer's assertion that this denial takes the form of *disavowal*, which "requires us to identify what is being disavowed, by whom, and for what reason,"[75] points to the plausibility of reading Hurston's ethnography of the Caribbean simultaneously as a product of black nationalism and also as seeking to deny the possibility of such revolutionary blackness taking place off the shores of "continental America."[76] I suspect that Hurston valued the notion of black revolution, but her identity as the only black female anthropologist within white academic and publishing worlds may have mandated her disavowal of Haiti as the seat of that generative racial revolution in her ethnographic work.[77]

There are many instances within *Tell My Horse* in which one can see Hurston grappling with a desire to create a narrative of black revolution against the desire to adhere to an international hierarchy that places the United States at its pinnacle. For instance, while taking stock of the gravitas of Accompong's[78] black revolutionary significance as the "oldest settlement of freedmen in the Western world,"[79] Hurston notes that in the twentieth century it appears to her as a failed civilization that has made little progress beyond its early freedom. Accompong is so backward, in fact, that it is Hurston who introduces the village to the modern cooking convenience of a stove. Noting that the women of the village are forced to cook over an open fire, Hurston suggests to the village leader, Captain Rowe, that they build a stove under Hurston's design and instruction. Once the stove is completed, Hurston tells readers that it was such a success and novelty that "many of the Maroons came down to look at the miracle." Whether or not Hurston is sincere in her desire to "save" the village women from having to inhale smoke every day, her narration of the stove's construction and significance to the village effectually conveys her modernity and the maroons' "primitiveness," a word she uses to describe them and their culture twice before she introduces the stove. The miracle of the stove, then, provides hard evidence for her earlier dismissal of the maroons' lack of progress: "I could not help remembering that a whole civilization and the mightiest nation on earth had grown up on the mainland since the first runaway slave had taken refuge in these mountains."[80] So while Accompong may be the home of the West's first black freedpeople, the United States is home to a mighty, modern civilization, of which Hurston is a part and product.

In stark contrast to the subject position of emcee that I argue Hurston employs in *Mules and Men*, she dons her traditional anthropological cap as participant-observer in *Tell My Horse*. For example, while collecting in Accompong, she rebuffs Rowe's offer to stage a ceremonial dance for her. Seemingly disgusted by the idea, Hurston writes that she declines Rowe's offer because she is too experienced to "fall for staged-dance affairs," and "self-experience has taught [her] that those staged affairs are never the same as the real thing."[81] I make note of this rebuff because it flies in the face of Hurston's use of performance to aid in the collection of materials for *Mules* but also calls into question my earlier argument regarding her interest in undermining the objective truth claims we usually associate with ethnographic collection. Additionally, Hurston's attention to hoodoo ceremonies and traditions in the American South was invested in creating a dynamic and modern black American subjectivity, while it appears that her aim in collecting in the Caribbean stands in stark contrast. And whereas she was an active participant in the experiences she documents in *Mules*, Hurston appears more of a passive observer in *Tell My Horse*: "I'd heard a great deal about their [the maroons'] primitive medicines and wanted to know about that. I was interested in vegetable poisons and their antidote. So I just sat around and waited," Hurston writes.[82] Again, we have the loaded language that privileges the West in her evocation of the "primitive," and Hurston is able not only to establish her own anthropological authority but also to reinscribe notions of "natural" and "authentic" primitivism with regard to her Caribbean subjects. Likewise, unlike when she is in New Orleans, Hurston is merely a participant-observer in Jamaica, waiting and encountering cultural truths with little admittance of the possibility of inauthenticity and performance that marked her earlier project. In short, we watch as Hurston re-creates herself as a black, international, intellectual, modern subject at the expense of blacks within the Caribbean. Our desire as scholars and critics might be to extend to Hurston some leeway when it comes to her ability to fashion a black community abroad. Many critics, in fact, have turned to Hurston's gender politics when her racial politics have proven suspect. I would argue that what one finds can be said of Hurston's relationship to nationalism must also be said of black female agency within a text such as *Tell My Horse*. I make this assertion in light of many less critical readings of *Tell My Horse* that emphasize its feminism begin by highlighting Hurston's opening remarks about voodoo in Haiti, which she characterizes as the unapologetically female religion of the people:

> Voodoo is a religion of creation and life. . . . "What is the truth?" Dr. Holly asked me, and knowing that I could not answer him he answered himself through a voodoo ceremony in which the Mambo, that is the priestess, richly dressed is asked this question ritualistically. She replies by towing back her veil and revealing her sex organs. The ceremony means that this is the infinite, the ultimate truth. There is no mystery beyond the mysterious source of life. . . . It is considered the highest honor for all males participating to kiss her organ of creation, for Damballa, the god of gods has permitted them to come face to face with the truth.[83]

This passage is inevitably an empowering moment in the text and marks it as a potential site for us to imagine Hurston as what Shameem Black would describe as a "cosmofeminist." Black defines cosmofeminism as the practice of feminist community building across national borders. Just as "cosmopolitanism attempts to encode an elusive ideal within imperfect histories,"[84] cosmofeminism attempts to make use of female biological similarity to enact transnational activism. And why not? As Houston Baker has argued, hoodoo in *Mules and Men* was a site for female empowerment,[85] so it would be easy to attempt to argue that Hurston's attention to voodoo marks a continued interest in creating feminist community abroad. Yet race and gender have always been foundational to formulations of nationalism. That is to say, these three work in tandem to produce particular notions of what it means to be a modern citizen, an especially contested category for blacks living in the United States during the twentieth century.

So whereas many critics document unifying potential not only among blacks of the diaspora but also among Hurston's ethnographic works themselves, I believe that the dissonances surrounding Hurston's representation of gender and community between *Mules* and *Tell My Horse* further illustrate my argument regarding her commitment to imagining black revolutionary action and black modernity, but only as it is carried out on American soil. From her emphasis on male spaces in her Jamaica section in her fifth chapter, which begins with the statement, "It is a curious thing to be a woman in the Caribbean after you have been a woman in these United States," Hurston resists an easy labeling of "feminist" in *Tell My Horse*. In fact, her fifth chapter hinges on a binarism that places the Caribbean's male chauvinism at odds with the "laws, privileges and pay and perquisites" given to every female American citizen at birth.[86] I believe this chapter's sentiment regarding superiority of black American women's equality seems especially confounding when one considers that Hurston wrote *Their Eyes Were Watching God*[87] while conducting her research in Haiti. *Their Eyes* takes place within the United States and centers on a single female protagonist, Janie. This novel both commiserates and contradicts the notion of Janie's grandmother that black women are the mules of the world. The majority of *Their Eyes*, then, is Janie's journey to humanity in spite of the systems and people who attempt to dehumanize her. It remains to be seen whether Hurston actually believes female humanity is impossible in chauvinistic Jamaica. While Daphne Lamothe contends that Hurston's treatment of Jamaican racial and gender politics is ironic,[88] I believe irony invites a too-positive critical intervention. Instead, Hurston's assessment of Caribbean gender politics performs the rhetorical work of blocking the reader's impulse to make contiguous the experiences of black women of the United States and those of the Caribbean. Again, in the face of her own contiguously written fiction and her established gender politics, Hurston is unwilling to permit that modern womanhood is possible outside the confines of the United States.

In spite of the moments that center around a form of black female agency that voodoo creates, *Tell My Horse* is also filled with moments of female dissonance and disunion that have the effect not of dissolving the feminist impulses present in Hurston's work but of removing the myth of easy black and female unification. Hurston's work defies our contemporary notions of diaspora and feminism in order to make a grander statement about the importance of local black cultures. Embodied within her writing is a sense of the black folk's particularity. Hurston resists the easy diasporic and gender alignments we as contemporary feminists might desire, in order to offer up a space for black Americanness carved out in relationship to Jamaican and Haitian "un-Americanness." The conditions under which black Americanness is carved in *Tell My Horse* is dubious, but Hurston's insightful understanding of her discipline and the ways in which ethnographic texts might be manipulated by African Americans who aim to orchestrate claims on modern American identity is profound. Hurston creates herself as American, black, and modern within *Tell My Horse* by highlighting Haitian and Jamaican primitivism.

In order to orchestrate such a feat, Hurston participates in a form of discursive imperial containment that makes *Tell My Horse* quite a complicated text. Diaspora, colonial anthropology, and American nationalism collide in *Tell My Horse* to produce not a fractured text but one that wants us to see value in blackness that rests on American nationalism. The latter objective certainly seems at odds with a progressive reading of Hurston's investment in diasporic thought—which seeks to unify people of African descent outside of the confines of the nation-state paradigm—but I would argue that such an objective may have never been Hurston's at all. Contemporary critics eager to either critique or "prove" Hurston's commitment to black diasporic visions might instead consider Hurston's use of the Caribbean not only as a foil for black American modernity but also as part of those fractures and fissures of black diasporic thought that make it a practice and not a reality. That is to say, Hurston's disavowal may sever the easy links that scholars often wish to present in order to provide, at the very least, the discursive space for antinational forms of black belonging, but what it leaves in the place of that perpetual absence is a sense of both the links and chinks in the chains of the black diaspora. Hurston may understand the impulse to move around the black Atlantic world as an African American woman, but as an American, she is still bound by mainland notions of modernity and power. More than that, she is invested in making headway in the long project of black belonging and citizenship within the United States. It is a pity that this project is carried out at the expense of her Caribbean racial counterparts, but acknowledging the ill effects of the project does not necessarily undermine entirely the utility of Hurston's work, when considered within the very particular frame of U.S. racial politics. Some critics may consider this act parochial, and that it is, but we might also consider the rhetorical moves necessitated by a nation, an academic discipline, and a publishing world for a black woman anthropologist in the early part of the twentieth century.

Langston Hughes once said that Hurston was the only person who could walk the streets of Harlem asking random people for the opportunity to measure their skulls. Such an intimate act and one that has the potential (and history) to amass a data set that could be misused to reinforce notions of black intellectual inferiority might seem at odds with a writer who imagined herself part of "the folk." Yet, as Hughes's remembrance highlights, Hurston was adept at working within the field of anthropology in a way that discouraged simple black objectification, at least when that collection was done in the United States. I am struck most by Hughes's description of Hurston's tendency to pick only the heads that she found interesting, because such careful selection may have been what allowed her to pursue a suspect science without making her black subjects feel like specimens, even if they were. There was a value in Hurston's selection process. And it is just this contradiction, between treating people as specimens and treating them as differently but equally modern subjects, that makes Hurston's ethnographic work critical. As we move further into the twentieth century, into a world in which U.S. global contact and influence become increasingly significant, Hurston's long career offers some insights into the lives and careers of a few other black writers. Richard Wright, whose career overlapped and then overshadowed Hurston's, as well as Himes and Baldwin, struggled with how to represent and be represented both inside and outside a country that increasingly marginalized their bodies and their bodies of work. Hurston's attempts, and the expense of such attempts, serve as a model for understanding how Wright, Baldwin, and Himes negotiated the conflicting calls of nationalism, gender, and race to produce some of the most interesting works of African American art in the midst of American expansion and as the United States struggled to live up to its stated ideals of freedom, justice, and inclusion.

2 / Escape through Ethnography: Literary Regionalism and the Image of Nonracial Alignment in Richard Wright's Travel Writing

What has my geographical position on earth got to do with the faults or merits of a book?

RICHARD WRIGHT[1]

I'm reading a book of the rituals for primitive people. Are there really any primitive people? Or, perhaps I ought to ask, if not all people are really primitive? Is it not that only conditions are primitive and not the people?

RICHARD WRIGHT[2]

"I am a rootless man," Richard Wright declares very early in *White Man, Listen!* (1957). It is a simple utterance meant to capture the tie between his statelessness and his humanity. "I declare unabashedly that I like and even cherish the state of abandonment, of aloneness; it does not bother me; indeed, to me it seems the natural, inevitable condition of man, and I welcome it," says Wright.[3] Many readers will note that Wright's statement is shaped by his acquaintance with French existentialism; but if we consider that his personal and literary roots are grounded in Jim Crow America—roots publicly solidified with the publication of his autobiographical novel *Black Boy* (1945)—the statement illuminates the complex relationship among geography, blackness, and humanity in Wright's work. The connectivity between these subjects is what Paul Gilroy, over a decade ago in *The Black Atlantic* (1993), challenged us to explore more deeply. For Gilroy, what Wright wrote while living in Paris symbolized black writing that contradicted the "ethnic absolutism" that has historically characterized black political culture.[4] Wright moved from the American South, then from Chicago, and then from New York to finally rest in Paris, where he lived until his death in 1960. Gilroy understands that movement—away from the particularity of African American life and culture in the United States to places and topics as far ranging as Spain and Spanish religion to Indonesia and Asian identity—as a move away from essentialism. Wright's movement might be seen as a series of moves away from "the real, true essence of things, the invariable and fixed properties which define the 'whatness' of a given entity," as Diane Fuss has described essentialism.[5]

But such an understanding of movement suffers from, among other things, being a broad-stroke association between movement and intellectual change. Such assumptive association has the destructive potential to inadvertently simplify and unify what was a series of troublesome physical, political, and artistic shifts in Wright's life and career as a writer. Gilroy argues that Wright's move from "an earlier exclusive interest in the liberation of African Americans from their particular economic exploitation and political oppression"[6] to more international themes signaled an evolution in his thought. For my own work, however, I am most interested in destabilizing contemporary Wright scholarship's impulse to commend the travel writings Wright produced between the time of his self-exile to Paris and his death in 1960 simply for representing a denationalized set of themes. The language of denationalization only privileges black thinkers/activists when they couple the concerns of African Americans with what are perceived to be more global concerns. While comparative analysis is fruitful for illuminating the ways in which black American culture is tied to a network of antiracist projects around the world, I worry that such privileging may inadvertently imply that African American cultural production and its analysis is not valuable in and of itself.

Thus, rather than assigning a pre- or post–African American interest to Wright's work, this chapter will explore what might be lost and gained by Wright's movement and disassociation from the United States. Paying close attention to tension among race, roots, and humanity in Wright's travel writing, I encourage a reconsideration of the uneasy literary ties that bound Richard Wright to American racial segregation, even in his most global writing. What follows, then, is an exploration of how "rootless" Wright remained tethered to U.S. racial constructs by the conventions of American literary regionalism and, by extension, American racial segregation's influence on his "black American writing." Moving past common criticisms that conceive of Wright's expatriation as either time spent alienated from African American concerns or as time spent nurturing a maturity that would take him from his provincial focus on African American culture, I argue that it might be more useful to consider his attachment to African Americans as exhibiting something deeper than alienation. When we consider the relationship between the publication history of Wright's autobiographical novel *Black Boy* (1945) and his struggle with American literary regionalism as evidenced in *The Color Curtain* (1956), we can begin to explore what it might have meant to be a black American writing within a global context during the Cold War era. This chapter takes seriously Gilroy's call for an increased focus on Wright's travel writing but concentrates on the role American racial segregation may have played in Wright's most geographically alien texts, *The Color Curtain* and *Black Power* (1954). My aim is to explore the possibility that Wright was not the complete "antiessentialist" at the end of his life that Gilroy contends. In fact, Wright remained into the mid-1950s deeply attached to an essentializing notion of African Americanness and blackness, in general, while simultaneously positing the necessity of racial-political nonalignment. The conflicting impulses to narratively essentialize black Americans while calling for their political nonalignment produced a fractured narrative around African Americanness that Wright found impossible to remediate but necessary to represent.

Black Boy solidified Wright's standing as one of the most important African American voices of the mid-twentieth century regarding U.S. race relations. As a coming-of-age story that highlights the importance of literacy and the possibilities guaranteed by life in the North, *Black Boy* places Wright in step with the black literary tradition dating back to slave narratives, a tradition that often underscores freedom's dependence on literacy and northern migration. Interestingly enough, however, as early as *Black Boy*, Wright prophesied not only his inability to escape the American South but also the possibility that sentiments born in southern soil might bloom elsewhere. "Yet, deep down, I knew that I could never really leave the South, for my feelings had already been formed by the South, for there had been slowly instilled into my personality and consciousness, black though I was, the culture of the South. So, in leaving, I was taking part of the South to transplant in alien soil, to see if it could grow differently, if it could drink of new and cool rains, bend in strange winds, respond to the warmth of other suns, and, perhaps, to bloom," Wright writes in the final pages of *Black Boy*.[7] His quest to transplant in alien, but not northern, soil signifies Wright's early understanding that uprooting would be necessary to achieve a sort of human dignity unheard of in America for black people.

Indeed, Wright's decision to characterize his final travel destination as "alien soil" becomes more interesting when considered in light of *Black Boy*'s publishing history. *Black Boy* is the truncated version of Wright's original but posthumously published novel *American Hunger*. If it had been published as Wright intended, with its deleted second section titled "The Horror and the Glory," *Black Boy* would have recounted his struggles as a black man in the American South *and* North. Unlike *Black Boy*, *American Hunger* ends not with Wright being delivered into the option-laden North but with literature and writing as his only true redeemer. Wright asks and answers,

> What had I got of out living in the south? What had I got out of living in America? I paced the floor, knowing that all I possessed were words and dim knowledge that my

country had shown me no examples of how to live a human life. . . . I wanted to try to build a bridge of words between me and that world outside, that world that was so distant and elusive that it seemed unreal. I would hurl words into this darkness and wait for an echo, and if an echo sounded, no matter how faintly, I would send other words to tell, to march, to fight, to create a sense of the hunger for life that gnaws in us all, to keep alive in our hearts a sense of the inexpressibly human.[8]

With these final words, Wright articulates his desire to use writing in order to catapult himself outside segregated America. For Wright, the United States placed blackness at the center of his identity, with no mention of his humanness. In *American Hunger*, Wright articulates a critical humanist agenda that became the foundation of his future writings. And as the ending of *American Hunger* makes clear, Wright perceives his humanist agenda as incompatible with an American reality.

Jeff Karem tracked the revision process that turned *American Hunger* into *Black Boy*, and what he uncovered is the story of how a few Book-of-the-Month Club judges coerced the revision in order to construct a positive U.S. national image. In the midst of World War II, two judges deemed it best not to offer as damning a critique of the United States' race relations as Wright offered in the last pages of *American Hunger*. Instead they encouraged him to cut the text to just before the protagonist, Richard Wright, leaves the American South for Chicago; this is done in order to "curtail his 'questing adventure' and confine his work to his 'roots,'" Karem notes.[9] "Confining Wright's autobiography to his Southern childhood . . . served to blunt the political impact of his work,"[10] Karem contends, and thereby confined Wright's "criticism exclusively to the South," producing a text that could "pay tribute to American ideals as a whole" and be "a national affirmation, not a national indictment."[11] Wright made the revisions the Book-of-the-Month Club suggested, and *Black Boy* went on to garner the club's prize and inevitable commercial and critical success: the royalties from *Black Boy* sustained Wright into the last years of his life. But Karem also argues that, as a result, Wright emerged "less an artist and more a conduit of factual and folkloric knowledge," and his text, once made regional, "ascribed authority to Wright based on the truths of his Southern past," thereby lessening his "threatening potential for the American present."[12] *Black Boy* is made a regionalist text and, as such, offers Wright no narrative access to the future. Wright is reduced to creating the "literature of memory."

In light of what Wright says as he closes *American Hunger*— "I would hurl words into this darkness and wait for an echo, . . . I would send other words to tell, to march, to fight, to create a sense of the hunger for life"—to have his words made impotent by generic restrictions undermines the power and potential with which he imbues himself as writer, as human. Wright wants his words to change the future, but his critics deaden them—this is important to note because they do this after they had acclaimed his gritty, naturalist novel *Native Son* (1940). But if we consider blackness the ultimate segregated region in the United States, to write from that position is to always be creating regional literature, an idea I elaborate on shortly. This is especially true during the 1940s, when the legal, economic, and psychic conditions of segregation shaped life in both the American North and South. Blacks literally and literarily occupied a space outside the confines of mainstream, white America. Unable to escape the critical expectation to produce regionalist writing—not with texts such as *Uncle Tom's Children*, *Native Son*, and *Black Boy* under his belt—Wright spends the rest of his career attempting to get out of regionalism's shadow. I argue that he does this in two ways in *The Color Curtain*. First, he leaves the United States and assumes the critical stance of being rootless and exilic. And second, he treats African Americans as regional characters within his own texts.

"A Basic Southern Occasion": Establishing Black as a Region

American literary regionalism is the genre of the alienated. It is a genre constituted by narratives about alien places and the people who inhabit them. Growing out of the late nineteenth- and early twentieth-century American realist tradition,[13] regionalism has historically been a literature defined by where and who it is not: urban, white, middle class, and male. As part of the print culture that constitutes the imagined community of the United States, regionalist texts perform the cultural work of bringing the margins to the center, allowing an anxious (urban, white, middle-class, male) readership to take stock of its national cultural holdings with the hope of allaying concerns regarding its own fragmentation. In the United States, the difference implied by regionalism, with its attention to vernacular language and "alien" landscapes, as Ann Kaplan has argued, allowed the nation to imagine a controlled reconstitution in the midst of societal upheavals such as war, urbanization, and immigrant influx. Additionally, regionalist texts allowed these "mainstream" readers the opportunity to solidify their sense of modernity and progress through reading fiction produced at the margins, in places and by people who exist outside the time and troubles of "cosmopolitan development."[14] To that same end, Eric Sundquist characterizes regionalism as the "literature of memory,"[15] which confines it to participating in the hegemonic cultural work of centralizing the reader's subject position and solidifying the temporal distance of the region and its inhabitants from the reader.

Many contemporary revisionists have tried to redeem regional writing from its pejorative status.[16] Yet revisionists tend to be overly concerned with the reception of "regionalist" writing. And while this is a valid concern, it rarely accounts for the sense of burden that a minority or female writer might experience in being associated with the genre. To that end, the burden of the particular has long been associated with African

American writers. Regionalism, with its attention to presenting the margins to the center, allowed numerous African American writers access to the publishing world, while at the same time keeping their representations segregated from the national narrative. "Regionalism made the experience of the socially marginalized into a literary asset, and so made marginality itself a positive authorial advantage," according to Richard Brodhead.[17] In the late nineteenth century, Charles Chesnutt was one of the first African American writer to earn literary recognition for his collection of dialect stories. Yet his authorial advantage was quickly undermined when he attempted to sell novels that tackled seriously the problems of the color line. The failure of Chesnutt's novels, books such as *House behind the Cedars* (1900) and *The Marrow of Tradition* (1901), proved the American readership uninterested in African American commentary on national issues. Likewise, the problem of a dual audience,[18] one black and one white, plagued James Weldon Johnson's ability to render racial protest into the novel form while being commercially viable and pleasing to a white audience that expected a "pleasant excursion into black life as local color."[19] So while many postbellum American writers entered the literary fold through regionalism, unlike their white, male contemporaries, most African American writers were later unable to orchestrate an easy escape from the genre.[20]

In the essay "Regional Particulars and Universal Statement in Southern Writing," writer Albert Murray senses the continued dangers of regionalism for the southern writer. Murray states that the southern writer must "[process] into artistic statement, [stylize] into significance" the "regional particulars—the idiomatic details, the down home conventions, the provincial customs and folkways."[21] Murray is pushing black writing out of the regional and into the universal to facilitate an escape from regionalist othering, because if the writer does not create a work of art that works "time and again, . . . has broad applicability," and "works in the world at large; . . . it has to be rejected as too exclusive, too narrow, or . . . too provincial. Too Southern," according to

Murray.[22] Still more direct, Murray says writers must treat "a basic Southern occasion as a basic American occasion which is in turn a basic contemporary occasion, and thus a basic human occasion."[23] Murray's statement encourages a move away from the particular to themes that will not alienate readers.

Because Murray addresses the particular, geographically specific situation of being a southern writer and writing about the South, his statement resists the easy replacement of "southern" with "black." However, we might be able to expand his concerns to African American writers, since African American literary (cultural) production has historically had the American South at its core. As Houston Baker notes, "black modernism is not only framed by the American south, but also is inextricable— as cognitive and somatic process of performing *blackness* out of or within tight spaces—from specific institutionalizations of human life below the Mason-Dixon."[24] So when Murray says "southern," he is talking precisely about the black southern writer. The parallel becomes more pronounced if we consider the drastic difference between issues raised by his statement on southern writing and by a white southern writer such as Flannery O'Connor. O'Connor makes it clear that the burden of being a southern, regional writer is no burden at all: "To call yourself a Georgia writer is certainly to declare a limitation, but one which, like all limitations, is a gateway to reality. It is a great blessing, perhaps the greatest blessing a writer can have, to find at home what others have to go elsewhere seeking. . . . And most of you and myself and many others are sustained in our writing by the local and the particular and the familiar without loss to our principles or our reason."[25] More important, however, is O'Connor's understanding that the region, particularly the South, needs no translation by or for northerners and is best when appreciated by the local inhabitants. While white southern writers may face the task of having their stories considered integral to the national narrative,[26] black writers face the task of creating black humanity. Unlike Murray, who feels the need to strive for a human story over a southern (black) story, O'Connor never questions the humanness of the art she produces. Since the burden of having once been property is not easily shaken off, Murray's striving for perceived humanness is part and parcel of the African American literary tradition, which began with Phyllis Wheatley's poetry, found itself articulated in Du Bois's *The Souls of Black Folk*, and continues to serve as motivation for many African American writers.

In this monumental way, Murray's view of regional writing differs from his southern peers such as O'Connor, Faulkner, and Twain, all of whom may have found their way to literary production through regional writing. For these southern white writers, the need to transcend the region in order to achieve humanity was not so pressing. Murray's statement exposes the deep-seated quest for humanness,[27] which is also tied to a quest for perceived universal themes and characterizations. Such humanity and universality is an achievement that holds the promise of desegregating the American literary canon. However, the quest for universalism at the expense of African American particularism does very little to deconstruct the literary racial hierarchy; it merely condemns those black texts that are perceived as aligning themselves with local articulations of blackness. Universalism continues framing "blackness" as a pejorative region without recognizing its complexity as a counterpublic sphere.[28] Understanding the fear of literary segregation is central to making sense of many black authors' quests for perceived literary universalism and is especially telling in the case of Richard Wright.

As early as 1937, Wright understood and articulated the stakes involved in the creative politics of African American letters in his essay "Blueprint for Negro Writing."[29] That is to say, he understood that there was an entire counterlife created by American racial segregation that shaped the scope and aims of black writing. In "Blueprint," Wright argues that this counterlife, though in many ways disabling, could be utilized to create a black social consciousness that exposed and changed black life in the United States. Because he was still living in the United States and was a member of the Communist Party—an ideological identity that he later disclaimed publicly with his 1944 *Atlantic Monthly* essay "I Tried to Be a Communist"—Wright saw black writing as part of a nationalist enterprise. In "Blueprint," he notes that "Negro writers must accept the nationalist implications of their lives,"[30] since these implications form the foundation of the reality of black life in the United States and will be the only avenue available to them for social change. Nationalism is double veiled in Wright's essay, then. First, Wright's reference to nationalism signifies the black counterpublic created by racial segregation:

> The nationalist aspects of Negro life are sharply manifest in the social institutions of Negro people as in folklore. There is a Negro church, a Negro press, a Negro social world, a Negro sporting world, a Negro business world, a Negro school system, Negro professions; in short, a Negro way of life in America. The Negro people did not ask for this, and deep down, though they express themselves through their institutions and adhere to this special way of life, they do not want it now. This special existence was forced upon them from without by lynch rope, bayonet and mob rule. They accepted these negative conditions with the inevitability of a tree which must live or perish in whatever soil it finds itself.[31]

The forced condition of racial separatism breeds a racial nationalism; it is foundational to what segregation can reap. This first meaning is best understood as fitting into the context of black nationalism, the separatist movement of the twentieth century. For this reason, though Wright's "Blueprint" was written nearly three decades earlier, it was reprinted in Addison Gayle's *The Black Aesthetic* (1971), and Wright served as a foundational thinker to many Black Arts artists of the 1960s and 1970s.

But even as Wright is making claims for black separatism, he is also referencing American nationalism and its importance in shaping the African American lived experience in the United States. Like Du Boisian double consciousness, Wright dictates that black writing must represent the particular "warping" experience of being black in the United States.[32] Moreover, Wright is clear that black nationalism is not a natural byproduct of the black soul but a reflection of those lives "whose roots are imbedded deeply in Southern soil."[33] In other words, Wright's brand of nationalism is firmly located in an experience of geography. "Blueprint" marks Wright's early understanding of the political and artistic importance of place in African American cultural production.

Yet, similar to Wright's desertion of the Communist Party due to the limitations it placed on black-centered progressive politics, he found the United States unfruitful soil for his psychological, physical, and artistic development. In 1947, he moved to Paris. Because Wright visited the United States infrequently from then until his death in 1960, it would be easy to argue that he abdicated his sense of responsibility to American race relations. But any such characterization of Wright would fail to understand that his post-1947 artistic vision fully embraced human possibility regardless of race and national confines. Or as biographer and critic Michel Fabre puts it, Wright believed that in order to save America he had to save the world.[34] From 1947 onward, Wright's creative and political blueprints—the two were never separate for him—ceased to be confined to the provincial landscape that he articulated in "Blueprint for Negro Writing." His time spent in France offered him access to an international human enterprise, but as I stated earlier, he continued to struggle with how and when to represent African American particularity. More philosophically, he struggled with the question of whether blacks could ever be received as truly human on U.S. soil.

Wright, Regionalism, and Segregation Transplanted to Alien Soil

In the spring of 1955, Richard Wright, U.S. émigré in Paris, flew to Bandung, Indonesia, to attend the Bandung Asian-African Conference. Bandung participants represented twenty-nine free and independent nations—among them China, India, Indonesia, Japan, Burma, Egypt, Turkey, the Philippines, and Ethiopia—for which the discussion of both nonalignment and Afro-Asian solidarity was critical. With the Cold War in full swing, as well as the fallout from the Korean War, Vietnam's struggle for independence, and the general push for decolonization by various African and Asia countries, the world of color was ripe for a conference promising change through solidarity. Wright iterates that he was drawn to Bandung by his status as a person of color and that he attended the conference in order to make an account of something momentous: the human race gathering to develop community, as his wife put it.

Bandung was part of a larger transnational political trend in Wright's life. From his involvement with Alioune Diop in the 1946 inauguration of *Présence Africaine* to the 1956 First International Congress of Black Writers and Artists, Wright was deeply involved in creating and honing what was to become the archive of Negritude. Collaborating, in person and/or writing, with Leopold Senghor, Aimé Césaire, Alioune Diop, George Padmore, C. L. R. James, George Lamming, the young Frantz Fanon, and various other black artists and thinkers, "the need to disseminate African culture was a priority for Wright."[35] The company he kept influenced his work by providing him another portal through which to address modernity's dehumanization. Thus, his time at the Bandung conference marked Wright's continued commitment to international activism that gave voice not only to members of the African diaspora but to disenfranchised people of color across the globe.

The Color Curtain is Wright's homage to Bandung's vision of Third World solidarity. It reads like an ethnographic document and centers in Wright's recounting of interviews he conducted with a few self-selected Asians and Euro-Asians. Wright describes his interview subjects by their representative types: colonial subject, Westernized Asian educator, full-blooded Indonesian, and so on. The text is part of the body of work known as Wright's "travel writings," which comprise *Black Power: A*

Record of Reactions in a Land of Pathos (1954), *The Color Curtain* (1956), *Pagan Spain* (1957), and *White Man, Listen!* (1957).[36] Consistent with his other travel writing, *The Color Curtain* illustrates Wright's skill as an ethnographer and journalist. Yet it is the lack of inflection Wright chooses to give the interviewees in the book that is one of the many fascinating aspects of this text. As John Reilly points out, "in none of his reported conversations does Wright make an attempt to preserve a sense of natural verbal exchange or to create verisimilitude. Instead he emphasizes the content of informal talk as though it were delivered without inflection, tone, or the dynamics of dialogue that provide 'color' and reveal animation. . . . They are spokespeople without unique voice."[37] This is an important feature of *The Color Curtain* because it might be used to mark a distinction from Wright's provincial (regional) African American texts, which always feature some element of dialect or highlight the black counterlife created by racial segregation. Reilly's critique of Wright's character renderings in *The Color Curtain* for their lack of "color" and uniqueness, qualities privileged within the regionalist text, can be best understood as symptomatic of Wright's departure from American regionalism. Wright's empirical voice situates him as a powerful narrator, unfettered by conventions of regionalism; in fact, Wright's voice takes the tone of ethnographer.[38]

Wright's decision to forgo the voice of regionalist for that of ethnographer is more complicated than substituting one genre for another, even if the genres are kin. However closely linked the two forms of writing may be, American literary regionalism consistently makes Wright the author-subject of the writing he produces. As a writer of regionalist texts, he is a writer whose black southernness is central to the perceived success of the subject matter. Conversely, through ethnographic travel writing, Wright creates "othered" subjects and situates his authorial voice as stemming from his astute understanding of ethnographic journalism and common interest, rather than from his own racial identity. For example, even though *The Color Curtain* is told in first person and recounts Wright's travels and interactions, his status as a participant-observer[39] requires that he is always officially an outsider to the material conditions he is recounting. By playing with the "insider-outsider" role that is foundational to participant-observation, Wright is able to toe the line between concerned activist and disassociated ethnographer. In either case, Wright's blackness grants him the "rapport"[40] necessary for this sort of ethnography: "In my questioning of Asians I had had one tangible factor in my favor, a factor no Westerner could claim. I was 'colored' and every Asian I had spoken to had known what being 'colored' meant," contends Wright.[41] But rapport is merely a trick of the participant-observer, because it is also Wright's blackness that keeps him from being fully assimilated into the narrative he creates concerning the Bandung conference.

Moreover, this role as "outsider" is crucial to Wright's own self-creation. According to S. Shankar, "the outsider . . . is the privileged possessor of an uncommon knowledge regarding power and society, as well as the agent capable of acting upon this knowledge. In Wright's consciously abstract and metaphysical argument in his book, the outsiders are agents of change, through not always for the better."[42] While Shankar is speaking of Wright's novel *The Outsider* here, I believe what can be said of that novel is equally true of Wright's more ethnographic writings. Thus, in disregarding his status as regionalist writer for that of outsider, Wright is able to exist outside of systems that seek to sever his creative agency. Wright is no longer merely a native informant-narrator. Wright's outsider status is what Gilroy privileges, but the role of African Americans in *The Color Curtain* makes clear that not everyone has access to the position of outsider.

There are three African American "characters" in *The Color Curtain*, all of whom are unassimilable into the milieu of Bandung in Wright's account—not that they are unmoved by the conference's goals; instead, they simply do not fit within the movement's framework due to their ties to American racial segregation. Additionally, unlike Wright, they have no authorial control over their characterization. For example, Wright tells the story of Mr. Jones, "a light brown, short, husky man who, according to American nomenclature, was 'colored.'"⁴³ Jones, a mechanic in Los Angeles, is so moved by the potential of the Bandung conference that he exhausts his life's savings to get to Indonesia. Wright, in one long paragraph, describes Jones as "colored" four times and as "obscure" once. Jones seems out of place at the Bandung conference. In fact, Wright notes that Jones "felt that he belonged to a 'colored' nation, that he was out of place in America, . . . so this brown man came thousands of miles to feel a fleeting sense of identity, of solidarity, of religious oneness with others who shared his outcast state. . . . And brown Mr. Jones, watching the wily moves of tan Nehru and yellow Chou En-Lai, understood absolutely nothing of what was going on about him."⁴⁴ Forgetting about the problem of our not hearing Jones's experiences in his own voice, Wright's closing statement hems Jones into the margins of the United States, while also disallowing him the privilege that Wright himself employs throughout the book: a necessary amount of objective removal, coupled with complete understanding of the global conversation and his place within it. For Wright, Jones is "obscure," meaningless to the larger discussion of anticolonialism and nonalignment at Bandung. And although it happens to be a problem of translation, the same problem Wright should have, Jones seems out of place precisely because he comes directly from Los Angeles and has no geographical distance that would separate him from American nationalism. Wright's representation of Jones illuminates how important geographical distance from the United States is to his conception of humanity and authorship.

Likewise, Wright makes an account of Adam Clayton Powell's experience at the conference. Powell, a well-known black pastor and congressman for New York, made his way to Bandung as the U.S. government's only official conference observer. Wright comments on the fact that Powell, a light-skinned black man, had to be introduced to conference participants as black because he was taken to be white. Whether or not Wright is attempting to slight Powell or merely "report the facts," Wright does intimate that some of the half-hearted response to Powell may be due to his perceived whiteness. He goes on to report that Powell's address "stressed the colored population of the United States" and that it "is to be recalled that, with the exception of Congressman Powell, no delegate or observer at Bandung raised the Negro problem in the United States."[45] Further, Wright describes the "Negro problem" as "child's play compared to the naked racial tensions gripping Asia and Africa."[46] As the content of Powell's speech, which stressed the importance and improvement of African Americans within the United States, might have prompted dismissal by Wright and the other conference-goers, Wright omits a detailed description of it in the final version of *The Color Curtain*. In short, not only does Wright's narration locate Powell's rhetorical failure in his visibly miscegenated and nationally segregated body—which is a product of the very particular condition of slavery and segregation in the United States—but Wright also determines that the concerns of African Americans have little global worth. This has the effect of reproducing the pejorative regionalizing of nation-based African American concerns.

Wright's emphasis on African American nonalignment is better illuminated when read through the lens of an earlier draft of *The Color Curtain*. In the developmental draft of the book, Wright treats Powell's speech and presence at Bandung more extensively. I will quote extensively from the draft as to give you a clearer sense of what Wright does with Powell's color, character, and American nationalism:

> Adam Clayton Powell is a Negro Congressman from New York; he is the pastor of one of the largest churches in the United States. His father was, he says, "a branded slave." Though classed by American standards as a Negro, Congressman Power is actually a white man, much whiter in terms of skin color than many whites that I've known. Now, Bandung too had its deep effect upon him. Bandung

called to something buried not too far beneath his hard, pragmatic mind; it called to his sense of racial and neo-national romanticism. . . . So Congressmen [sic] Powell flew to Bandung, coming as fare [sic] as the Philippines in a Unites States Bombing plane; their [sic] he teamed up with the Philippine delegation and, while on his way to Bandung, began holding press conferences to "defend the position of the United States as it regards the Negro problem." So far, not matter whether regards his errand as useful or not, his attitude makes sense.

But, *once in Bandung, seeing the dusty faces of colored statesmen, Mr. Powell not only sought to defend and define the position of the United States on the Negro problem, but he became the spokesman for "American's 23,000,000 colored people."* He was, of course, including the Puerto Ricans, Mexicans, and maybe some others.

I'm not critical of Mr. Powell's efforts, though his efforts were not to my style, smacking too much of high-pressure salesmanship and public relations.—/two hardy, frisky arctic animals utterly unknown in the tropical latitudes of Bandung. The astounding aspect of Mr. Powell's appearance at Bandung was that he felt *the call, felt its meaning.* . . . At the very moment when the United States was trying to iron out the brutal kinks of its race problem, there comes along a world event which reawakens in the hearts of its "23,000,000 colored citizens" the feeling of *race,* a feeling which American life had induced deep in their hearts. If a man as sophisticated as Mr. Powell felt this, then it is safe to assume that in less schooled, more naïve hearts it went profoundly deep. (Indeed, I wonder why Congressman Powell stated he spoke for only 23,000,000 colored people? There are about 40 or 50 million colored people in the New World and had the Congressman spoken for all of them, he could have demanded that he be placed on the Democratic Ticket as a vice-presidential candidate in the next general elections!)

But let us go back into the conference hall and listen to the speeches by heads of delegations.[47]

I think it becomes painfully clear from this earlier draft that Wright did not much like Adam Clayton Powell. In this early draft, we can see Wright more clearly stating that did does not consider Powell to be truly black; he is also questioning Powell's motives by calling him a "high-pressure salesman" who is as alien to Bandung as an arctic animal in the tropics. Moreover, this early draft clarifies Wright's true beef with Powell: he is merely politicking on behalf of the United States. While in the final draft of *The Color Curtain* Wright tells us that Powell's discussion goes unregistered by his Asian and African audience, the early draft does not take such a clear stance. The speech does not figure into this early draft, in fact. What it most telling, then, is Wright's easy movement away from Powell's example: Wright leaves Powell outside the conference hall and enters to hear speeches by heads of delegations that he presumably feels belong at Bandung. This shift, literally leaving Powell outside the conference, once coupled with the final version of text, in which he tells us Powell's speech fails to move the audience, illustrates my argument regarding Wright's disavowal of African American proximity to American nationalism, even when it appears to be taken by the excitement of the new world order being offered by Bandung.

The final example we will examine of Wright's segregated inclusion of African Americans and their concerns within his text centers around a conversation Wright has with a white American reporter. One evening while in his hotel room, Wright hears a knock at the door, finds a young white woman standing on the other side, and proceeds to invite her into his room. It is a move that feels for me—as someone who has read *Native Son*—oddly inappropriate but one that I read as necessary for Wright to narrate in order to punctuate his own racial liberation. Soon after the white journalist enters, she reveals that she is seeking his advice because she believes her black roommate, whom she describes as being a "black, *real* black [woman]" might be practicing voodoo.[48] She describes the black woman's nightly ritual involving a blue light and the scent of something burning. After a few questions, Wright determines what the black roommate does not want her white roommate to know: that she is straightening her hair with a hot comb and a Bunsen burner once the lights go out. It is a simple misunderstanding that has powerful ramifications for Wright's textual representation of black Americanness. Because the exchange continues with Wright informing the white journalist that her black roommate straightens her hair simply because she is self-loathing,[49] the interaction could be read as Wright's attempt to represent the American racial allegory, which highlights white American benightedness with respect to black Americans. Wright offers this black woman's "shame" to the white journalist (and readers) as an object lesson in the international colored population's inferiority complex, a topic with which he feels the conference is reckoning. Yet, when the white woman asks what she can do to change this, he responds by saying, "Nothing. It's much bigger than you or I. Your father and your father's father started all this evil. Now it lives with us. First of all, just try to understand it. And get all that rot about voodoo out of your mind."[50] Wright does to these female journalists, Mr. Jones, and Powell what the Book-of-the-Month judges did to him just a decade earlier: he regionalizes them by confining their concerns to a temporal past, thereby blunting the force of African American (and semiprogressive, white) resistance to U.S. racial segregation.

How does one make sense of the faith Wright has in the power of an event such as Bandung alongside his seeming lack of active engagement with the American racial allegory that he represents as out of place in *The Color Curtain*? Considering Wright's pan-African work in Paris and his investment in international activism, his decision to narrate the interaction with the journalist is complicated by his apathy regarding the potential of his object lesson. Because Wright and this white woman talk in his hotel room, the conversation is segregated outside the confines of the primary conference space. As with Wright's critique of Powell's speech to the Bandung attendees, American racism is too specific to be explored on the international public stage for Wright, and possibly for the Bandung participants. Instead, Wright recreates the intimacy of American racial segregation in his hotel room. I believe that African Americans' continued geographical and intellectual association with the United States compels Wright to deny them integration into the narrative framework of global solidarity and nonalignment. Such integration is only accessible to those who forgo association with the geography and politics of the United States.

Even after Bandung, it is difficult for Wright to rhetorically fuse the particular concerns of African Americans in the United States with his growing interest in the more "universal" theme of human struggle. His tendency to marginalize African Americans in *The Color Curtain* is indicative of his continued negotiation concerning the textual "value" inherent in African American cultural production located in the United States. Concerned with the "discursive economy of Wright's text," Shankar imagines a metaphorical economic system in which the "value-coding" of a text originates from outside the text.[51] Shankar contends that in Wright's earlier publication *Black Power*, unable to make sense of his own blackness while in his ancestral home of Africa, he oscillated between relegating colonial Africa to prehistory and embracing the continent's potential for a modern anticolonial revolution.[52] Under this textual value system, Wright is caught in the trap of participating in an economy that privileges Western rationalism and textual production, while also wanting to rearticulate such coding. For Shankar, the resulting tension between the West and the non-West is palpable in Wright's *Black Power*.

Framing a Diaspora of Difference in *Black Power*

As I argued briefly in the preface and as I have demonstrated in my analysis of Wright's representation of African Americans in *The Color Curtain*, Richard Wright's life outside the United States might be best seen as an exercise in attempting to resist being locked into a particular subject position based on his racial and national identity. If the quest for humanity in a modern world characterizes Wright's international movement, then his 1953 visit to Africa's Gold Coast (present-day Ghana) marks a moment in which Wright attempts to locate the nature of black modernity through an *intraracial* lens. This is especially important considering that the majority of Wright's work explores interracial relations, be they American or international. Let me underscore that Wright's decision to visit and write about Africa was not motivated solely by a desire to embrace Africa as his ancestral home. Wright's intentions were part of a large intellectual and political project for Third World solidarity and the development of a politics of nonalignment within the Third World—a political stance that he articulated more fully in *The Color Curtain*. In the midst of the Cold War, Wright's decision to visit Africa had as much to do with blackness as it had with developing a growing transnational community of dissent against Communism and Western imperialism. Wright's visit coincided with the Convention Peoples Party, led by Kwame Nkrumah, in its push for the Gold Coast colony's independence from England. At some level, then, *Black Power* seeks to warn the Western world of the potential threat that African independence posed to the West and the Western world's fight against Communism. "The Western world has one last opportunity in Africa to determine if its ideals can be generously shared," Wright argues in the book's introduction, titled "Apropos Prepossessions."[53] He goes on to note that he is writing the book in order to show the Western world "how others see and judge" it.[54] The West can either respond favorably to Africa, in Wright's eyes, or risk the wrath of a black continent.

If Wright's rationale for writing *Black Power* was to document what Africa might mean to the Western world, he states that he is also going to understand what Africa means to him, a self-identified but socially constructed person of African descent: "I wanted to see this Africa that was posing such acute questions for me and was conjuring up in my mind notions of the fabulous and remote: heat, jungle, rain, strange place names. . . . I wanted to see the crumbling slave castles where my ancestors had lain panting in hot despair."[55] The rationale for his visit has the potential to create an uplift narrative of black diasporic solidarity. But any potential for the text to fall into a totalizing narrative of black diasporic connectivity—one in which Wright is engaged in a homecoming at the joyous moment the country seeks its own independence and moves into a modern world—is quickly bypassed. This is no modernist narrative of racial unification and closure. Even as he plans the trip, Wright questions his ability to identify with the people of Africa: "*Africa!* Being of African descent, would I be able to feel and know something about Africa on the basis of common 'racial' heritage? Africa was a vast continent full of 'my people.' . . . Or had three hundred years imposed a psychological distance between me and the 'racial stock' from which I had sprung?"[56] His described excitement about the trip is always undergirded by a "vague sense of disquiet" that gets represented throughout the travel narrative with ellipses and a lack of analysis at crucial moments of potential connection.[57] Wright is often unwilling to unify his personal experience in the Gold Coast by providing readers with an extensive explication; instead, he often opts for cringe-worthy descriptions in which, prompted by the sights, sounds, and smells of his travels in the African country, readers find him shuddering, retreating, sweating, and even suffering from dysentery. The fact that the narrative is oddly rich in scatological references demonstrates that Wright does not process going "home" as easily as we would expect from such a cosmopolitan traveler.

Since the publication of *Black Power*, Wright's rendering of Africa and African people has been critiqued for issues ranging from Wright's ethnographic impulse to his insistence on Western notions of modernization. However, as Manthia Diawara points out, "Wright was for Africa" and initiated a conversation between African Americans and Africans that was founded not on racial identification but on "the desire to win freedom for oppressed people all over the globe."[58] Wright may have been for Africa, but he continued to be haunted by what it would mean for him to be "of" Africa: "My problem was how to account for this 'survival' of Africa in America when I stoutly denied the mystic influence of 'race.'"[59] Due to his ideological point of view, which sought to expose the social construction of racial inequity, Wright was unable to make jibe the sights and sounds of his American "home" with those he finds in Africa. He continues to ponder the relevance of the connections throughout the text.

Wright's competing impulses to show Africa to the Western world and to show Africa to himself illustrate *Black Power*'s potential to undermine an essentializing version of black diasporic identity that denies black ethnic and national fragmentation in order to promote the uncritical promise of uncompromised black unification. What Wright creates in *Black Power*, often at the expense of traditional "African culture," is a more dynamic vision of black diaspora. Or, as Kevin Gains notes, "the difficulties Wright's text poses for us are actually illuminating insofar as we read them as expressions of Wright's struggle for critical perspective and political solidarity in diaspora."[60] Thus, *Black Power* might be best understood as a text that illustrates how the road to black diaspora is full of pit stops and backtracking.

In fact, Brent Edwards contends that "points of misunderstanding, bad faith, unhappy translation" must be considered part of the bedrock of black diasporic studies.[61] Edwards theorizes diaspora as a set of rhetorical practices composed of not only successful communication but also a fair share of miscommunication and visible seams in the fabric of meaning shared between black communities. He refers to these tears by the French word *decalage*, which, mimetic of the term's significance to diasporic studies, refuses easy translation into English.[62] The gaps in understanding between the two diasporic representatives become the very nature of what it means to be part of the black diaspora: misunderstanding, miscommunication. Thus, *decalage* opens the door for us to consider Wright's *Black Power* as not merely a dismal example of Wright's tendency (as some critics have accused him) to disown his blackness in favor of whiteness[63] but instead an occasion to consider the rhetorical missteps that make Wright's work symbolic of black diasporic thought. *Decalage* introduces ambivalence, multiple meanings, and untranslatability into the narrative of black intraracial discourse and assures that Africans and African Americans maintain what Earl Lewis has termed overlapping diasporas.[64] Rather than lumping communities into a single diasporic experience, overlapping diasporas acknowledges the multiplicity within the diasporic experience, as well as the way differing ethnic, cultural, and national diasporas intersect.

But how does one frame a text so that it is able to speak to the issue of black coalition across cultures or nations, while also maintaining an ambivalence that guarantees a dynamic sense of blackness? More importantly, how does Richard Wright portray blackness within *Black Power*? He does so by representing the text through the use of multiple prefaces. *Black Power* approaches "Africa" at least five different times before Wright ever lands on the Gold Coast. Each approach offers the reader a different portal of entry into Africa: visual, poetic, epistolary, methodological, or explicative narrative. These portals authenticate Wright's inquiry without providing a monolithic episteme of Africa. Moreover, Wright frames "Africa," his own entry into the Gold Coast, and the reader's entry into his text with a series of competing concepts that illuminate multiple sets of problems that will occupy the text. As Brent Edwards has suggested, frames "imply a certain transitionality or instability if not rupture" of meaning within the text of blackness.[65] The frame, then, is a formalistic strategy that guarantees that Wright is able to shift the nature of blackness, both African and African American, into an unstable textual paradigm. From the miniaturized copy of a letter from Nkrumah, which certifies that Nkrumah knows Wright and authenticates Wright's research travel to the

Gold Coast, to a map of the northwest coast of Africa, Wright suggests a variety of relationships between himself, Nkrumah, "Africa," blackness, and the world. For the final section of this chapter, I will examine Wright's use of the photographic image as framing.

Upon opening *Black Power*, one is greeted by a picture of Nkrumah and a caption that reads, "Kwame Nkrumah, Prime Minister of the Gold Coast." Actually, the image contains two pictures of Nkrumah: one in which he wears a Western-style suit and another of a smiling man dressed in what appears to be traditional Ghanaian attire. The former is superimposed on the latter, leaving the reader to contemplate the implied relationship between the two images. For instance, should we assume that the two pictures suggest that Nkrumah is equally at ease in the "modern" Western world and the "traditional" African world? Or should we allow the scale of the images to shape our reading? The scale of Nkrumah's Westernized image is significantly smaller and appears marginal to and decentered from the image of Nkrumah in traditional wear. Yet the Westernized Nkrumah rests above the latter. Should we perhaps assume that this positioning of the images implies movement or progress? While Nkrumah's traditional heritage looms large, maybe it is only a matter of time before a more Western version of the prime minister expands and overtakes the larger version—or vice versa? The questions, and thus the readings, can proliferate because the images relate but lack exposition.

The ambiguity of the meaning regarding the Nkrumah images, rather than detracting from the power of the text, encourages a more dynamic reading of Wright's *Black Power*. Lacking a context for the images of Nkrumah, one's eyes are drawn across the page, over the binding of the book and onto the book's title: *Black Power: A Record of Reactions in a Land of Pathos*. The experience of reading, of attempting to make meaning out of signs, encourages readers to link the likeness of Nkrumah and the promise of Wright's feelings and reactions suggested by the book's subtitle. Nkrumah and Wright exist in possible substitutional relationship to one another. It is a bold move considering that the body of the text reveals a lack of relationship between Wright and Nkrumah, since Wright feels desperately out of place where Nkrumah smilingly appears to be at home.

Yet another layer of ambiguity must be added to the function of images in *Black Power*. The implied substitutive union between one black man's images and another black man's feelings might lead one to believe that Wright is invested in creating that totalizing narrative of black community. However, one need only take into account the other image of a black man that exists in the first edition of the text: the image of Wright on the back dust jacket. In this closing frame, a serious-looking, suit-clad Richard Wright looks over his shoulder, askew at the camera. He is sitting at a desk and appears to have been "caught" in the act of writing. Unlike Nkrumah—who, if attire dictates psychology, is caught between the Western world and African tradition—Wright is resolutely "modern," a Western man. It is the juxtaposition between the images of Nkrumah and Wright that undermines the very substitution that the early image's proximity to the book title suggests. Additionally, whereas Nkrumah's image exists without an explicit historical context, Wright's dust jacket image contains a modest biography:

> Richard Wright was born in 1908 on a plantation near Natchez, Mississippi. He moved to Memphis, then to an orphanage, and to the homes of various relatives. Deciding to write, he went to Chicago and got his first success with UNCLE TOM'S CHILDREN in 1938. Since then he has become famous as the author of BLACK BOY, NATIVE SON, and the powerful denunciation of Communism appearing in THE GOD THAT FAILED. Mr. Wright has been living with his family in Paris since 1946.[66]

What is important about this history, however, is the way it denies a temporal and geographical substitution between Wright and Nkrumah. Wright is born in America, not Africa. Coupled with Wright's image, the facts of his birth and the importance of American geography to his artistic production attempt to deny the relational substitution implied by the earlier association between image and text. These frames compete to create and deny the totalizing narrative of "race" and black diaspora in Wright's text. In the end, they create a narrative that values intraracial difference as much as it values the possibilities implied by proximity and contact.

The use of photography as a means to capture and create difference did not go unutilized by Wright. If "to collect photographs is to collect the world" and "to appropriate the thing photographed,"[67] as Susan Sontag suggests, then the photographs Wright took during his trip to the Gold Coast are of the utmost importance when considering his relationship to the nearly decolonized African nation. Much like the images that pepper the bound copy of Wright's *Black Power*, the hundreds of photographs Wright took during his visit to the Gold Coast tell a story of Wright's relationship to the ethnographic eye and the "critical distance" such an eye can create. The photographs range from portrait and candid images to landscapes, all taken by Wright's own hands, and are telling. One of the most telling is an image taken of a young child eating a cracker while resting on his walking mother's back. The image might go unnoticed if it were not for the typewritten caption that Wright attaches to the picture, which reads, "The Young Can Change: This mother, no doubt, loves her *fufu*, but her baby is nibbling a European cracker. And if he is frowning, it is not because the cracker does not taste good."[68] This odd caption speaks to the project Wright is most interested in exploring in *Black Power*: the possibility of African modernity. Like Hurston, who I have previously argued created the Caribbean as primitive foil meant to highlight the black American's modernity, Wright creates the promise of modernity for the African child. But this is true only if the child is willing to forsake the nourishment of his tradition, represented by his mother's traditional *fufu*, for the nourishment of Western culture. The young African child, carried in the outmoded transport of his mother's back, rests on the cusp of change, unlike his mother, who is doomed to her own African past.

Wright's eye for the nonmodern African woman is probably most poignantly seen in an image Wright titles "An African Bathroom," which carries with it the following caption:

> The above photo was taken with a telo-photo lens at a distance of more than 40 yards. This teen age girl is taking a bath preparatory to going to church. The background is the kitchen. It is early morning and there are no prying eyes to disturb her toilet. To the left is a big black, cracked pot which has been discorded [sic] but not removed. Africans never throw anything away. Wornout articles are simoly [sic] to one side. Later in the morning the space in which this girl is standing will become a scene of washing, cooking, eating, sewing, carpentering. . . . It will be a tableau in which everything will be happening at once.[69]

The caption references an image Wright has taken of a naked young woman who is washing herself. No one but Wright, and now us, can see the young woman's private activities because they occur at a time when it appears others are away from a space that Wright tells us becomes public later in the day. In the flicker of a shutter, Wright is able to penetrate the private actions of a young woman and, I would argue, affirm his own sense of impenetrability—not only does Wright appear in none of the Gold Coast images he takes, but the vast majority of the candid images are of women and children in traditional dress. The young woman is captured into Wright's "imprisoning reality,"[70] which renders her an object of his eye, be it from forty yards away. His distance, oddly far and yet too intimate when centered on the young woman, speaks to his simultaneous desire to capture and to remain alienated from her and the experience he details in the caption. And the camera is what allows Wright to be both intimate with and alienated from the young woman. As Susan Sontag points out, photography

has so many narcissistic uses, [and] is also a powerful
instrument for depersonalizing our relation to the world;
and the two uses are complementary. Like a pair of binoc-
ulars with no right or wrong end, *the camera makes exotic
things near, intimate and familiar things small, abstract,
strange, much further away.* It offers, in one easy, habit-
forming activity, both participation and alienation in our
own lives and those of others—allowing us to participate,
while confirming alienation.[71]

Sontag speaks directly to what Wright is able to accomplish in
his role as photographer. His "An African Bathroom" begins to
tell the visual and textual story of his appropriation of the young
woman's body in order to render a particular story about African tradition, which must be separated from the African future
and Wright's own present. That is to say, by drawing attention to
his use of the telephoto lens technology, Wright makes us aware
of his ability to make the young naked woman appear near,
while also making himself seem much further away—from her
and from the African past to which she becomes associated in
the image. Wright uses apparatus and technique to create the
sort of ethnographic distance that he desires.

Thus, "An African Bathroom," much like Hurston's Jamaican kitchen, rests on Wright's ability to wield a technological
advantage over the African women who populate his photograph collection. Just as this particular image captures a young
woman's nakedness, it also appears to capture a community's
failure to conform to bourgeois notions of single-function
spaces, cleanliness, and privacy; an African bathroom is also
a trash dump, kitchen, dinning room, workshop, and general
meeting place. This multifunction location highlights the lack
of modern conveniences that would signal to a Western viewer/
reader that the tableau that Wright mentions is a modern one.
And unlike the little boy eating the cracker in the previous
image, the young bathing woman and her community is offered
no chance to join the West. Her nakedness and lack of privacy

link her with a past that refuses to be discarded, even once it is unusable. The lens, images, and Wright's explanation of his ability to stay far removed from the refuse that marks the life of this young woman, even during her "bath time," rests on the "close association between dirt and sex in Western culture,"[72] which are both associated with women, according to Phyllis Palmer. While I am not suggesting that there is an absolute erotic desire on behalf of Wright toward the young woman, I would like to suggest that her nakedness and the sexuality that it implies commingle with the "untidy" surroundings in order to affirm the ethnographic distance that is achievable through photographic distance by Wright. "An African Bathroom" affirms my sense that Wright uses the ethnographic form and the camera lens to create an account of his own inaccessibility to knowledge subjection. Wright's Gold Coast images suggest that there is salvation for Africa, but it comes through consumption of the West, not through being consumed by it.

In the end, reading Richard Wright's *Black Power* is an exercise in contradiction. Readers are encouraged to consider black community that is created not by "race" but by political alignment and vision. Such contradiction is achieved through Wright's employment of multiple lenses that offer the reader metonymy without relationship, feelings without rationalizing, and the possibility of being African American without being tied to either America or Africa. The vision of black diaspora that Wright offers at the end of *Black Power* is one that links African Americans and Africans via having both once been colonial subjects: "I am an American and my country too was once a colony of England."[73] The black experience is evacuated from black diaspora, but community persists. His insistence on racial distance is disconcerting, at best, but it does open up the possibility for a more "global" understanding of alignment.

Wright's relationship to African Americans and regionalism in the international context typifies the vexed position that the black American writer must often occupy in order to make his or her writing matter in the present and, more importantly, in the future. The years Wright spent in Europe were dogged by accusations that ranged from his having an outdated sense of U.S. race relations (because his post–*Black Boy* writings failed to capture the racial nuance created by the burgeoning Civil Rights Movement in the United States) to a sense that his internationalism had taken him too far from his expertise in African American life. Torn between two creative worlds—a world that depicted African Americans in the United States and a world that depicted the modern human condition of oppression in all its variations—Wright found little solace in his attempts to bridge them. From his imagined magnum opus "Celebration," which he envisioned would tie his novel *Savage Holiday* (1954) and two unwritten novels that explored the lives of Montezuma and a pathological New York teenage girl, respectively, to his travel writings,[74] Wright met with constant critical disinterest in the Unites States. Publishers, editors, and his own literary agent spent the last years of Wright's life trying to get him to go back "home," at least creatively. Confounded by negative reviews and the general push to move him back into the *black region*, Wright asked his agent, "What has my geographical position on earth got to do with the faults or merits of a book?"[75] In reality, geography was destiny for Wright. It was the thing both from which he ran and to which he clung as a writer, as a man. Looming financial instability—his *Black Boy* royalties were bound to give out—gave critics' concerns more weight than they might have had, and Wright continued to his death trying to make the regional mesh with his global perspective.

Paul Gilroy commends Wright for his ability to resist ethnocentrism and for his willingness to live between insider and outsider status. But I hope that I have shown that such resistance on Wright's part was not without its own share of racial essentialism, in the form of regionalizing and political segregation of African Americans in *The Color Curtain*. Likewise, Wright was not left unmarred by his attempts to desegregate his creative vision, as is evident from a warning he received from his agent Paul Reynolds just two months before the *Color Curtain*'s

American publication: "It seems to me—and of course I'm only guessing now—that as you have found greater peace as a human being, living in France, and not being made incessantly aware that the pigmentation in your skin sets you apart from other men, you have at the same time lost something as a writer. *To put it another way, the human gain has been offset by a creative loss.*"[76] Obviously, the exchange rate between the particular and the antiessential for African Americans is not as easy or as complete a transaction as Gilroy describes. Wright may have transplanted but was not exactly able to cultivate African American concerns in the alien soil. His example begs us to think more critically about how best to give textual value to African American regional particularism without forgoing the possibility of African American global agency.

3 / Deconstructing the Romance of Ethnography: Queering Knowledge in James Baldwin's *Another Country*

And if the word integration means anything, this is what
it means: that we, with love, shall force our brothers to see
themselves as they are, to cease fleeing from reality and begin to
change it.

JAMES BALDWIN[1]

In August 1970, sitting across from Margaret Mead, James Baldwin recalls a run-in with the employees of a Tallahassee bank who had refused to cash his $250 check. Three months into researching a story on the American South, Baldwin was broke and desperate for money that might ward off any vagrancy charges that would land him on a chain gang. With real or imagined cops at his heels, Baldwin says that he could not allow racism to keep him and his money separated: "I saw everybody in that bank before they would cash that check. I was determined that they were going to cash that check or lynch me." On the particular day he is remembering, Baldwin says that for the second time in twenty-four hours he found himself at the window of a young, white, female teller who had previously refused to cash his check. Yet, on this day, the teller was forced to work with him. Baldwin recalls for Mead the look of mystification that fell over the Florida teller's face and speculates on its causes: she was mystified not only by his access to such a large sum of money but also by his ability to meet her gaze. Baldwin contends that the teller's "American sense of reality" was shattered and only recoverable through the creation of a narrative that could negate Baldwin's Americanness. He tells Mead, "The only way she would understand that black boy in the bank was to tell herself, 'He doesn't know any better; he's from Paris.' Otherwise she was going to be haunted to her dying day."[2]

Baldwin becomes a "French-issued" black American in the mind of the teller, and some readers might be inclined to think that this newly coined and ambiguous identity would be the sort of counteridentity desired by a self-described exile such as Baldwin. However, in addition to exploring new citizenship possibilities as an internationally mobile black subject, at the core of Baldwin's remembrance is a desire to explore the power of African American national removal (even if only semipermanent) and the conditions under which one might make a return. Thus, the personal anecdote functions in a number of ways for Baldwin. First, the remembrance provides a public platform for him to ponder the way living outside the United States changes how he relates to mid-twentieth-century American racial hierarchies. At the heart of his story is the conflict between his sense of autonomy and personal agency gained through having lived outside America and his place within a southern American racial fabric upon his return. His anecdote connects him to the fairly commonplace narrative tradition of the black American who returns to a segregated nation after having lived or traveled abroad: the return to the United States involves an attempt to socially, economically, and psychologically confine black citizens through the practice of racial segregation. In "The Price of the Ticket," Baldwin illuminates this racial-national dilemma more clearly:

> The romance of treason never occurred to us for the brutally simple reason that you can't betray a country you don't have. (Think about it.) Treason draws its energy from the conscious, deliberate betrayal of trust—as we were not trusted, we could not betray. And we did not want to be traitors. We wished to be citizens.
>
> *We:* the black people of this country, then, with particular emphasis on those serving in the Armed Forc-

es. The way blacks were treated in, and by, an American
Army spreading freedom around the globe was the reason for heartbreak and contempt. Daddy's youngest son,
by his first marriage, came home, on furlough, to help with
[Daddy's] funeral. When these young men came home, in
uniform, they started talking: and one sometimes trembled, for their sanity and for one's own. One trembled, too,
at another depth, another incoherence, when once won-
dered—as one could not fail to wonder—what *nation* they
represented. My brother, describing his life in uniform,
did not seem to be representing the America his uniform
was meant to represent—: he had never seen the America
his uniform was meant to represent. Had anyone? Did he
know, had he met, anyone who had? Did anyone *live* there?
Judging from the great gulf fixed between their conduct
and principles, it seemed unlikely.
  Was it worth his life?[3]

Baldwin uses his stepbrother's service experience to get at the
conundrum of freedom and national belonging (or citizenship)
that seemingly not only eluded African American servicemen in
a pre-civil-rights era but also produced a trembling incoherence
in the black subjects who merely bore witness to the return of
the service members. In other words, Baldwin's remembrance
highlights the ways in which the lives of African Americans
who travel abroad and of those who do not are equally changed
by the confrontation of the black American subject who must
reconcile national and international subjectivity. More importantly, they must collectively consider what the value of black
life is to the nation.

  Baldwin's anecdotes about his own arrival at the Florida bank
and his remembrance of his stepbrother's return after service
abroad touch on commonplace themes in black American narratives of internationalism and national reentry. Moreover, what
is most interesting about these two remembrances is the way
that Baldwin appropriates the very stylized "arrival scene" that

is common to many classical ethnographies and travel writings,[4] further linking his art to the historical and textual origins that shaped Mead's discipline. Keep in mind that this stylized arrival narrative traditionally provides the reader with a sense of the difference between the ethnographer and the culture that he or she will interpret and gives the reader a sense of the ethnographer's ultimate ease in integrating the cultural space of analysis. Both the serviceman's and Baldwin's arrivals are marked with a certain amount of racial dissonance, which compel us to consider the difference race makes to perceptions of national belonging, especially when played out through the traditional ethnographic arrival narrative. For instance, while the Florida teller and even the genre of ethnography would like to stylize Baldwin's presence in Florida as an "arrival," Baldwin narrates it simply as a return to the United States' particular racial experience. His narrative seeks to highlight not the return but the disorder his very existence causes in the white imagination. Baldwin had been in Florida for nearly three months, he tells Mead, but the Florida teller must imagine him at the point of entry in order to make sense of his impertinence and wealth. His return, then, is a return to a racial hierarchy that seeks to place him in its most debased position. Moreover, the distinction Baldwin is attempting to narrativize is best understood as a distinction between the exceptionalism of a "first encounter" and the monotony of a black "homecoming," which inevitably entails a return to that place which has been known, felt, and/or experienced as a black man living within the United States. Whereas the "arrival" is sure to bring the unexpected, the "homecoming" many times brings the resumption of a known life. In that sense, Baldwin's story is an assertion not of his exceptional status as a black American international but rather of a return to a familiar national racial incoherence. The same must be said of servicepersons and the family and friends that greet them.

This tradition, then, speaks to the second function of Baldwin's remembrances. Through his ongoing conversation with Mead, we come to know that Baldwin believes his own self-assurance (which unnerved the Floridian bank teller) must be linked to the larger national unease brought about by the Civil Rights and the growing Black Nationalist Movements of the late 1960s and early 1970s. To more fully explore why I am drawn to this particular exchange between Mead and Baldwin, I would like to pay closer attention to a moment in the conversation when we are able to receive the payoff of Baldwin's labor of remembrance. Baldwin tells Mead that upon his return to the United States he realized that the shattering of the "American sense of reality" had to do in part with a collective reaction to the fact that "all of a sudden, the niggers, *our niggers*, are not acting like *our niggers* have always acted. And of course, *they* don't know that *our niggers* were never what *they* thought *they* were."[5] What is most striking about this passage is Baldwin's decision to assume the voice of white Americans when he refers to blacks as "our niggers," while also shifting to a voice in opposition to white America in using the pronoun "they" to refer to white Americans. So what first appears to be simple autobiography becomes an occasion to reproduce a set of conflicting voices and concerns that speak to larger American social conditions. I want to make clear that this grammatical instability does not render these subjectivities equal by any stretch of the imagination—how could "they" ever be equal to "their niggers." Instead, it speaks to the imagined mobility of the subject that might generate a variety of points of view. This generative potential of points of view is something I will explore in more depth later in this chapter, but ultimately Baldwin illustrates the permeability of a whiteness that necessitates the "nigger construct" and draws attention to how such permeability serves as the only way to undo the chains of the "nigger construct" that continues to plague the United States. Moreover, it again speaks to Baldwin's sense of the commonplace narrative he is attempting to construct around the assertion of black citizenship in the face of black international mobility.

Even sitting across from Mead in the early 1970s, Baldwin was enacting a sort of "homecoming," as he had already proven his capacity on numerous textual occasions to occupy the subjectivities of men and women across racial, sexual, gender, and national lines. From the novel *Giovanni's Room* (1956) to one of his many essays such as "Many Thousands Gone" (1951), his rhetorical shifts in pronoun, point of view, and racial positioning are part of a longstanding project to deconstruct an objectivity that maintains the divisive notions of "belonging," "whiteness," and "citizenship." In other words, Baldwin is, at some level, using the moment he sits across from one of the most important cultural documenters of the twentieth century to model the necessary capacity of each American to mix autobiography, multivocal narrative, and social critique.

Genre disruption is key to understanding Baldwin's literary work for social change. Rather than merely offering a critique of the white establishment, which Baldwin inevitably does, he also creates for himself a rhetorically dynamic subjectivity that is able to unabashedly assume a particular voice in one breath, only to critique this voice with another voice in the next breath. So in this 1971 conversation with Mead, in which he models the capacity to think and speak from the position of a variety of people, Baldwin presents us with an important theme: the significance of the (real and fictional) writer who is able to occupy, represent, and understand multiple points of view. More important than merely being able to shift points of view, however, is Baldwin's careful articulation of an artistic/social critical voice that has also done the work of self-reflection. Baldwin is not interested in creating characters or nonfiction personas that have shirked the hard work of locating and reckoning with their own role in the social systems they wish to either analyze or represent. This may seem a simplistic task, seeing as the nature of fiction relies on the ability of the writer to convincingly create perspectives not his or her own; and although Mead fancied herself *both* an anthropologist and a literary artist,[6] Baldwin is still attempting to model this objective mobility in the face of one of anthropology's greatest researchers. It is not simply the performance of perspective flexibility that I find provocative in this exchange. I suggest that Baldwin chooses to flex his narrative muscles in front of Mead because of her work as a trained ethnographer.

Thus, in this chapter, I focus on Baldwin's fictional attack on the mode of ethnographic knowing that is incapable of the sort of grammatical shifting Baldwin performs in his discussion with Mead—the sort of ethnographic knowing that must rely on the sharp boundaries between the "native" and the "ethnographer" because to do anything less would risk the sanctity of the knowledge produced and hierarchies affirmed by an adherence to dichotomies.

Baldwin's critique of the static nature of the classical ethnographic "eye"/"I" is best illustrated in his novel *Another Country* (1962), in which he portrays the possible deadly repercussions when one lacks the ability to embrace shifts in point of view and the capacity for self-reflection. Baldwin's refrain in "Price of the Ticket"—"go back to where you started, or as far back as you can, examine all of it, travel your road again and tell the truth about it. Sing or shout or testify or keep it to yourself: but *know whence you came*"[7]—is one that he would utter throughout his career. The impulse of this refrain compels the individual to understand his or her own subjectivity and motivations in order to truly know his or her place within the world. This is not knowledge obtained by living in a vacuum but rather the sort of knowing that comes from accepting "the real reason for [one's] journey."[8] This travel metaphor that allows Americans in Baldwin's vision to know from *whence they came* is one that his story to Mead resists and that flies directly in the face of outward exploration enacted by not only anthropologists but most white Americans, according to Baldwin. Thus, in order to uncover more fully Baldwin's critique of a type of outwardly focused knowledge, I explore how *Another Country* offers a critique of what I describe as the "romance of ethnography," which functions to entrap and endanger all characters that are unable both to shift out of and to fully reckon with the racial and sexual realities of their lives within a desegregating United States. In *Another Country*, we see the rejection of the ethnographic eye that encourages the search for knowledge elsewhere through the creation of participant-observation relationships that are meant to probe the black subject. Instead, what Baldwin offers at every turn in the narrative is a model of how to resist such knowledge production on the part of racialized and marginalized others, a model that also serves as possible pedagogical instruction in self-knowledge for members of the white majority. People of color cease to become easily entered "regions" of knowledge.

The Romance of Ethnography

I do not want to suggest that Baldwin's turn to experimentation in grammatical stability is particularly novel. In fact, Kamala Visweswaran has argued that negotiations of positionality have marked the ethnographic work of many feminist anthropologists during the twentieth century. Visweswaran suggests that early twentieth-century female anthropologists, especially those of color such as Zora Neale Hurston, produced what are often referred to as experimental ethnographies during a period that predates the postmodern crisis in anthropology of the early 1980s. For instance, Visweswaran notes that Hurston's autobiography, *Dust on the Tracks*, "reads less as a straightforward autobiography than as an ethnography of the community of which Hurston was a member."[9] Baldwin thus joins Hurston and other African American thinkers who attempted to attack the monomythic notion of black American identity cultivated throughout the twentieth century by professions such as qualitative sociology and anthropology. Much like sociological studies' influence on American public policy,[10] Lee Baker reminds us, "anthropological discourse on race feeds into the larger discourses out of which it is itself constructed. For example, lawmakers have used anthropology to write legislation that shapes public policy, and journalists have used it to produce media that shape public opinion. The discipline of anthropology, in turn, is validated by this sort of appropriation."[11] We should think of Baldwin's work as a competing narrative meant to upstage, or at least to contend with, mid-twentieth-century national discourse that often relied on sociological and anthropological tracks to create and then manage "the crisis" of the black family and black culture, more generally.

Within black literary studies, then, the disciplinary tensions between sociological and anthropological examinations of black culture and cultural production have been embodied more often than not in the tension between Richard Wright and Zora Neale Hurston. As I mentioned in chapter 1, these two writers, who feature centrally in my understanding of black literary production in the mid-twentieth century, are often placed at odds due to their differing opinions about which disciplinary approach is best for exploring America's so-called "Negro question." I have resisted on previous occasions in this book the tendency to see them as adversaries, opting, rather, to see them as people with different racial-national projects. I will continue to do so rather than to allow the professional differences between anthropology and sociology to overshadow the fact that Hurston, Wright, and now Baldwin encourage us to think about the importance of taking a critical stance toward traditional ethnography. I want to focus on this site of similarity in order to offer a possible explanation as to why Baldwin might have taken such a critical position against the practice of participant-observation in his novel *Another Country*.

In order to begin thinking through the legacy of ethnography, I turn very briefly to the preface and introduction to the Anglo-Polish anthropologist Bronislaw Malinowski's *Argonauts of the Western Pacific* (1922). Early in this important anthropological text, Malinowski both outlines the inherent superiority of the ethnographic work produced by the trained professional and gives student ethnographers suggestions on how to guarantee that their time in the field will produce quality ethnographies. Warning his colleagues and students that, while "there is still a large number of native communities available for scientific study, within a generation or two, they or their cultures will have practically disappeared."[12] Much as I argued in chapter 1 on Hurston regarding Boas's push to send Hurston to the American South before black culture was "destroyed" by modernity, Malinowski encourages his colleagues and students to go into the field before the "natives" disappear. His sense of the "richness" of fieldwork sites and urgency is telling of the ways in which the discipline of anthropology understood itself in the early part of the twentieth century as engaged in a race against time to document and preserve the cultural hierarchies set in place by colonialism. Colonialism itself shapes and was shaped by the discourses and geographic investments of the people Malinowski deems amateurs. Along those lines, he goes on to contend that since the opportunity to conduct field research is fated, researchers must understand that it is not by "magic" but by patience and "systematic application of a number of rules of common sense and well-known scientific principles"[13] that one can begin to separate valuable fieldwork and, by extension, ethnographic texts from texts produced by amateurs such as explorers, missionaries, or colonial administrators.

Although these amateur figures are seen as interlopers to the scientific discipline that Malinowski seeks to create for himself and his colleagues, they in fact produce "adjacent and antecedent discourses" to that of the professional ethnographer.[14] Their travelogues, diaries, government/administrative reports, and novels serve as distant models to the ethnographic form. Malinowski adamantly distances himself from these genres through a belief in and a constant conjuring of the scientific method in the introduction to his ethnography. Yet these antecedent and adjacent cultural surveyors, although often colonial to their cores, do provide a set of narrative techniques (characterization, authorial voice, thick description, etc.) that tie traditional ethnography to fiction writing—an important linkage that I come back to later in this chapter.

In a twist that may read as a progressive articulation of cultural relativism, Malinowski goes on in his *Argonauts* introduction to contend, "Ethnology has introduced law and order into what seemed chaotic and freakish. It has transformed for us the sensational, wild and unaccountable world of 'savages' into a number of well ordered communities, governed by law, behaving and thinking according to consistent principles."[15] Malinowski may differ from a colonial administrator or a missionary in his sentiment regarding the antiquated nature of the use of a term such as *savage* when referring to native populations,[16] but his cultural relativism does nothing to undermine the lines that separate the "native" from the ethnographer. In fact, the very science that transforms a "savage" into a "native" is the same science that mandates one pick a fieldwork location so far from "home" that one will not be inclined to "fly [home] at any moment for recreation" because "the native is not the natural companion for the white man, and after you have been working with him for several hours, seeing how he does his gardens, or letting him tell you items of folk-lore, or discussing his customs, you will naturally hanker after the company of your own kind."[17] Malinowski imagines "the field" as a sort of prison or desert-island form of isolation that the ethnographer must embrace due to the purposefully insufferable distance between the ethnographer and his or her actual home. So while Malinowski is clearly separating his discourse regarding the "primitive other" from that of his nonprofessionalized Western counterparts through embracing close proximity and the sort of prolonged interaction supposedly cultivated through participant-observation, he clings to what he describes as the natural segregation between the native and the so-called "white man." Traditional modern ethnographic writing, thus, rests on proximity between the native and the ethnographer (i.e., the employment of participant-observation) but also maintains a commitment to preserving the differences between the two bodies and cultures: although cast away[18] in the field for an unspecified amount of time, the ethnographer's intention is always to return home in order to interpret what he or she saw.

Malinowski's directives on field behavior, and his sense that copious note taking and participant-observation could guarantee a productive account, work to produce a narrative that highlights the ways in which classical Western ethnography succeeds in producing a "discursive order whose territorial and visual forms of authority are those of the modern state."[19] By that, I mean to say the distance and proximity of the ethnography to the subjects of analysis maintains a power hierarchy that affirms the authority of the ethnographer's ability to gaze and make sense of his or her "field site." Yet one continues to wonder how these plans play out "on the ground." Theoretically speaking, the role of order and hierarchy is much more complicated than a simple description of the "authoritative" ethnographer who can participate and observe and then leave "the field" exactly as it was when he or she entered. This air of distance is, however, the foundation of classical ethnography and is thought to be necessary both for maintaining integrity while the ethnographer is in the field and also central to facilitating his or her inevitable flight from "the field." And while ethnography has undergone a series of postmodern shifts since Malinowski's day, there continues to be the expectation that the ethnographer will maintain a critical distance in every sense, especially sensually.

Sensual distance, or to put it more bluntly, celibacy, is a mainstay of ethnographers while in the field. In fact, it was not until the posthumous publication of Malinowski's field diary, *A Diary in the Strict Sense of the Term* (1967), that it was revealed that "sexuality was anything but unproblematic for Malinowski."[20] The discursive demand for celibacy in the field rests on the ethnographer's need to maintain the status of "objective observer, free from the distracting desires"[21] which might wrongfully shape his or her interaction with subjects and, thus, contaminate fieldwork results. Yet a growing number of anthropological ethnographers have become interested in theorizing the role of sex and sexuality in the field, suggesting that absence of sex within the discourse of ethnography does not actually mean that ethnographers are not having sex or that desexualizing the ethnographer is even possible, especially for women and gay people who are already read as sexualized subjects.[22] In fact, Andrew Killick suggests that the dominant narrative of the asexual ethnographer only serves to more firmly establish the heterosexual male privilege of the ethnographer. Killick goes on to contend that regardless of the ethnographer's racial or sexual orientation, his or her stance is always that of the "hetero-sexual-masculine subject position" as long as the field is mythologized as "a place to be penetrated by the heroic figure of the lone anthropologist in search of self-renewal."[23] Moreover, the desexualizing of the ethnographer, coupled with the eroticizing of the ethnographic Other, reinforces traditional tropes of field that present the ethnographer as entering into "a stronghold of cultural secrets," a "breeding ground of experience," or "virgin territory to be penetrated by the ethnographer's interpretive thrust."[24] Giving a whole new meaning to "mind fucking," Killick suggests that we might read the trope of the asexual ethnographer as a means to reinforce the narrative of the white male's privilege to feminize the fieldwork site and those who inhabit it.

If the relationship between the ethnographer and subjects is one of denied sexual tension, then this relationship provides us with an occasion to consider the role of sex in knowledge produced by social sciences dedicated to translating human difference. It is no accident that James Baldwin would take on the concepts of love, sex, sexuality, and race as he imagined the social and interpersonal effects taking place in the United States as the country ended state-sanctioned segregation. *Another Country* is a text that asks many questions, and one that gets asked repeatedly by a variety of characters is "Do you love me?" It is a question that is not difficult for many of the characters in the novel to answer, but it is difficult to know the significance of the answer. By that, I mean to suggest that Baldwin is questing after something more meaningful than the "yes" or "no" of love and romance in this novel. Of what does love make one capable? In other words, *Another Country* asks its readers to consider what love means to a nation in the midst of racial and social upheaval.

Writing *Another Country* was painful for Baldwin. Written among his various homes in the United States, France, and Turkey, the novel took years for him to finish. Besides the deep biographical nature of the text—David Leeming suggests that Rufus was a composite of Baldwin and a close childhood friend—the novel also tested Baldwin's capacity to explore the possibilities of love and life in 1950s American culture. The novel's action is set in New York City's Greenwich Village, "the place of liberation,"[25] and characters of the novel are forced to meet the national social shift head-on at the very intimate level of interpersonal and sexual relationships. In addition to the racial politics that dictate the ways in which characters engage, the novel is also home to an explicit queer sexual sensibility, well before such a sensibility found itself publicly expressed in New York City's 1969 Stonewall resistance. With the honest reckoning of the painful intersection of race, gender, and sexuality as the thematic backdrop for much of the plot's action, many of the novel's early critics found the text to be offensive.[26] One must speculate that the bad press stemmed from the fact that, although *Another Country* carried on many of the same themes that had been present in *Giovanni's Room*, the novel located these themes squarely within the United States, making the text too radical to be this close to "home."

Another Country follows the sexually complicated, interracial relationships among a set of artist friends who are brought together after one—Rufus Scott, an African American jazz drummer—commits suicide. After Rufus's death, his best friend, Vivaldo, and Rufus's sister, Ida, embark on a difficult love affair that is complicated by Vivaldo's inability to see past his own white liberalism. He loved Rufus and loves Ida but refuses to acknowledge his own white male privilege in ways that would allow him to understand the quotidian racism that killed Rufus and limits the life options available to Ida, a black woman: "*You don't know, and there's no way in the world for you to find out, what it's like to be a black girl in this world*, and the way white men, and black men, too, baby, treat you. You've never decided that the whole world was just one big whorehouse and so the only way for you to make it was to decide to be the biggest, coolest, hardest whore around, and may the world pay you back that way."[27] In this quote, Ida makes clear to Cass, the novel's other female character, that the dual constraints of race and gender confine her possibilities in ways that are both unimaginable and unknowable to someone who will not share her experience. This experiential significance is important for Ida to highlight because it affirms the text's foreclosure of easy affinities, even when characters share the same gender and sex. Ida is refusing to be known, not merely because she refuses the power of racial integration but because she refuses affinity that would render her history and experience a silent expense of integration. Similarly, the relationship between Ida and Vivaldo is further strained because she cannot forgive Vivaldo and the other white characters of the novel for their insensitivity to her brother's blackness and all it might signify in mid-twentieth-century New York. Although Vivaldo and other white characters in the novel perceive Ida to be too sensitive to racial difference and inequity, Baldwin creates in Ida a character hardened by American racism but open to love. This combination makes it difficult for Ida and Vivaldo to find their romantic footing because she is a "lover" who refuses to forget. Seemingly anticipating postracial discourse that mandates silence around racial history and racial hurts due to injustice, Ida stands firm in her desire not to be known but to be acknowledged.

As I expressed earlier, the novel rests on questions of love and romance, their simultaneous possibility and impossibility. Many critics have thus approached the unwieldy and sprawling novel with an attempt to make meaning from the relationships that are so central to it. According to William Cohen, *Another Country* ultimately adheres to a "liberal humanist ideology of salvation and love"[28] that relies on a relatively fixed and incontestable axis of gender and race in order to affirm the possibility of change starting with the individual. As Cohen suggests, the novel ultimately fails to deliver to the racialized and gendered subject a radical means for traversing the social categories of difference; the novel chooses instead to highlight the importance of love between individuals.

Moreover, Cohen critiques the novel for making salvation available only to the gay, white male and achievable only through white, queer masculinity. Baldwin fails to create space in his text for women and queers of color, according to Cohen. While Cohen chooses to critique this possible reality in the novel, I would like to suggest that because of Baldwin's refusal to make black people solely responsible for the moral development of whiteness and white people, it makes sense that one of the most important examples of knowledge production and salvation for whiteness would happen between and among white men. Because although Baldwin may seem to suggest to his namesake nephew in "My Dungeon Shook" that black people are responsible for helping white people, whom he calls their "lost, younger brothers," to "see themselves as they are, to cease fleeing from reality and begin to change it,"[29] this letter to his nephew is actually meant to teach his nephew the importance of black survival, not the importance of white moral development. Much like Cohen, Kevin Ohi marks a similar frustration with Baldwin's novel but differs from Cohen's suggestion that there might actually be a form of transcendence available to anyone in the novel, regardless of race, class, or gender. Ohi opts instead to read Baldwin's refusal to deliver on the promise of liberatory self-knowledge as an affirmation of the unrelenting push resulting from some sort of unspeakable and unknowable trauma.[30] While Ohi closes his reading by suggesting that an existential unknowability is central to the novel, Ernesto Javier Martinez argues that Ohi's reading fails because it does not "do justice to the novel's complex understanding of identity and knowledge."[31]

Martinez suggests that knowledge production in the novel rests on characters' ability to use identity constructs (race, sexuality, class, gender, etc.) as a means of self-understanding but that characters' narrative success rests on their ability to risk metaphorically "killing" those aspects of their identity that might mire them down: "the possibility for human flourishing is both founded on and mired by the identities that we have made and that have been made of us; . . . the task in front of us, then, is not to avoid this fact but to engage it and to do so with the only resources we have, our capacity for self-reflection and our courage to change," writes Martinez.[32] In all these critical readings, critics in some way take seriously the possibility that knowledge might be gained—even Ohi ends by going back on his essay's argument to say something akin to "knowing that it is difficult to know is knowledge in itself."

I would like to return now to my earlier discussion of romance and ethnography in order to suggest another possible relationship to knowledge and difference that Baldwin might be forging in *Another Country*: the denial of interpretation around categories of difference. While many critics of the novel seem interested in questions about knowledge and confusion, offering a variety of ways to make sense of why some characters stay confused or why some others seem knowledgeable, I would like to suggest that Baldwin is deeply invested in the means of knowledge production in the novel. More than merely pointing out to readers that the modern condition is one of existential crisis, Baldwin has the white characters in *Another Country* remain confused because they are too in love with the idea of knowing.[33] More particularly, they are in love with the idea of knowing "Others." I do not want to suggest that Baldwin is foreclosing the possibility of knowledge and human connection—I would, in fact, argue, similar to Martinez, that self-knowledge is Baldwin's preferred mode for fostering human connection. Instead, I am suggesting that Baldwin is highly critical about the conditions under which knowledge is obtained. Paying particular attention to the character of Vivaldo, I argue that Baldwin issues a highly damning critique of the white liberal gaze, ultimately suggesting that such a gaze is deadly when applied to the black subject.

When *Another Country* opens, the reader finds a depressed and downtrodden Rufus roaming Manhattan. Rufus is financially, spiritually, and morally bankrupt, and it takes nearly eighty pages of flashbacks for readers to learn that he is in this state because of love. Having fallen in love with a working-class, southern, white woman named Leona, Rufus is driven to domestic and personal abuse because he is unable to manage his racial grief. Baldwin describes Rufus as the kind of black man who never learned to love his own blackness. In fact, in a classic move on Baldwin's part, Rufus's ability to value blackness is only brought about through time spent out of the United States while serving in the navy. Returning home from service, Rufus presents his sister, Ida, with an Indian shawl he picked up in England. Looking at Ida wearing the shawl, Rufus is struck by her beauty and the beauty of black people more generally:

> He had never seen the beauty in black people before. But, staring at Ida, who stood before the window of the Harlem kitchen, seeing that she was no longer merely his younger sister but a girl who would soon be a woman, she became associated with the colors of the shawl, the colors of the sun, and with a splendor incalculably older than the gray stone of the island on which they had been born. . . . Ages and ages ago, Ida had not been merely the descendant of slaves. Watching her dark face in the sunlight, softened and shadowed by the glorious shawl, it could be seen that she had once been a monarch. Then he looked out of the window, at the air shaft, and thought of the whores on Seventh Avenue. He thought of the white policemen and the money they made on black flesh, the money the whole world made.[34]

The passage suggests a number of things about Rufus. Most obviously, it illustrates the importance of mobility in facilitating the sort of self-worth that might have made Rufus a more confident and less volatile lover of himself and of whites. Yet this sort of self-worth is withheld from Rufus, as it lies in the Indian shawl's non-American origins. Even as he gazes at his sister and is taken by her beauty, he removes this beauty from their Harlem apartment and locates it in a time and place that is inaccessible to both of them: idealized Africa. The shawl ultimately allows Rufus to see what Ida might have been had she not been born in the United States, a descendant of slaves. If she had instead been born generations ago in Africa, she would have been saved the trauma of being black in America. So as Rufus's eyes shift from this idealized vision of Ida and onto the streets of Harlem, he is reminded that the reality of black life in the United States ensures that Ida will not be a monarch but, instead, a whore. Moreover, he is reminded that he will be powerless to protect or support her. Now, the novel is fairly ambivalent about whether or not Rufus's, and later Ida's, sense of black abjection is justified—both Leona and Vivaldo use white liberal sentiment in an attempt to variously divest Rufus and Ida of their racial traumas[35]—but the passage does seem to point to a deep sense of loss that is irrecoverable within the confines of the United States. Rufus's and Ida's "black radical consciousnesses"[36] have little effect on their white liberal partners' ability to truly understand them and, by extension, the black experience.

When Rufus kills himself less than ninety pages into the novel and Leona is driven mad by the violence of the love that she and Rufus shared, the narrative, interestingly, makes way for more love. Picking up where Rufus and Leona leave off, Ida and Vivaldo begin their own interracial love affair in the wake of Rufus's death. Seemingly less broken than Rufus, Ida proves to be a much more sturdy lover than he had been.

Yet Vivaldo continues to expose his own lack of understanding of blackness throughout the novel. In fact, in addition to Vivaldo's lacking the capacity to understand, his quest for knowledge and the control that knowledge can produce stands at the heart of Baldwin's critique in the novel. In other words, through narrative repetition, Baldwin insists that love is foundational to knowledge; yet there is something off in the love Ida and Vivaldo share. For example, after making love to Ida for the first time, Vivaldo feels a deep disconnection between them. While she sleeps, he ponders what has just happened: "She was in his bed but she was far from him; she was with him and yet she was not with him. In some deep, secret place she watched herself, she held herself in check, she fought him. He felt that she had decided, long ago, precisely where the limits were, how much she could afford to give, and he had not been able to make her give a penny more" (*Another Country*, 172). In an extended scene in which Baldwin makes use of free indirect discourse, Ida's orgasm becomes a litmus test measuring the state of their relationship, as well as a metaphor for Vivaldo's capacity to exert control over the trajectory of their relationship. Vivaldo describes Ida as resisting him through her attempts to manage the "limits" of their relationship. He is aggravated by her unwillingness to give herself over to him completely because he believes that orgasm is commensurate with submission. And in an odd twisting of what is already an awkward metaphor, Vivaldo looks on Ida in postcoitus sleep and thinks that she may only intend to "frustrate him; to frustrate, that is, any attempt on his part to strike deeper into the *incredible country* in which, like the princess of fairy tales, sealed in a high tower and guarded by beasts, bewitched and exiled, she paced her secret round of secret days" (173, my emphasis). Most provocative in this scene is Vivaldo's use of the language of exploration as he imagines his complete sexual conquest of Ida. Vivaldo imagines Ida's unwillingness to be more *deeply struck* as a purposeful attempt to keep him out of that *incredible country* of her life. Lest one be swayed into thinking that Vivaldo's imaginings are merely an example of his romantic naiveté, as I noted earlier, the ethnographic gaze relies on an understanding of its subject as an object that might be "penetrated by the heroic figure."[37]

Moving away from Vivaldo's daydream, briefly, to an earlier set of moments in the novel, I would like to explore Vivaldo's pre-Ida relationship to blackness, black women, and black spaces because I think it speaks to what is at stake between Ida and Vivaldo. To say that Vivaldo has a penchant for black women would be an understatement. For many years, Vivaldo traveled to Harlem, where he "dropped his load and marked the spot with silver," in search of a simple exchange of sex for money (*Another Country*, 132). Ultimately the exchange proves to be more emotionally costly than his white liberal guilt can handle, so Vivaldo stops going uptown looking for sex from black prostitutes. However, the novel presents Vivaldo's uptown jaunts as instigated by a search for something more than sex:

For several years it had been his fancy that he belonged
in those dark streets uptown precisely because the history written in the color of his skin contested his right to
be there. He enjoyed this, his right to *be* being everywhere
contested; uptown, his alienation had been made visible
and therefore, almost bearable. It had been his fancy that
danger there was more real, more open, than danger was
downtown and that he, having chosen to run these dangers, was snatching his manhood from the lukewarm
waters of mediocrity and testing it in the fire. He had felt
more alive in Harlem, for he had moved in a blaze of rage
and self-congratulation and sexual excitement, with danger, like a promise, waiting for him everywhere. (132, original emphasis)

What first appears to be movement initiated by a simple car-
nal lust is revealed to be a larger, more extensive quest for white
cultural relevancy and individualism.[38] In other words, Vivaldo
enjoys the excitement, danger, sexual potential, and novelty of
Harlem because he can enjoy what he describes as his right to be
everywhere, even where his presence is most contested. Because
Harlem, like the ethnographic field, is a space that Vivaldo
always has the option of "opting out of" at his whim, it becomes
a space for Vivaldo to test his life and his own sensuality through
close proximity to racial difference. Serving purely as a location
for the enhancement of his sensual being in the world, Vivaldo
moves into the "plot space" of Harlem because it "enables the
narcissistic project of the ethnographer's encounter with himself, his renewal of himself."[39] Harlem, as well as the black people
who live there, are ultimately a necessarily expendable *detour* on
Vivaldo's quest for manhood.

The repercussions of such a self-serving quest for manhood
are dire for black people in the novel. Rufus dies because Vivaldo believed that "they were friends, far beyond the reach of
anything so banal and corny as color" (*Another Country*, 133).
Underlying this quest for manhood is the idea that Vivaldo

might actually learn or uncover something important by traversing this space of contestation. Yet Baldwin denies him any such knowledge. Vivaldo's trips to Harlem produce only "one or two marijuana parties, one or two community debauches, one or two girls whose names he had forgotten, one or two addresses which he had lost. He knew that Harlem was a battlefield and that a war was being waged there day and night—but of the war's aims he knew nothing" (133). He has nothing to show for his time spent in Harlem, which might make some readers question whether Baldwin is actually issuing a critique of the treatment of blackness and black spaces that fall under an ethnographic gaze. As Andrew Killick again points out, "The 'savage,' whether we call her an informant, narrator, interlocutor, or whatever political correctness demands, has been reduced to a function of the plot-space traversed by the anthropologist-as-hero. That plot-space, the field, serves mainly to enable the narcissistic project of the ethnographer's encounter with himself, *his* renewal of *himself* through the penetration of feminized, other space."[40] The plot-space of Harlem, then, traversed by Vivaldo-as-hero serves mainly his narcissistic project of affirming his own self-worth.

The emptiness of Vivaldo's narcissism is nowhere more apparent than in his writing. Again, this connection between Vivaldo and the ethnographic gaze suggests that Baldwin is implying that such a gaze when applied to black people is absolutely useless and may, in fact, be dangerous. After the novel devotes a number of pages of remembrance to Vivaldo's time in Harlem and his relationships with black people, mainly Rufus, Vivaldo returns to his home. Like an ethnographer who returns home after a long and fruitful trip into "the field," Vivaldo soon sits down to write about his experience: "He sat down again at his worktable. The page on the typewriter stared up at him, full of hieroglyphics. He had read it over. It meant nothing whatever. Nothing was happening on that page. He walked back to the window" (135). All of Vivaldo's living and observing is for naught because he is unable to create meaning on the page, as is evidenced by the use of the word "hieroglyphics" to describe his writing—Vivaldo is producing an ancient text that remains unreadable to even him. In a way, Vivaldo's failure as a writer is indicative of Baldwin's refusal to grant him authorial power. Well before the late twentieth-century crisis in ethnographic authority, Baldwin is imagining ways to silence the authority of a dominant heteronormative voice when depicting matters of race and racial difference. We see Vivaldo on numerous occasions—for instance, contemplating writing, watching and making mental notes regarding other people's lives, painting scenes in his mind, and ascribing meaning to others' lives. Yet we never see Vivaldo write, and it appears he may not even be able to read for cultural comprehension. Baldwin denies Vivaldo any potency as a writer and interpreter.

In contrast, let us return to the sexual relationship between Vivaldo and Ida, which one critic wrongfully describes as "a haven from [the racial] brutality" that might befall Ida as a black woman living in the United States.[41] As I noted earlier, the morning after the first recorded sex act between Vivaldo and Ida leaves Vivaldo feeling unmoored. When Ida awakens, she and Vivaldo exchange awkward pleasantries inquiring into whether either of them has ever before loved someone like the other. In other words, they are attempting to determine if the other has ever slept with someone of the other race. Both admit to having had interracial sex before but affirm to each other the uniqueness of what they have. As an affirmation of this uniqueness, the two engage in another sexual encounter. This second encounter is different for Vivaldo than their first "frustrating" sex. The language employed to describe the second encounter—"dangerous," "breaking through," "cruelly," "forced," "bared teeth," "viciously," "pushed her to the edge," "throbbing," and so on—speaks not only to the erotic battle taking place between Ida and Vivaldo but also to Vivaldo's desire to own Ida in the patriarchal way that he felt had eluded him during the first encounter. Between these two scenes, Baldwin uses Ida's orgasm, first its illusiveness and then its fulfillment, as a way to measure Vivaldo's sense of his ownership over her:

"He had never been so patient, so determined, or so cruel before. Last night *she had watched him*; *this morning he watched her*; *he was determined to bring her over the edge and into his possession*, even, if at the moment she finally called his name, the heart within him burst. This, anyway, seemed more imminent than the spilling of his seed" (177, my emphasis). More than his own orgasm, Vivaldo desires to be the last word on Ida's tongue. As the sex scene closes, Vivaldo first watches the "the tall, dusty body, which now belonged to him," then falls asleep and wakes up to find Ida cleaning his apartment and making coffee (179).

It seems rather humorous to imagine that causing an orgasm could spell ownership, "but the idea that boundary and passage stand for sexual intercourse does not preclude the possibility that sex is itself a metaphor for something else—perhaps for a dominant, 'heroic' relation of self to the other."[42] In the case of Ida and Vivaldo in *Another Country*, sexual fulfillment for Vivaldo comes only when his manhood is affirmed through complete sexual domination. Moreover, "sexual imagery is nevertheless a powerful means of conceptualizing [the self-other distinction], through identifying the self with the penetrating male hero. The act of 'interpreting' the other then constitutes not only a symbolic sexual penetration, but the construction of the self as masculine and dominant."[43] In light of this, I am suggesting that Vivaldo imbues the sex act, particularly sexual domination, with the remedy to his earlier incapacities: the first being his inability to acquire a firm grasp on blackness through entering it as one would "enter the field" and the second being his incapacity to return home and write up his "findings." Thus, this ownership of Ida and the need to figure himself a hero become Vivaldo's only claims on the authority of interpretation. Moreover, the metaphorical/literary domination is acted out through heterosexual domination. Placed in the landscape of sexuality, we can begin to see Baldwin's critique of the romance of the ethnography.

Is it possible to produce knowledge in *Another Country*? As I stated earlier in this chapter, many critics have attempted to make sense of *Another Country*'s complicated and slightly unfulfilling narrative and plot by suggesting the various ways in which Baldwin uses knowledge and confusion as a method for social critique. While I agree with Ernesto Martinez's argument that "Baldwin's characters are on the verge of knowing something fundamental about how oppression in the United States functions in their lives,"[44] I disagree with his underscoring of the "suicidal sensibility" that he believes shapes the text. In other words, I do not believe that Baldwin is arguing that individuals need to relinquish (kill) those aspects of their identity that keep them from knowing more about themselves and the social order. Baldwin's intervention comes much sooner than at the moment of having to make a decision about what one will allow oneself to know about oneself, others, and the world around one. Instead, *Another Country* asks what happens when characters assume that they have the right to know what they are not told and/or what is not told to them. If one reads the novel as a crisis in ethnographic authority, then one can begin to see Baldwin making space in knowledge production to include a more democratic, less heteronormative relationship to knowledge and power. Understanding one's right to know is the largest question of the novel. In an attempt to further flesh out the ways in which Baldwin is attempting to create alternative relationships to knowledge and power through narrative, I would like to turn to another relationship in *Another Country*: this time, Vivaldo's sexual relationship with Eric.

Eric is a queer, white, American actor who is recently returned from France to take a role in a Broadway play. On the verge of fame, Eric returns to find the city and friends he once knew changed by the death of Rufus. We also learn that before he left the United States for France, Eric had been connected to the rest of *Another Country*'s ensemble through Rufus, with whom he had a sexual relationship that threatened to end as badly as Rufus and Leona's. Eric functions as the queer male foil to Vivaldo's heteronormative ethnographic gaze. We are led to believe that it is his sexuality that proffers Eric the ability to do the sort

of self-reflexive gazing that leads to self-truth. From his childhood as a queer boy in the American "deep South" (he is from
Alabama) to his return to New York after time spent in France,
Eric is a character at war with himself in order to know the very
nature of love and his life. Unlike Vivaldo, who looks on lovers
with the sense and desire to own them, Eric is deeply invested
with a desire to know himself. Whom does Eric love, and why
does Eric love them?

When Eric enters the novel, we find him oceanside in France,
sitting naked in the garden and watching his lover, Yves, frolic
in the sea. While the scene calls to mind a queer garden of Eden,
the dialogue between Yves and Eric suggests that their time in
France has not been effortless. It is, instead, comparable to Eric's
time in the United States:

> "You are afraid of trouble in New York. Why?"
> "I'm not *afraid*, Yves. But I *have* had a lot of trouble
> there."
> "We have had much trouble here, too," said Yves, with
> his abrupt and always rather shocking gravity, "and we
> have always come out of it and now we are better than ever,
> I think, no?" (*Another Country*, 190)

What becomes apparent in this passage is that Eric's unease
about returning to the United States is an unease that has little
to do with the differences between nations and more to do with
the relationships he had while in the United States. Eric's return
to the States is structured as a return to a space in which he has
to make his sense of himself mesh with the sense his friends (fellow American citizens) have of him. If Paris is a place in which
the "discontented wanderer is thrown back on himself—if his
life is to become bearable, only he can make it so" (215), then
France offers very little escape from the similar work that one
does when in the United States. Additionally, these quotes set
the tone for the major difference between what might be con-
strued as "the field" for Eric and "the field" for Vivaldo. While
Vivaldo visits Harlem to feel differently about himself, as if the

space would transform him or affirm him by virtue of his presence in it, Eric finds that in France he is forced more deeply into himself. This difference in the function of space and identity seems telling as we consider what sort of knowing each man produces.

Eric sees his return to the United States as necessary because "it was time [to come home]. In order not to lose all that he had gained, he had to move forward and risk it all" (229–230). Many critics turn to this quote when they want to instill in Eric a sense of knowledge that surpasses that of many other characters in the novel, and especially when he is compared to Vivaldo. Eric notes that he has to go home because he had to end his three years of "avoiding" and is at risk of becoming an "exile" if he does not return to the United States (184). Like Baldwin's return and run-in with the Florida bank, Eric's return serves some symbolic use: it returns him to his geographical and racialized past, which is shaped by sexual encounters with black men that made him "a man" (206). These early encounters are important to Eric's present because they are what allow him to do the required self-reflexive thought needed for change. Eric, thinking about his first gay sexual experience, which happened with a black man, thinks, "What had always been hidden to him, that day, revealed and it did not matter that, fifteen years later, he sat in an armchair, overlooking a foreign sea, still struggling to find the grace which would allow him to bear that revelation. For the meaning of revelation is that what is revealed is true, and must be borne" (206). This passage may frustrate the reader, as we are never sure what is revealed. Kevin Ohi suggests that this knowledge is figured as a trauma, not as liberation, and that Eric must bear it.[45] Thus, Eric's return to the United States and the return of his childhood memory of gay sexual initiation are linked not as moments of liberation but as moments of reckoning. What is produced from this reckoning is the creation of more self-work that Eric will spend the rest of his life doing. In this sense, I would like to suggest that Baldwin links queer sexuality, knowledge, and self-worth in ways that work in direct opposition to the romance narrative that we saw enacted with Vivaldo and Ida. Rather than producing some sort of final revelation and resolution, that queer self-knowledge is an ongoing and frustrating process is key to true knowledge in Baldwin's novel.

But the notion of self-knowledge is alien to Vivaldo. For instance, in the moments right before he and Eric will make love for the first time, he tells Eric that he cannot decide "whether [Eric] want[s] to make everybody as miserable as [he is], or whether everybody *is* as miserable as [he is]" (*Another Country*, 338). Eric replies by suggesting that Vivaldo frame the question differently: "How happy are *you*? That's got nothing to do with me, nothing to do with how I live, or what I think, or how miserable I am—how are *you* making it?" (338). What Vivaldo reads as misery is actually the effect of self-inquiry (self-reflexivity) that has allowed Eric to move through the world of the novel requiring very little from other characters. Although Eric does manage to take part in the dissolution of Cass and Richard's marriage when he chooses to have an affair with Cass, he does this knowing that it will have repercussions with which he will have to deal (289). But more than modeling for Vivaldo the importance of turning inward the outward glance, Eric's reply suggests that one has to enter into oneself in order to be able to truly know. Knowledge is, thus, not something that comes about through penetrating the minds or experiences of others but rather comes through entering the world differently.

By closely linking knowledge to gay sex in this novel, Baldwin is aligning the possibility of knowledge acquisition with those who allow themselves to be penetrated. Yet, returning to Killick's argument regarding the role of penetration and the ethnographer and the ways in which sex can become a metaphor for the ethnographic process, it seems rather important that Baldwin save the sex scene between Vivaldo and Eric for the end of the novel, when novelist conventions promise a climax that resolves the crises of the novel. After establishing their mutual love and fear of Rufus, Vivaldo and Eric realize that they have cared for and loved each other from afar for many years. But this is not until the morning that they make love for the first time. And while we know that Vivaldo has had gay sex before, "it was his first sexual encounter with a male in many years, and his first sexual encounter with a friend" (284), as well as the first time he has sex with a man that he loves. Baldwin does not deny the importance of love in meaningful sex, but he does shatter the heteronormative narrative of romance that once shadowed Vivaldo's daydream of sex between himself and Ida. On the contrary, the very act of gay sex becomes a mystery to Vivaldo:

> He kissed Eric again and again, wondering how they would finally come together. The male body was not mysterious, he had never thought about it at all, but it was the most *impenetrable of mysteries* now. . . . This was as far removed as anything could be from the necessary war one underwent with women. He would have entered her by now, this woman who was not here. . . . Now, Vivaldo, who was accustomed himself to labor, to be the giver of the gift, and enter into his satisfaction by means of satisfaction of a woman, surrendered to the luxury, the flaming torpor of passivity, and whispered in Eric's ear a muffled, urgent plea. (386)

The sex scene continues until orgasm. While most critics are taken by Vivaldo's shifting to thoughts of Rufus in the midst of the sex act—Vivaldo begins to wonder if Rufus felt or did the same thing as he when he had sex with Eric—they become interested in Vivaldo's seeming guilt and/or latent sexual desire for Rufus.[46] I believe it is actually fairly clear that Vivaldo has sexual feelings for his friend and for men more generally, and thus I am more interested in the other person "present" in the sex scene: Ida. Right before the moment of orgasm, Vivaldo remembers how "Ida, at the unbearable moment, threw back her head and thrashed and bared her teeth. And she called his name" (*Another Country*, 386). The present sex scene continues to an orgasm that has Vivaldo repeatedly calling out Eric's name, in a moment that recalls his own desire to have Ida call his name when he makes her orgasm, thereby linking her penetration to his own. If we take seriously the importance of penetration to the establishment of a heterosexual-masculine position inherent in the traditional role of ethnographer, then Vivaldo is divested of the power he sought to establish earlier in the text through his relationship with Ida. Although Vivaldo will never assume the identity of a gay man,[47] he is forced to change his relationship to Ida and to blackness, since she is the only living stand-in for such an identity concept in the novel.

I would like to place Baldwin's triangulation of Ida, Vivaldo, and Eric's sexual relations within the rather recent tradition of queer discourse of race, shame, and sexual penetration. I do this not merely to point out that Baldwin was an early innovator of intersectional thinking on sexuality, gender, and blackness but also to point out how Baldwin's triangulation offers us an insight into how he generatively imagines nonnormative knowing. *Another Country*, then, might be read as a precursor to thinkers such as Leo Bersani, who, at the height of the white male AIDS crisis of the 1980s, argued in his essay "Is the Rectum a Grave?" that the national aversion to gay sex, and sex more generally, rests on the moral taboo associated with penetration, which is seen as "passive" and thus associated with womanhood.[48] Bersani is much less sophisticated than Baldwin, and down right offensive, in his inability to consider blackness and gayness commingling in a single body. But Bersani's sense that gay sex is somehow shameful and demeaning because its close association with female subordination provides a clear overlap with Baldwin's emphasis on penetrative gay sex as a mode of self remaking, especially for Vivaldo. Moreover, Bersani calls for the embrace of demeaning, the feminine, in sex as a means to "practice nonviolence."[49] In the end, I see the inherent value in Vivaldo's sexual "debasement" because it allows him to finally cease to do the debasing work of getting to "know" others. Instead, Vivaldo's self-debasement allows Baldwin to show us how to value white, male debasement as a means for freedom.

Ida and Autoethnographic Resistance

Many critics have argued that Baldwin too easily rests all the queer power and potential in the white gay male,[50] denying the possibility of black queerness, lesbianism, or even lives for women outside of heteronormative gender roles. So I do not wish to suggest that Baldwin posits that the only character in *Another Country* capable of resisting the authority of the ethnographic gaze is Eric. As a matter of fact, Ida resists Vivaldo's quest to own and know her at every turn, which causes no end of drama in their relationship. In a rather tumultuous moment symbolic of Vivaldo's callous sense of ownership of Ida, he tells her he wants to take her home to Brooklyn to meet his parents. Vivaldo is doubly motivated to take her there: first, he would like to shock his parents, and second, he would like to share his entire life with Ida, which means integrating her into his family circle. Yet Ida is unwilling and uninterested in "the education of [Vivaldo's] family" (*Another Country*, 279). She does not care for their personal growth; she tells him that she is not "about to be bugged by any more white jokers who still can't figure out whether [she's] human or not. If they don't know, baby, sad on them, and [she hopes] they drop dead slowly, and in great pain" (279). Ida cannot be characterized as anti-integrationist since she is dating a white man, but she also refuses to facilitate white moral development by going home with Vivaldo. She is, in short, a great mouthpiece for some of the most interesting ideas regarding the role of black voice and black identity in an increasingly integrating world. She refuses to take on the role of specimen that will usher Vivaldo's family into the new age of American race relations, and she will not teach them how to treat her like their equal. This fight illustrates a clear articulation on the part of the novel's only living black character that cultural translation is not the job of African Americans.

Vivaldo's push to know Ida is what is ultimately their undoing. His approach, which I have established as reenacting an ethnographic romance of penetration, leaves little room for actually knowing what she wants, needs, and deserves. In a racist-sexist world, Ida needs more than love and the promise of a happy ending. Vivaldo continues to be enticed by the romance plot of his relationship because it distracts him for having to confront the truth of his own life, as Eric told him is necessary. Even after having had sex with Eric, Vivaldo continues to try to enact a certain romance narrative with Ida:

> What in the world did these songs mean to her? For he knew that she often sang them in order to flaunt before him privacies which he could never hope to *penetrate* and to convey accusations which he could never hope to decipher, much less deny. And yet, *if he could enter this secret place*, he would, by that act, be released forever from the power of her accusations. His presence in this strangest and grimmest of sanctuaries would prove his right to be there; in the same way that the prince, having outwitted all the dangers and slaughtered the lion, is ushered into the presence of his bride, the princess. (313, my emphasis)

Again we see Vivaldo trying to wrap a fairy-tale plot around his understanding of the significance of black cultural production in Ida's life. If he could escape the romance plot, he might gather something interesting about himself and his own relationship to black culture, rather then merely speaking in terms of illusive fairy-tale subjects.

Ida's resistance to love takes on a greater significance, especially when placed in the context of the novel's larger critique of the heteronormative romance plot. So when Cass suggests that Ida and Vivaldo get married because their love is strong enough to set them "free," Ida responds by saying, "Love doesn't have as much to do with it as everybody seems to think. I mean, you know, it doesn't change everything, like people say. It can be a goddam pain in the ass" (346). Ida will not allow a love that fails to acknowledge the ways in which she feels she has been scarred by the country as a black woman: "Some days, [Cass], I wish I could turn myself into one big fist and grind this miserable country to powder. Some days, I don't believe it has a right to exist. Now, you've never felt like that, and Vivaldo's never felt like that. Vivaldo didn't want to know my brother was dying because he doesn't want to know that my brother would still be alive if he hadn't been born black" (351). Ida is able to reveal to Cass that the national ignorance regarding racial inequity—embodied by Vivaldo in this passage—produces violence against the black citizen. Again, simply ending racial segregation through social interaction and sexual integration will not end the violence that kills men such as Rufus. In other words, although Rufus and Vivaldo were best friends, Vivaldo failed to truly engage with the things that made their friendship impossible. We learn through Ida's retelling of Rufus's cause of death that love and leaving the country are not enough to solve the American racial dilemma.

I would like to suggest that Ida's resistance to a love plot meant to give Vivaldo complete access to her cultural and spiritual soul, along with Vivaldo's newly accessed (sexual) identification with Ida as someone who can also be "penetrated," produces the sort of shift the narrative needs to progress and conclude. While the narrative does not change the relationship between Ida and Vivaldo—readers have no idea if they will stay romantic partners—but we do get the sense that they are different with each other. After Ida reveals to Vivaldo that she has been cheating on him with a television executive that has promised her a leg up in her career, she and Vivaldo are forced to reckon with not only her cheating but also his silence on her cheating. Ida requests that he let her finish her story, thereby forcing Vivaldo to know the things he does not want to know, the things that stray from the fairy-tale narrative that he extracts from her through cajoling and asserting his own heroism (417). Finally, it is Ida's decision to damage the romance that sets them free. The results are breathtaking.

After having been informed of the truth, Vivaldo is able to conjure a "detail that he needed for his novel, which he had been searching for for months," and he finds his mind "illuminated, justified, clarified" in ways that it had not been for months, simply because he has now listened to the stories of another and has not attempted to impose his own voice and/or escape the ways in which the story implicates him (427). What he gets, however, is not a happy ending: "He had finally got what he wanted, the truth out of Ida, or the true Ida; and he did not know how he was going to live with it" (430). But I would argue that Baldwin's refusal to end the story with hope and revelation—Vivaldo is unable to say "I love you" because "the words would not come" (430)—mark his divestment of the romance plot as a means of change and salvation in a desegregating nation. Moreover, Ida makes it clear that she does not want his understanding, and she does not want him translating her emotions into his language, into a pattern that he can manage. His promise to "not understand" allows him to lose the innocence that had made it impossible for him to write in the past (431). We watch him sit down, but what Vivaldo will write remains to be seen. Instead, we are given the impression that it will have to be something that implicates him and requires him to accept his responsibility for the status quo.

As I consider the awkward and unfinished relationship between Vivaldo and Ida at the end of *Another Country*, I am further reminded of the importance of Vivaldo's debasement and its tie to blackness and womanhood. Their lack of communion, their sure disunion, galvanized by Vivaldo's embrace of penetrative gay sex, speaks to the important connection between "black" and "queer."[51] As Kathyrn Stockton argues in *Beautiful Bottom, Beautiful Shame: Where "Black" Meets "Queer"* (2006), self-debasement does "not create harmonious communities of like-minded black or similarly identified same-sex queers"; it creates, instead, "a kind of social solitude of people who are set, in some deep measure, apart from each other—but in an apartness they create together and in which they are held."[52] Stockton's treatment of shame and debasement as central to the concepts of "queer" and "black" helps us to understand that Baldwin's use of Vivaldo's debasement does not mean to create a cohesive community—black and white, male and female, gay and straight; rather, discordance between these binaries might constitute communities under a more positivist vision. There is no marriage or long-term union in store for Vivaldo and Ida— not because Vivaldo has had sex with another person but because Baldwin's narrative stays true to the danger of the romance plot when exploring racial and sexual knowing. Various distances in the novel are opened wide with no promise of closing, and one is given the sense that such is the way that it should be.

I began this chapter with a set of remembrances that Baldwin shared with Mead regarding what it means to be a black man returning to the United States from abroad and the way he highlights how he is different or changed by the experience. Baldwin ties his response to racial oppression back to larger social justice movements taking place within the United States. The result of his refusal to accept his newly coined status as "French" is that he is able the weave together the relational similarities between African Americans in the United States and those outside the States around issues of black social justice. Moreover, these social justice movements of which Baldwin was a part throughout his adult life, whether living in New York City or Istanbul,[53] make it impossible for a romance plot of national interracial union to take hold without a great degree of national reckoning. One can neither escape to another country nor refuse to acknowledge the past and past damages done. It is again in Baldwin's letter to his nephew that he articulates that a black person's role in integration is not merely to accept white people or to educate them in black humanity but to force them, through a critical love (not romance), "to cease fleeing from reality and begin to change it."[54] Following Baldwin's refusal to make black culture and cultural production into a "knowable object of analysis," the next chapter will explore how Chester Himes distorts the geographical site of blackness (Harlem) in an attempt to completely deny white access to black subjectivity.

4 /　Ethnography of the Absurd: Chester Himes's Detective Fiction and Counterimages of Black Life

For my part, judging from what I have so far seen (and I don't think anything I shall see henceforth will change it) I like America best; I like it despite its faults, and there are many; perhaps I like it because of them. I am what America made me, and the longer I stay away the more I discover how much of America is in me and how much of me is in America.

CHESTER HIMES[1]

In January 1957, Marcel Duhamel[2] approached Chester Himes to write a crime novel for the Gallimard publishing house's *Série noir*.[3] Himes, who, like so many of his African American contemporaries,[4] had left the United States four years earlier to live in Europe, was finding it difficult to sustain himself financially and agreed to write for the *Série noir* because the publisher advanced him a thousand dollars on the novel.[5] And while Himes had no qualms about writing strictly for money, the success in France of the novel *La reine des pommes*[6] encouraged him to continue writing in the genre.

Ultimately Himes came to believe that the genre of detective fiction offered him, and other African American writers as well, the optimal outlet for expressing the violence of black life in the United States: "American violence is public life," he wrote, "it's a public way of life, it became a form, a detective story form. So I would think that any number of black writers should go into the detective story form. As a matter of fact, I feel that they could be very competent. Anyway, I would like to see a lot of them do so."[7] More importantly, because the series was both written for a French audience and first published by French publishers, the detective series delivered Himes from the same American publishing industry that made it impossible for Richard Wright to exercise full creative control over his artistic vision. And more than delivering Himes from the same fate of Wright, financially and creatively, writing in France allowed Himes to move away from the stagnant genres of realism and protest that he took up in his early novel *If He Hollers Let Him Go* (1945). The French, in turn, were drawn to Himes's Harlem novels because the novels fed them the "spectacle" and "sensationalistic details about U.S. race relations and African American urban life" that had historically fascinated French intellectuals.[8] His generic distance, coupled with this ability to continue to be financially solvent due to his representation of a version of urban black American life for a French audience hungry for hyperbole, marks Himes's detective writing in interesting ways that I will take up throughout this chapter. So in addition to the literal distance separating Himes from the United States, Duhamel's invitation to Himes freed him to create some of the most interesting and rich African American–authored crime fiction of the twentieth century.

While Himes did not invent African American detective fiction,[9] his work within the genre makes him one of the most prolific and committed African American writer before Walter Mosely's rise to the helm of black detective fiction. As the most well-known mid-twentieth-century African American detective writer, Himes had his detective novels cover varied topics, themes, and characterizations concerning urban black life. From rogue police officers and cross-dressers to dope and sex fiends, the men and women who populate Himes's literary accounts offer readers a version of the black experience that is grim and dirty, but always vibrant and moving. Moreover, the fabric of life that Himes weaves into his depiction of an unremitting black Harlem is complex. It is a complexity that depends on Harlem's *local color*. Or, as Himes more aptly states, "I put the slang, the daily routine, and complex human relationships of Harlem into my detective novels, which I prefer to call 'domestic novels' for that reason."[10] In other words, creating Harlem as a domestic space, a space of "home," a space where inhabitants can be themselves, is crucial to Himes. And Himes's Harlem cycle—his "domestic novels"—which consists of eight novels[11] written between 1957 and 1969 with Harlem as a primary setting, depict a very intimate space. Like any domestic space, then, these novels grant a type of knowledge power to people with firsthand knowledge of the place. In fact, in Harlem, knowledge power is commensurate with how much time one actually spends there. Those who are inhabitants always occupy the role as most knowledgeable and most able to negotiate Harlem, even though it is a recognizable police state, which requires limitations on their mobility and autonomy.

Thus, in this chapter, I am interested in exploring how Himes manages to make Harlem a home to its black inhabitants, while also creating a set of narratives that highlight the location as a place under siege by the white power structure. As Manthia Diawara argues in his essay "Noir by Noirs," Himes's detective series remains a radical critique of black American life because of his insistence on never shying away from racial protest, even when he seems to swing toward potboilers of the noir tradition. Riffing off the noir tradition, which itself rests on the visual glorification of whiteness through negative association of evil with blackness, Diawara notes that Himes's detective novels, though not part of the realist/protest tradition for which he became relatively famous, are radical because, "for Himes, Black people are living in hell and White people in heaven not because the one color is morally inferior to the other, but because Black people are held as captives in the valley below the towers of Riverside Church. The noirs in Himes's text are Black people trapped in the darkness of White captivity, and the light shed on them is meant to render them visible, not White."[12] Similar to Diawara's sense that Himes sought to create a productive black narrative out of the rubble of white oppression, I seek to explore how Chester Himes, writing from Paris, attempted to create an alternative black identity by re-creating the black American ghetto from abroad. In this chapter, I will focus on four of Himes's novels and explore how Himes's works engage similar themes of cultural translation and ethnographic description that have been examined in previous chapters.

Unlike Hurston, Wright, or even Baldwin, Himes's intervention into the discourse of black cultural translation is done exclusively through the novel form. Thus, his detective protagonists, Grave Digger Jones and Coffin Ed Johnson, who remain constant over the set of Harlem-based detective novels, function as participant-observers by virtue of spending the entire detective series translating the motivations of black criminals to a larger white police force. I argue that Himes, much like Baldwin, is critical of participant-observation's capacity to produce any sort of realistic representation of black life. Himes thus disrupts this technique by rendering the detectives more and more ineffectual as he moves closer to the final installment of the series. With my concluding discussion of Himes, I usher my readers into the moment just before the Black Arts Movement and the rise of black nationalist thought. The very act of black cultural translation is fated for Himes, and the death of the participant-observer is foundational to understanding Himes's detective series as a whole.

In the midst of the dichotomy between participant-observer and the observed community, Himes makes use of a set of black detectives who function as both native informants and participant-observers to the absurd violence of black Harlem. They serve to create a "document" of blackness that only an "outsider" would believe. I want to stress here that I believe Himes employs an ironic relationship to the ethnographic function of his novels for his audience of white (French) readers—as the novels always had first runs in France. This ironic relationship moves the novels into the realm of absurdity, the unbelievable but entirely founded; hence as the chapter title suggest, Himes creates ethnography of the absurd that seeks to document not black life with any realism but black life under the arresting pressure and violence of white oppression. In the end, the detective series provides readers, depending on their race, a varied experience of what is "real" about black culture: is it the violence of black people, or is it the violence of urban segregation and living under a police state? Thus, this notion of the "real" and the verisimilitude expected of ethnography is where I will center my analysis of Chester Himes's detective fiction. And what better place to set the "real" than the "home"? Himes's decision to frame his detective cycle as a "domestic series" invites us to consider that those who are not part of the domestic space lack the intimacy, familiarity, and, thus, a certain amount of agency within Harlem. Within the Harlem cycle, more often than not, those who lack that familiarity are white police officers. This shift in power within Harlem is what Himes prized most about his novels. As Wendy Walters suggests, taking her cue from Himes himself, detective fiction was Himes's way of intervening in a national narrative that had rendered the average African American powerless. "Himes's detective novels," writes Walters, "allow him to control the site of nostalgia, briefly to imagine refashioning U.S. race relations and law enforcement practices."[13] Acting as the patriarch of this domestic sphere, Himes attempts to use the detective novel to remedy the problems inherent in U.S. race relations and the Jim Crow system, both of which have contributed to the formative conditions of a space such as Harlem in the mid-twentieth century. Thus, by confronting the racism of hard-boiled detective fiction, Himes takes a shot at the white establishment; or as Megan Abbott suggests, "Himes's use of hardboiled conventions to present a vision of black masculinity takes on added resonance for . . . hardboiled fiction is a historically racist tradition with a long history of taking great pains to ignore, diminish, or stereotype black men."[14]

From *A Rage in Harlem* to *Blind Man with a Pistol*,[15] Himes conceives of Harlem as a space where two black police offers, "Grave Digger" Jones and "Coffin Ed" Johnson, have the power to solve crimes and to protect black citizens from themselves and, more importantly, from the white police force. Yet this depiction of these detectives changes over the course of the detective series, making it harder for readers and the black community of Harlem to see them as much more than another hand of white power. In this sense, they become native informants that must be eliminated in order for Himes's imagined Harlem to survive outside of complete ordering of their lives by the white state. In addition to imagining and sketching out the deaths of his native informants, I argue that Himes also creates a category of "policed men," who function to subvert the power structure that polices Harlem.

More than challenging power structures, Himes's detective fiction requires readers to reconsider the "facts" of blackness. Confronted with a landscape of violence and sexual perversity that have historically been represented as synonymous with black American life filtered through a white supremacists' America, Chester Himes's detective fiction poses the problem of realism for many of its readers. The violence of Himes's work rests on readers' belief that anything can happen in Harlem, a refrain that Himes's protagonists Grave Digger and Coffin Ed often repeat. Himes's understanding of white racism and his knowledge of what Christopher Breu has termed the "fantasy of correspondence" encouraged Himes to write Harlem as a space where violence and sex are not only natural but expected. Under the fantasy of correspondence, "fiction and everyday life are presented as inextricably bound together, meanings from the one shaping and reformulating those from the other and vise versa."[16] If black violence and sexuality in Himes's works are perceived as inextricably bound due to racial expectations produced by white racism, then we must consider the work Himes does to undermine those very expectations. I believe that it is at the moment when readers are expecting racial verisimilitude, the hallmark of ethnographic writing, that Himes delivers hyperbole.

Mapping Harlem: Refusal of the Knowable Region

Chester Himes's detective novels are sketched over symbolic multilayered maps of Harlem. We can begin to imagine a realistic city grid on which characters are placed and over which they move. For instance, in the first pages of Chester Himes's *Rage in Harlem* (1957), the first installment of his Harlem detective cycle featuring his now-famous detectives Grave Digger Jones and Coffin Ed Johnson, readers are given the exact location of these main characters: "They were standing around the kitchen table. The window looked out on 142nd Street. Snow was falling on the ice-locked piles of garbage stretching like levees along the gutters as far as the eye could see."[17] Himes's attention to "the real" landscape of Harlem is one of the ways in which he begins to craft his ethnography-inspired series as a set of texts meant to deceive his readers into believing they are being given "the truth." By placing characters within the Harlem landscape, Himes demonstrates not only that Harlem is populated with African Americans but that the life events of these novels' characters correspond to a very real space.

But it becomes clear fairly early that Himes is not particularly invested in realism. In fact, Himes's detective fiction is filled with senseless murders and characters engaged in farfetched schemes such as a "Back to the Plantation Movement." Yet through it all, he remains true to representing a varied urban experience and, most importantly, its accompanying racism—a practice that defines the experience in terms of its absurdity[18]—by relying on geographical realities. Himes considered the absurdity of his texts as indicative of their realism: "My books are as authentic as the autobiography of Malcolm X. But I don't strain after authenticity when I'm writing them. I sit there laughing at the people, I believe in them so completely."[19] While we have come to accept the collaborative narrative produced between Alex Haley and Malcolm X to be an "autobiographical" account of Malcolm X's life, the complexity of genre (autobiography, biography, interview, and/or fiction) marked by the Haley-X collaboration makes Himes's play on authenticity most interesting. Himes's laughter is hard to place, but it is much more central than whether he is telling a true story about black Harlem in his detective stories. It is Himes's ability to laugh at

French readers gobbling down black hyperbole and his ability to laugh at an American racial system that produces black hyperbole that Himes seems to desire to capture. As Kevin Bell points out regarding the stakes of Himes's detective novels, "Himes's novels are rather an improvisational rethinking of time and event that, in their irreverent defusing of the definitional and in their cinematic poetics of discontinuity, explore and eviscerate the American culture industry that produces 'race,' 'gender,' and other categories of cultural identity solely to exploit them."[20] In other words, Himes's texts seek not to replicate through realistic representation the identity categories that create, confine, and manage black life in the United States but rather to laugh directly in the face of those who believe in and or value such oppressive categorization and devaluing of black life.

However, playing with notions of a "realistic" portrayal of black city life requires more than just adding black characters to streets that really exist. Instead Himes's aim is to provide a varied collection of experiences that resonate with those that might exist within any cityscape—for example, racism, police brutality, poverty, violence, crime, the quest for civil rights, friendship, and community. Himes addresses the violence of racism with attention to how a community might provide a safety net. Written and published on the heels of the Supreme Court decision in *Brown v. Board of Education* (1954), Chester Himes's detective fiction plays out versions of the turmoil of U.S. race relations.

The term *domestic*, consequently, has a twofold resonance: it illuminates Himes's quest to depict a symbolic black space that is home to its residents, and it underscores the very intimate story of African Americans living under a police state—a story with which he became familiar during the time he spent as a prison inmate.[21] The tension present in Himes's fiction between Harlem as home and Harlem as police state is another iteration of the insider/outsider debate that has shaped other chapters of this book. Himes attempts to articulate this tension as follows: "When I describe life in Harlem, the people live in poverty and moral misery, but retain a capacity to enjoy every moment. Most of the characters are petty criminals or victims, and many of them have only a hazy perception of the oppression they suffer, or any understanding of the link between racism and economic exploitation. Of course, all of this is part of the fabric of their lives, and they aren't thinking about it. They're far too busy surviving."[22] Himes is somewhat patronizing here of Harlem residents' ability to understand racism as the cause of their socioeconomic oppression, but his confidence in the group's ability to continue to create a rich fabric of life in the face of oppression is visible in his novels. As Raymond Nelson notes, "without sacrificing his bitter moral outrage, without taking his eyes from the ugly wound at which he has relentlessly pointed for some thirty-five years, he brightens his sordid criminal Harlem with the wild comedy, eccentricity of character, and exotic low-life that he inherited from the celebratory black writers of the twenties. . . . They are at once depraved and funny, grotesque and amiable, absurd and pragmatic, agonized and witty."[23] Ultimately, understanding the resilience of Himes's characters is key to making sense of the dark and violent detective novels and the role they play in intervening in the national narrative of race relations. Throughout the detective series, he tries to use Grave Digger and Coffin Ed to explain the home space of Harlem.

To explore exactly how Himes intervenes in the national narrative of blackness, this analysis will deal specifically with Himes's *A Rage in Harlem* (1957), *The Real Cool Killers* (1959), *Run Man Run* (1959), and *Blind Man with a Pistol* (1969). I have selected these particular texts because they represent a cross-section of themes that can be found throughout the Harlem cycle. Most important, topography and the policing system are thematic focuses for Himes. Additionally, the texts have been selected because their publication dates (1957–1969) and the deteriorating success of detectives Grave Digger and Coffin Ed in solving crimes coincide with the reality of a deteriorating national belief in the possibility of racial equality for African Americans. By the time Himes writes *Blind Man with a Pistol* in 1969, the nation is being torn apart by race riots (which Himes includes in the text), and the novel's depiction of the ineptitude of Grave Digger and Coffin Ed invites a discussion of contemporaneous national race relations that rest on assimilation and cultural translation.

In much the same way as Ralph Ellison depicts the dichotomous relationship between the symbolic spaces of Harlem and not-Harlem in *Invisible Man*, Chester Himes is interested in Harlem's role in creating and sustaining a form of African American urban identity. In the face of outsiders who would like to define and control this space, Himes centers the narrative action of his novels within Harlem. And excluding *Run Man Run*, the space of not-Harlem plays a minor role, at most, in the novels. This outside space, instead, is often referenced only to mark Harlem's boundaries; it exists for Himes as Harlem's antithesis.

But what and where is Himes's Harlem? The answer to this question is complicated. On the one hand, Himes's Harlem exists on the map he creates through his incessant recital of street numbers and landmarks. Himes is invested in re-creating an accurate verbal map of Harlem, and it is made up of streets, cross-streets, and major landmarks. On the other hand, this map is formed out of his memories of the real space—and as we shall come to see, these memories are far from accurate. The description, which I quote at length, demonstrates Himes's ability to delineate and his interest in re-creating a verbal map of Harlem.

> Where 125th Street crosses Seventh Avenue is the Mecca of Harlem. To get established there, an ordinary Harlem citizen has reached the promised land, if it merely means standing on the sidewalk.
>
> One Hundred and Twenty-fifth Street connects the Triborough Bridge on the east with the former Hudson River Ferry into New Jersey on the west. Crosstown buses ply up and down the streets at the rate of one every ten

minutes. White motorists passing over the complex toll bridge from the Bronx, Queens or Brooklyn sometimes have occasion to pass through Harlem to the ferry, Broadway or other destinations, instead of turning downtown via the East Side Drive.

Seventh Avenue runs from the north end of Central Park to the 155th Street Bridge where the motorists going north to Westchester County and beyond cross over the Harlem River into the Bronx and the Grand Concourse. The Seventh Avenue branch of the Fifth Avenue bus line passes up and down this section of Seventh Avenue and turns over to Fifth Avenue on 100th Street at the top of Central Park and goes down Fifth Avenue to Washington Square.

Therefore many white people riding the buses or in motor cars pass this corner daily. Furthermore, most of the commercial enterprises—stores, bars, restaurants, theaters, etc.—and real estate are owned by white people.

But it is the Mecca of the black people just the same. The air and the heat and the voices and the laughter, the atmosphere and the drama and the melodrama, are theirs. Theirs are the hopes, the schemes, the prayers and the protest. They are the managers, the clerks, the cleaners, they drive the taxis and the buses, they are the clients, the customers, and the audience; they work it, but the white man owns it. So it is natural that the white man is concerned with their behavior; it's his property. But it is the black people's to enjoy. The black people have the past and the present, and they hope to have the future.[24]

Himes maps, very specifically, the boundaries of Harlem: it is located in upper Manhattan, starting about 110th Street (above Central Park); it is bordered on either side by water, the Hudson and the Harlem rivers; and it is linked to the rest of the city and boroughs by a network of bridges, ferries, streets, and subway tunnels. It is a precise map whose grid is rendered with an accuracy that Himes, through frequent visits to Harlem during his expatriation, spent years developing. Himes's devotion to his maps offers readers a clear sense of the space within which the characters of his novels interact and, more importantly, live (or die, more often than not). Like early map makers that Michel de Certeau references, Himes attempts to represent Harlem with the "totalizing eye"[25] of the "white man."

But more than just detailing a map of Harlem, Himes's attention to Harlem's contours—from the natural and man-made structures that mark its boundaries to the apartment buildings and historic landmarks that fill the space—creates a sense that every recess of Harlem is knowable from this particular perspective. The totalizing serves at a meta-level to add a grandness to the space, suggesting that every line has some symbolic importance to the plot and character. Even his choice to call Harlem "Mecca," a symbolic space in its own right, serves as a signal to readers that the site holds a power and is a refuge for its inhabitants.

However, the Harlem that Himes describes in his domestic series is the Harlem of his memory. Himes makes no secret of the fact that he was not a Harlem resident. "I didn't know what it was like to be a citizen of Harlem; I had never worked there, raised children there, been hungry, sick or poor there," Himes writes. "The Harlem of my books was never meant to be real; I never called it real: I just wanted to take it away from the white man if only in my books."[26] Similarly, Himes recounts in an interview an incident involving a black college professor who attempted to chastise him for being inaccurate and, as a result, an inauthentic spokesperson for the black condition. Himes responds to the accusation by stating that he "had created a Harlem of [his] mind; that [he] had never attempted to be a spokesman for any segment of the black community."[27] Each of these quotations brings to bear, once again, the question of realism in Himes's work.

How is the gap between realism and memory bridged, especially when that memory has no substantive experiential

138 / ETHNOGRAPHY OF THE ABSURD

base? Responding to Himes's admission that he had never lived in Harlem, Michael Denning suggests that Himes's stories should be considered "topographies of this unreal city [Harlem], a mapping of its symbolic landscape." "The Harlem of his [Himes's] topography assaults the imaginary Harlem of the stories of white America," according to Denning.[28] His assessment of Himes's novels, and Himes's own assessment of those same novels, encourages readers to think of the domestic detective cycle as a guide to understanding a *type* of urban black experience. The creation of the Harlem cycle is an attempt to reappropriate a space that, as Himes describes it, is owned by white people. So the Harlem domestic series is both an assertive representation of the African Americans community's hold on its past, present, and future and Himes's own attempt to take hold of a narrative that has been the "property" of a white imagination for too long. Thus, from abroad, Himes repeatedly returns to the United States via the Harlem of his imagination. To think of Harlem as a symbolic space where various allegories of U.S. race relations in circulation during the mid-twentieth century can be explored from an African American perspective allows for the simultaneous commingling of realism and the "unreal," a combination that is the foundation of the surreal. More important, however, is the fact that Himes meets the myth of blackness concocted by a racist society not with reality but with another myth. And this may well be the most important point of Himes's novels: not that they tell a real story of black life but that they represent the imposition of a black-authored myth over that of white-authored myths of blackness.

From Harlem streets, apartments, basements, restaurants, bars, and crime scenes to the police station, Himes's domestic detective novels offer readers varied glimpses into black life in Harlem. But this is, after all, hard-boiled detective fiction, so much of the action in the Himes Harlem series takes place "off the beaten path." Unlike the classical detective story, the

ETHNOGRAPHY OF THE ABSURD / 139

hard-boiled genre into which Himes writes features a hard-boiled city space that consists of "empty modernity, corruption, and death" and is a "wasteland," a "man-made desert or cavern of lost humanity"[29] made possible by American racism. Moreover, readers are given access to marginal spaces, but, more importantly, they are shown the ways in which marginal spaces can be manipulated by characters. This is incredibly important because it becomes the most obvious way in which Himes begins to articulate a critical stance against the ethnographic impulse of mapping that results in the totalizing map that I spoke of earlier. Readers soon find that Harlem is not at all what is on the map. We see the insides of pot dens, abandoned funeral parlors, criminal hideouts, and brothel bedrooms more frequently than we ever see the inside of "respectable" homes—occasionally characters will visit family and friends who live outside of Harlem, but they always seem out of place. In fact, Grave Digger and Coffin Ed, who live on Long Island or Queens depending on what book one reads, are rarely placed in their homes. What begins to develop, then, is an understanding that these marginal spaces within Harlem are metonymical to a greater Harlem. As with Himes's description of Harlem as a space that outsiders often travel around or "pass through" on the way to someplace else, so it is with these marginal spaces. They are overlooked and underused; they are dangerous. Himes's novels are filled with descriptions of Harlem spaces that are "dark, deserted, dismal, . . . eerie, shunned and unpatrolled at night, where a man could get his throat cut in perfect isolation with no one to hear his cries and no one brave enough to answer them if he did."[30] In many ways, Himes's Harlem is exactly the Harlem of the white imaginary—it is violent, dirty, and filled with seemingly unredeemable residents.

Looking eastward from the towers of Riverside Church, perched among the university buildings on high banks of

the Hudson River, waves of gray rooftops distort the perspective like the surface of the sea. Below the surface, in the murky waters of fetid tenements, a city of black people who are convulsed in desperate living, like the voracious churning of millions of hungry cannibal fish. Blind mouths eating their own guts. Stick a hand in and draw back a nub.
  That is Harlem.
  The further east it goes, the blacker it gets.[31]

More often than not, Himes describes Harlem as a cesspool filled with cannibalizing, black piranhas. It is a fearful place, then, because it resists knowability, even when it appears to be peddling the most archetypical images of black urban destitution.

  And this is the very image of Harlem that Himes wishes to expropriate. He redeploys this version of Harlem by recasting the milieu. Whereas Harlem appears at a distance to be a fetid ocean of tenements, in Himes's Harlem no space is exactly what it appears to be. What we come to learn is that the verisimilitude of the verbal map Himes created was merely a façade. There is no such thing as verisimilitude in Himes's Harlem. Himes's attention to perspective—being at a distance versus being in the midst—creates a system whereby those who never enter these marginal spaces are never able to decipher the complicated ecosystems these spaces support. Most of these marginal spaces serve a multiple array of functions for the true residents. For instance, in *A Rage in Harlem*, Goldy, the cross-dressing, nun-impersonating brother of the tale's protagonist, conducts all his business in the back of a tobacco store, "which fronted for a numbers drop and reefer shop."[32] Additionally, this shop serves as the hangout for a group of delinquent boys. Adding another layer, Goldy uses his room in the back to shoot up speedballs and to hatch his own confidence games. As a result, readers are shown not only the underbelly but the potential depth of every space in Harlem. One can never be sure what is authentic about the people or the places in Harlem. Himes continues to explore the multiplicity of Harlem spaces in *Blind Man with a Pistol*. The novel opens on a sign in the window of a long-condemned house that reads, "Funerals Performed." Neighbors have noticed an onslaught of black nuns entering and exiting the building but have investigated no further because they assume that the building is being used as a convent: "The colored neighbors just assumed it was a convent, and that it was in such bad repair seemed perfectly reasonable in view of the fact that it was obviously a jim-crowed convent, and no one ever dreamed that white Catholics would act any different from anyone else who was white."[33] Soon after the nuns' foot traffic is noticed by the neighbors, another sign appears in the window: "Fertile womens, lovin God, inquire within."[34] It is not until this sign appears in the window that the police are moved to investigate the space. What they find inside is an old black man named Reverend Sam, his eleven wives, and more than fifty naked children eating at a trough. The smell of feces (actually a stew of pig's feet, chitterlings, and other animal bowels) plagues the air. Questioning reveals that Sam is a Mormon, has fathered all fifty children, and likes to keep twelve wives for religious purposes—hence the sign in the window for fertile women. Sam's hypersexualized household— the detectives make note that the genitalia of Sam's young sons appear to be elongated—plays into antiquated stereotypes concerning black sexual prowess. In a bout of post-Moynihan surrealism, Himes does little to dispel this myth and others concerning the viability of a traditional African American family. In fact, we find later that Sam is part of an illegal child-smuggling ring. His children are being given away to whites for purposes that remain unclear.[35]

What begins to take shape is the expected narrative of black sexuality, family disorder, and foul living conditions. But Himes distorts and hyperbolizes—makes absurd—this

142 / ETHNOGRAPHY OF THE ABSURD

well-known narrative until it becomes unrecognizable to (white) readers[36] expecting a certain version of black identity. Even the white police officers are forced to admit the implausibility of what they find in the condemned house; they are frustrated by questioning Sam and his family because all their answers are too expected, too stereotypical. And herein lies the power of this particular symbolic space. Reverend Sam's "home" is both what whites expect and what they believe cannot exist. I would like to suggest that Himes reclaims black sexuality and the black home and family by creating a space so foul and unimaginable that it is untouchable by the white community. Police are expelled because they have no language to interpret what they have seen.

In addition to creating a hyperbolic vision of black identity, Himes uses the strategy of drawing attention to the ways in which Harlem creates palimpsestic spaces—new spaces built on old ones, with the new space never fully erasing the place that came before. Similar to his use of Goldy's "office" to illustrate how Harlem consists of many spaces that are used for a motley of purposes by a cross-section of Harlem residents, in *Blind Man with a Pistol* Himes explores how these spaces remain in constant circulation. Unlike the empty tenements in which Richard Wright's Bigger Thomas hides out in the Chicago-based *Native Son* (1940), Himes's Harlem is fully occupied. And, more important, like a Middle Eastern city, Harlem is built on itself, but the imprint of the past is never far from the surface. It is this imprint that outsiders find confusing.

One such palimpsestic space is the auto-insurance office of Seymour Rosenblum. Himes writes that a sign that reads, "CHICKEN AUTO INSURANCE, Seymour Rosenblum," was often misunderstood by white motorists driving through Harlem. The text goes on to note, "white motorists thought that the Negro speaker was selling 'chicken auto insurance' for Seymour Rosenblum. They could believe it. 'Chicken' had to do with the expression, 'Don't be chicken!' and that was the way people drove in Harlem."[37] However, the "chicken" part of the sign was left over from a bankrupted restaurant's sign that had been replaced by Mr. Rosenblum's insurance company. And even more importantly, the history continues to be layered. Besides glossing a history of the vexed relationship between blacks and Jews in Harlem, Himes posits this site as one of racial revolution. The genuine use of this space at the moment the narrative takes place is for Marcus Mackenzie to preach the gospel of brotherhood. Mackenzie, a black preacher, is convinced that the answer to the U.S. race problem is for black and white people to march half naked through the streets of Harlem. However farfetched Mackenzie's plan, his concern for an answer to the race problem in the United States underscores the relationship between national politics and Harlem's symbolic spaces. In this layered history, each layer influences the one that will come after it. History of space and race is the unavoidable truth of Himes's use of stratified spaces in the domestic series.

Refusal of a Knowable People

Just as Himes is unremitting in his quest to question and consider mainstream notions of Harlem as a region that might be easily definable and knowable, he is equally concerned with disrupting notions of identity. For that reason, there are two types of men in Himes's detective fiction: police men and policed men. To say that these positions follow racial lines would be to undermine the complicated racial scenario that Chester Himes creates in each of his novels. Because Grave Digger and Coffin Ed are black police officers and, at least at the start of the domestic series, control Harlem with violence and guns, as well as control the white precinct's relationship to black Harlem, the typical "white police officers against black residents" scenario is hard to sustain in these books. Himes constructs narratives in which the process of detection and policing are at times unsystematic and unreliable. Moreover, policing Harlem is a practice that requires community involvement—sometime voluntary, sometimes coerced by violence—both black and white. As a result, Digger and Coffin's aim is to work within the police system to make it impossible for white police officers to perpetuate race-induced police brutality in Harlem. Digger and Coffin are the only police officers who have geographical, physical, and intellectual access to Harlem residents, and thus they function as native informants to the police force. As Wendy Walters points out, "their license for brutality is based on the police department's utter reliance on them as skilled readers of Harlem's behavioral and linguistic codes."[38] Likewise, Stephen Soitos believes that Digger and Coffin are "doubleconscious detectives in the sense that they themselves are trickster figures who bridge the white and black worlds, using both to their advantage."[39] The black detectives, then, are mediators between the black and white worlds. However, rather than simply supplying the white police force with black victims, they act as "community protectors." Grave Digger and Coffin Ed complicate notions of black criminality with their insistence that Harlem residents are not all criminals, and this complication is something encouraged within the novels. When Himes was asked if he thought Grave Digger and Coffin Ed were "sellouts" to their race because they policed Harlem with violence, he responded by saying that he had created them as idealized versions of black police. "I replaced a stereotype," said Himes. "I've taken two people who would be anti-black in real life, and made them sympathetic."[40] Unlike the white police, they are able to protect Harlem because they care. So, while they are representatives of the law, early in the series they are just as interested in protecting Harlemites as they are in solving crime. They exist in a liminal space between insiders and outsiders that is hard to maintain as the series draws closer to its end, closer to an attempt to make a black nationalist statement, as I will describe in more depth in this book's conclusion.

In no other of the domestic novels is Grave Digger and Coffin Ed's commitment to protecting black Harlem more apparent than in *The Real Cool Killers*. This novel centers on the death of a white man in Harlem. As the story progresses, we learn that the white man who has been murdered was a sexual pervert with a penchant for beating underage black girls. Grave Digger and Coffin Ed's investigation is juxtaposed with a larger, white police investigation of the same murder. But whereas Grave Digger and Coffin Ed are interested in getting to the bottom of the murder, the white police officers cling to racial stereotypes and rely on excessive violence to little avail:

> Uniformed [white] police stood on the roof, others were coming and going through the entrance; still others stuck their heads out of front windows to shout to other cops in the street. The other front windows were jammed with colored faces, looking like clusters of strange purple fruit in the stark white light.
>
> "You can see for yourselves we're looking for the killer," the chief said. "We're going through those buildings with a fine-toothed comb, one by one, flat by flat, room by room. We have the killer's description. He's wearing tool-proof handcuffs. We should have him in custody before morning. He'll never get out of that dragnet."[41]

Rather than investigate the events leading up to the white man's murder, the white police force initiates a massive manhunt, and every black person in the ghetto is treated like the potential killer.[42] The police let racial slurs fly and violence ensue, but they are unable to detect *who done it*. The white police investigation is impeded at every pass by the Real Cool Moslems, a group of teenaged delinquents who disguise themselves as Arabs[43] when on the streets of Harlem. Most of the Harlem community knows the boys' true identities, but the police are unable to coerce this information out of any residents. In fact, when they end up in the hideout for the Moslems and come face-to-face with the group and its leader, who later incriminates himself as the murderer, the police are still unsure of the group's identity.

In the midst of this manhunt, we find Grave Digger and Coffin Ed given the charge by their lieutenant to get to the bottom of the murder. "You know Harlem, you know where you have to go, who to see," the lieutenant tells Grave Digger. Their familiarity with Harlem is valued and allows them to conduct a less oppressive (if no less violent, however) search for the white man's murderer. According to Michael Denning, the central role of Coffin Ed and Grave Digger in Harlem "comes not as we have seen, from their position as heroes or centers of consciousness, but as mediators, between black and white, life and death, law and crime."[44] As Denning points out, the two detectives are successful because they can solve crimes for the white establishment and, in so doing, keep the Harlem community safe from the white establishment. It is Grave Digger who, after all, uncovers the sex ring surrounding the white murder victim.

But Grave Digger and Coffin Ed are not Harlem residents; they live in one of the outer boroughs when not engaged in crime detection. Like traditional participant-observers, they go "home" every night. As a result, their ability to read the codes of Harlem life are not always consistent. As Grave Digger admits, "But this is Harlem. Nobody knows all the connections here."[45] For instance, throughout *The Real Cool Killers*, the Real Cool Moslems are able to keep hidden from Coffin Ed that his daughter is part of their gang and that she is the lover of a prominent gang member. His daughter, Evelyn (a.k.a. Sugartit, when she hangs out in Harlem), remains undetectable to him because no one will let him in on her moniker. Coffin Ed spends the bulk of the novel questioning after Sugartit, who we learn was to be the next sexual victim of the white man whose murder ignites the novel's investigation. The web of disguises and code names makes it difficult for anyone outside Harlem to decipher the multiple relationships that exist among residents.

Moreover, by the time Himes writes *Blind Man with a Pistol*, Grave Digger and Coffin Ed are as confounded by black

Harlem as some of their white colleagues are. Again this novel revolves in many ways around the murder of a white man in Harlem. And again the reason behind the murder is sexual—he is killed while soliciting gay sex. However, unlike the earlier novels in the series, Grave Digger and Coffin Ed are unable to resolve the mystery. Citywide politics intervene—the murder victim has unexplained ties to government officials—and the search for the murderer is called off by city officials. *Blind Man with a Pistol* is the story of a Harlem in transition—it is a space where even the best black detectives cannot make sense of the power dynamics with which they are presented. "All we're doing is losing leads. We're as bad off as two Harlem prostitutes barefooted and knocked up," an exacerbated Grave Digger confesses to his lieutenant.[46] The lieutenant responds by telling them that they have been in Harlem too long, that they are no longer able to detect with fresh eyes the changing Harlem milieu. Grave Digger and Coffin Ed are forced to watch crimes go unsolved, riots break out, and a confused blind man kill innocent people in a Harlem-bound subway train. *Blind Man with a Pistol* marks the end of Grave Digger and Coffin Ed.

Yet Chester Himes had been offering counterpoints of authority for a long time. As early as *A Rage in Harlem*, there are signs that point to the fact that the two black detectives are not the only people policing Harlem. The dope-loving, nun-impersonating Goldy provides a site of counterauthority in *A Rage in Harlem*. An undercover officer of sorts, Goldy spends the bulk of his time on the Harlem streets gaining familiarity with the residents and monitoring their behavior. When his brother, Jackson, comes to him for help in finding his girlfriend, Imabelle, and retrieving the money he has lost to a group of grifters, Goldy is quick to realize that Jackson has been exploited by both the grifters and Imabelle. Like any good detective, though, Goldy checks his leads. And it is his methods that are most indicative of the ways in which white power structures can be circumvented by those who are outside the structure: "So he [Goldy] put on his gray wig and white bonnet and went down to the Harlem branch post-office on 125th Street to study the rogue's gallery of wanted criminals." Through studying the pictures and visiting the "dice games, the bookie joints, the barbecue stands, the barber shops, professional offices, undertakers', fleaheavens, grocery stores, meat markets called 'The Hog Maw,' 'Chitterling Country,' 'Pig Foot Heaven,'"[47] Goldy begins to piece together the narrative of fools gold, confidence games, and murder. Goldy occupies the position of both policed and police men, making it difficult to draw a distinction between the two.[48] Here Himes begins to introduce the unknowable black subject.

Run Man Run is another novel in which Himes offers a counternarrative to the traditional policing story. The novel begins when a drunk, white cop walks into an alley convinced that three late-night porters in a luncheonette have stolen his car. He proceeds to kill two of them in cold blood and then shoots the last. This third porter, Jimmy, escapes before the police officer, Walker, can murder him. The novel chronicles Jimmy's quest to remain alive after implicating Walker in the murders. Although readers know from the start that Walker is guilty, the characters in the novel are harder to convince. Everyone thinks Jimmy has gone insane, and Walker uses this misrepresentation to his advantage to track Jimmy throughout Harlem. The novel ends with Walker's brother-in-law solving the mystery, leaving Jimmy free to start a life with his fiancée, Linda Lou.

But the tone of *Run Man Run* is different from that of the detective novels featuring Grave Digger and Coffin Ed. It is much more typical in its depiction of white-on-black violence: a white cop controls the narrative of black violence, even when the black man happens to be innocent. However, the novel attempts to intervene in the traditional narrative of police power by having Jimmy decide to pursue Walker. Inverting the police-policed scenario, Jimmy decides he must kill Walker in order to free himself. And after making this decision, there is a moment in *Run Man Run* when Jimmy stands in front of a bookstore in Harlem and reads the book titles of various Harlem Renaissance writers whose books are displayed in the window. He is standing there waiting to buy an illegal gun, and it is at this moment, while reading the titles of black-authored books, that Jimmy feels secure:

> Suddenly he felt safe. There, in the heart of the Negro community, he was lulled into a sense of absolute security. He was surrounded by black people who talked his language and thought his thoughts; he was served by black people in businesses catering to black people; he was presented with literature of black people. Black was a big word in Harlem. No wonder so many Negro people desired their own neighborhood, he thought. They felt safe; there was safety in numbers.[49]

Literature becomes a sort of palliative from the stresses of policing. Moreover, literature is implicated in the reclamation of not only the space in which African Americans live but the lives they lead there. Literature reminds Jimmy that Harlem is his "safe space," his Mecca, and he has to fight for his right to control its narrative. "I'm going to kill the schizophrenic bastard," exclaims Jimmy, "and keep on living myself."[50] I would like to draw further attention to this quote because it affirms this study's sense that these texts rest on the cusp of a nationalist impulse that Himes was attempting to develop but not exactly fully able to orchestrate in his writing.

Ultimately, Jimmy's plan to confront Walker backfires because Walker is able to shoot faster than Jimmy—his police training has made him a far better shot. Walker leaves Jimmy for dead and makes his way back downtown to kill the final witness to his original crime. He is, however, apprehended by Brocks, his brother-in-law, who also happens to be the police detective assigned to the case. Himes, in a last attempt to make apparent the corruption of the police system, has Walker and his brother-in-law plot a final counternarrative to the one that Jimmy will tell in order to guarantee that Walker enters an insane asylum rather than a prison:

> "What happened to you that night?"
>> "I don't know. Just drinking too much I suppose."
>> "No," Brock said. "It was more than that."
>> "Maybe too many women," Walker said.
>> "No, not that either," Brock said. "Are you sick?" he asked.
>> Walker stared at him blankly for a moment. "You mean insane?"
>> "No, I mean sick physically," Brock said. "Syphilis or cancer or something like that."
>> Walker broke out in a sudden boyish laugh. "Not that I know of, unless I have syphilis of the brain."
>> "That could be," Brock said.
>> "What do you think they'll do with me?" Walker asked.
>> "It was a break for you that you beat up those two women," Brock said. "That will probably get you into the nut house."[51]

The power of the white police narrative takes priority once more. In fact, Brock even intimates that he had attempted to fix the case so that no one would ever know that Walker had killed the black men in the luncheonette: "I thought you'd know I wanted you to get rid of the gun; I thought you'd have sense enough to see that."[52] Unwilling to accept the final story, Walker goes for his gun to kill Brock, and Brock kills him instead.

The novel closes with Jimmy recovering from another non-fatal gunshot wound, inflicted again by Walker. And while his plan to police the police has failed, Himes's readers are given the sense that Jimmy's actions, successful or not, are important. Jimmy's drive is to tell his story. He tells his girlfriend, "But I want to explain to you [why I went after Walker]. You got to know." To take control of a narrative that has seemingly spun out of control is what is at stake for Jimmy—and Himes, for that matter—in *Run Man Run*.

Through the use of ethnographic techniques such as topographical realism and characters meant to function as participant-observers and native informants, Himes highlights the tension between what black American culture might look like from afar and how it might be experienced from within. As Breu argues, Himes holds up "a funhouse mirror to the racial and sexual imaginary of postwar American culture, reflecting back, in distorted and often parodic ways, the already fantastic sexual fantasies of a white supremacist American culture."[53] I believe he attempts to intervene in a well-known narrative in which African Americans have been cast simply as powerless criminals. They have traditionally been unable to imagine themselves as viable agents for self- and community protection, but from Goldy to the Real Cool Moslems and Jimmy, Chester Himes's detective cycle offers counterimages of black-white power dynamics. As Himes states in the quote that serves as the epigraph to this chapter, "I like [America] despite its faults, and there are many; perhaps I like it because of them." Moreover, he tells us that his connection to the United States would find him for the rest of his life. I think this statement, made in spite of the fact that he spent the rest of his life living in France and Spain, signals to us Himes's continued intellectual investment in thinking through and speaking into the inadequacies of the American racial system. This is not to say that he was not able to find a home outside the American racial landscape; rather, it is to take seriously Himes's own sense that that system, warts and all, was one that would allow and compel him to create art. More important, however, Himes's artistic commitment to the United States propelled him to explore a community under siege and to create art that recognized the importance of community involvement and multiplicity that traditional ethnographic accounts of black urban life cannot represent.

Conclusion: Look Down! The Black Arts Affirmation of Place and the Refusal to Translate

What the Black Man must do now is look down at the ground
upon which he stands, and claim it as his own. It is not abstract.
Look down! Pick up the earth, or jab your fingernails into the
concrete. It is real and it is yours, if you want it.

—AMIRI BARAKA[1]

More than a decade after the landmark desegregation case of *Brown v. Board of Education* (1954), three years after the Civil Rights Act of 1964, and in the midst of the Vietnam War, on July 29, 1967, President Lyndon B. Johnson issued Executive Order 11365. The United States government was in a state of admitted confusion with regard to its relationship with African American citizens and urban race relations. The executive order called for the formation of an advisory commission to investigate the urban "disorders" taking place in black communities across the nation. Johnson charged the commission with figuring it out: "What happened? Why did it happen? What can be done to prevent it from happening again?"[2] These three questions were to inform the investigation and shape the form of the report. By March 1, 1968, the committee released the outcome as the *Report of the National Advisory Commission on Civil Disorders*, better known as the "Kerner Report."

From the moment one opens the report, it is clear that the Kerner Commission understood the 1967 summer of civil unrest as part of a history of African American racial protest. Beginning with recent events, the commission stipulated that the 1963 Ku Klux Klan bombing of the Sixteenth Street Baptist

Church in Birmingham, Alabama, that killed four young black girls and the 1965 violence that rocked the Watts neighborhood in Los Angeles after police assaulted a black motorist should both be considered precursors to the 1967 racial unrest that raged throughout the nation.[3] The commission did not understand exactly what motivated the unrest, nor did they seem to have the capacity to assess the expectations of the black people from over one hundred cities who sought to express their anger through this collective turmoil, but the commission was at least able to contextualize a long history of African American discontent. Providing a historical sketch of the accumulation of three hundred years of racial injustice, the commission contended that it provided this history "not [to] justify, but to help explain, for black and white Americans, a state of mind."[4] The report moves from the colonial period to enslavement, to emancipation and Reconstruction, to state-sanctioned segregation, and finally to the "disorders" in order to illustrate that African Americans have protested their inequality from the time of the nation's founding. The story that the Kerner Commission wanted to tell, however, frames the Black Power Movement as derivative and marginal, while also depicting black unrest as merely the growing pains of a people frustrated by their lack of complete U.S. national inclusion. The commission concluded by stating,

> The central thrust of the Negro protest in the current period has aimed at the inclusion of Negroes in American society on the basis of full equality, rather than at a fundamental transformation of American institutions. There have been elements calling for a revolutionary overthrow of the American social system or for a complete withdrawal of Negroes from American society. But these solutions have had little popular support. Negro protest, for the most part, has been firmly rooted in the basic values of American society, seeing not their destruction but their fulfillment.[5]

The commission's sense of the uniqueness and impact of what we have come to call the Black Power Movement is surprisingly minimal. As Lisa Collins and Margo Crawford explain, "The idea that African Americans in the United States could understand themselves as constituting a viable nation—and a potentially glorious and righteous one at that—fell beyond the commissioners' faith."[6] Whereas the report describes those who were perceived as advocating black power as having "retreated into an unreal world,"[7] the commission frames the urban unrest as an exercise in the affirmation of America's central ideals. This notion is in direct opposition to the foundational beliefs of many black power activists and writers of the period, who imagined forming their own nation within the United States as the only way to access the "real" world.

Just as the commission sought to diminish the power of black consciousness in a nation that risked "moving toward two societies, one black, one white—separate and unequal,"[8] many black writers of the period fully embraced the promise of national separation. Poet-critic Amiri Baraka (né LeRoi Jones) asserted in his 1965 remembrance of Malcolm X's influence on black culture that "we [black people] do not want a Nation, we are a Nation. We must strengthen and formalize, and play the world's game with what we have, from where we are, as a truly separate people. America can give us nothing."[9] As a formidable thinker and artist of the Black Arts Movement (BAM), Baraka's assertion of the importance and viability of black nationalism stands in direct contrast to the Kerner Commission's conclusions regarding race and American nationalism. Not only does Malcolm X—along with more historical black nationalist figures such as Marcus Garvey, Frantz Fanon, and W. E. B. Du Bois— provide Baraka with an intellectual model for black cultural separatism, but Baraka implied that art and the imagination are central to the formation of a vibrant space of black health and/ or well-being.[10] Separatism and art are linked. As James Edward Smethurst points out, there was very little practical separation between the artistic and ideological wings of the philosophy of black determinism: "Black Power and Black Arts circuits were often the same, not just ideologically, but practically. Black organizers/artists might set up Black Power meetings . . . in different cities while on some sort of performance tour. Conversely, one might be in town for a big meeting or political convention and put on readings, concerts, plays and so on."[11] Linking the centrality of art to severing the ties that bind black Americans to mainstream American society, Baraka suggested, "The Black Artist's role in America is to aid in the destruction of America as he knows it."[12] Black art is further espoused as fundamental to the black nationalist ideological agenda by Addison Gayle in the canonical BAM anthology on black artistic production and critical evaluation, *The Black Aesthetic* (1971). In his introduction to the anthology, Gayle critiqued the literary landscape that has historically required black artists to work with the "white public in mind," measure their production by its acceptance or rejection by white people, fill their art with "half-truths," season their work with the "proper amount of anger," and ultimately assure the white audience that they "believed in the principles of Americanism."[13] Black arts and black aesthetics stand in direct contradiction to this past relationship, Gayle explained: "The Black Aesthetic, then, as conceived by this writer, is a corrective—a means of helping black people out of the polluted mainstream of Americanism, and offering logical, reasoned arguments as to why he should not desire to join the ranks of a Norman Mailer or a William Styron. To be an American writer is to be an American, and, for black people, there should no longer be honor attached to either position."[14] For Baraka and Gayle, art is a way for black artists to move away from an unproductive conversation with the white public and toward a productive conversation with black people regarding black life. BAM artists imagine a life in which the measure of art's significance must be determined not by its own beauty but by how much more beautiful "the poem, melody, play, or novel made the life of a single black man."[15] I open this conclusion with the Kerner Commission's report so that it might function as a touchstone for understanding the Black Arts Movement and to provide a historical context for the sort of ideological and artistic shifts that take place among the generation of writers that populate *Black Regions of the Imagination* as well as those that come after them. I believe BAM represents the culminating movement away from the particular sorts of relationships to international mobility and ethnographic cultural translation that, as I have argued throughout this book, shaped some of the writings of the twentieth century's most celebrated African American writers. I do not wish to imply that the report or the urban uprisings for which the report attempts to account were the catalysts for the Black Arts Movement; instead, the report might function as a gateway for understanding the cultural climate and the literary and cultural stakes that necessitated a shift in the foundational concerns of African American letters. In other words, the conditions of blackness in the United States reached an apex that contributed to an art movement shift that continues to shape the concerns of black artistic production.

And while many African Americanists have been hesitant to embrace the lasting importance of the Black Arts Movement, due in part to its ideological imperative and gender/racial essentialisms, the movement serves, at the very least, as a discursive opening for us to consider what the proactive embrace of black art versus cultural translation looks like. What might a call for cultural resistance and nation making within a nation look like when carried out through black artistic imagination? As Smethurst reminds us, "The Black Arts movement made a considerable impression on artists and intellectuals too young to remember its events firsthand. Many of the more explicitly political hip-hop artists owe and acknowledge a large debt to the militancy, urgent tone, and multimedia aesthetics of the Black Arts movement and other forms of literary and artistic nationalism."[16]

Likewise, the literary and social importance of the Black Power and Black Arts Movements did not go unnoticed by the generation of writers that matured in the decades before the

1960s and 1970s, the type of writers on which *Black Regions of the Imagination* has focused. We should remember that Richard Wright captured the energy surrounding Ghana's decolonization by titling his book on that subject *Black Power* (1954), well before Stokely Carmichael uttered the words in Mississippi during the 1966 March Against Fear. And although Eldridge Cleaver famously accused James Baldwin's work of containing the most "grueling, agonizing, total hatred of the blacks" and "the most shameful, fanatical, fawning, sycophantic love of the whites that one can find in the writings of any black American writer of note in [his] time,"[17] Margo Crawford encourages us to think more generously and generatively about Baldwin's capacity to produce a black power narrative. Through an insightful reading of Baldwin's *Tell Me How Long the Train's Been Gone* (1968) and photographs taken by Black Arts photographer Bob Crawford during a 1969 black cross-dressing ball, Margo Crawford compellingly argues that *"Tell Me* is Baldwin's 'Black is Beautiful' novel."[18] *Tell Me*'s marrying of queer black culture and black cultural nationalism help to expose and remind us of the "latent male homoeroticism in the cultural nationalism of the Black Arts Movement."[19]

Along similar lines, I would like to add Chester Himes's posthumously published novel, *Plan B* (1993), as further evidence of the ways an earlier generation of black writers attempted to move into a literary and historical moment in which black cultural translation was outwardly rejected. At one level, I am suggesting that the way in which we periodize African American literature should always be under scrutiny and at risk of revision. This sort of period permeability can been seen in Smethurst's work on the Black Arts Movement, which reveals how the Old Left, Popular Front, and New American Poetry generate "the continuities (and communities) of radical politics and poetics that would provide a matrix for the emergence of Black Arts institutions and ideology in a variety of locations across the United States."[20] On another level, I suggest that, much as the Black Arts writers were influenced by earlier political and artistic trends, these earlier artists were also influenced and moved to produce art shaped by the ideals of black power. Much as *Tell Me* might be considered Baldwin's (failed) "black is beautiful" novel, we might do well to ponder the significance of *Plan B* as a (failed) black power novel.

The Best Laid Plans

Around the same time that the racial unrest spreading across the United States compelled President Johnson to create the Kerner Commission, far off in Spain, Chester Himes had begun writing *Plan B*. In 1967, Himes excitedly wrote to his friend John Williams that he was embarking on his "wildest and most defiant" Harlem detective novel. In it, he planned to kill off his two beloved detectives, Coffin Ed Johnson and Grave Digger Jones. The novel would be his most defiant because it would tell the story of "an organized black rebellion which [was] extremely bloody and violent, as any such rebellion must be," according to Himes.[21] Two years later, he wrote to Williams, telling him that he was "not near finished with [the story]—and then on the other hand it might never be published."[22] Nearly three decades after Himes's initial letter, Williams begins his book review of Chester Himes's *Plan B* by deriding the novel as a "disaster," saying that reading it is like "catching Himes with his fly open or wearing soiled and rumpled mismatched pants and jacket, when he usually was well turned out in a neatly tailored suit."[23] The rest of Williams' review is no less scathing:

> *Plan B* remains a puzzle to me, because it does not begin to make clear the crucial, connected point Himes discussed back then: "It's a calculated risk, you know, whether they would turn and try to exterminate the black man, which I don't think they could do. I don't think the Americans have the capacity, like the Germans, of exterminating six million. I don't think the white American man could. Morally, I don't think he could do this." I characterized that as a "jive morality." I disagreed with Himes then and do now.

Only once in *Plan B* does the author arrive at this point,
where American morality is put to the test, in a couple of
lines of dialogue at the novel's strange and disappointing end. And this is precisely why I believe the book will
always be an incomplete testimony to his beliefs.[24]

In the decades between Himes's initial excitement and Williams's review, Himes periodically abandoned, wrote, revised,
and imagined *Plan B*. It, however, remained unfinished at the
time of his death in 1984. Still, Williams seems to hold Himes
accountable for the posthumous publication of a book that had
remained holed up in a drawer until it was happened upon by
his biographer and critic, Michel Fabre. After Himes's death,
Fabre (rightfully or wrongfully) helped to realize Himes's vision
of black liberation. I would argue that despite the novel's obvious lack of polish, character development, plot symmetry, and
cohesive narrative, and its rather hurried conclusion, considering Himes's *Plan B* provides a proper ending to *Black Regions of
the Imagination*. In fact, all these qualities signal an imperfect
end to one generation of black writers just as a new generation
constructs new possibilities for creating black writing.

Plan B at its core tells the story of a subversive and violent black
uprising that is conceived of and funded by Tomsson Black. Black,
who serves prison time for raping the wife of a wealthy white
man, embarks on a long-term plan of revenge that involves the
reclamation and conversion of an old plantation into a hog farm
known for producing the world's best chitterlings. Black's company, CHITTERLINGS, INC, functions as a profitable front allowing
him to funnel weapons to random black people across the nation
in the hope that they will take up arms against white America.
To maintain his anonymity, Black remains deeply entrenched
in the world of America's wealthy white elite, even becoming a
go-to person for the white establishment when it is faced with race
issues related to the national upswing in black-initiated violence.

Yet Black's character and plan are not revealed until much
later in the narrative. The majority of the early portion of the

text is spent establishing the genealogy of the inhabitants of the land on which CHITTERLINGS, INC, is built. The land was once occupied by the Harrison and Macpaisley families—a group of degenerate whites who lack the intelligence to turn a profit on the land and who become more sexually perverse with every generation—and the land's capacity to encourage the fecundity of razorback hogs becomes the symbolic residual of the perversity and danger of the plantation system itself. Black's CHITTERLINGS, INC, is impossible without the Harrisons and Macpaisleys—not because the families were particularly good at cultivating the land but precisely because they were awful at it, and, as such, Black's "Plan B" had been hatched generations ago and takes over a century to come to fruition. As Skinner and Fabre, Himes's biographers, note, "*Plan B* thus remains an incandescent parable of racial madness as well as a retrospective of American racial history."[25] Much like the long history of race relations and racial violence explored in the Kerner Report, Himes establishes a long and layered history that serves as the foundation for much of the violence that unfolds in *Plan B*.

And so *Plan B* begins with racial, sexual, and class violence, illustrating the intersectionality of all these categories within any narrative of black liberation. The novel begins in a Harlem apartment, where a black couple, T-Bone and Tang, has just received a box that contains an automatic rifle along with an anonymous note that reads, "WARNING!! DO NOT INFORM POLICE!!! LEARN YOUR WEAPON AND WAIT FOR INSTRUCTIONS!!! REPEAT!!! LEARN YOUR WEAPON AND WAIT FOR INSTRUCTIONS!!! WARNING!!! DO NOT INFORM POLICE!!! FREEDOM IS NEAR!!!"[26] Himes uses this letter to set the tone and to create the mystery of the novel: Who sent the rifle? Why did they send the rifle? And from what exactly will the black reader of the note be freed? Whatever the answers to these mysteries, Tang cannot control her excitement at the thought that on the other side of the barrel lives her liberation. For Tang, liberation takes the form of the freedom from having to selling her "pussy to whitey" (9). Her boyfriend/pimp, T-Bone, on the other hand, wants nothing to do with the violent liberation promised by the automatic rifle; he is, instead, absolutely fine subsisting off the profits that come from selling Tang's body to "poor white trash" (10). In fact, T-Bone is so taken aback by Tang's willingness to take up arms that he accuses her of "lissening to that Black Power shit" and threatens to tell "whitey" on her (10).

T-Bone ultimately murders Tang in a fit of rage because he cannot abide by the personal danger that he imagines her longing for liberation might invite on him. Himes's opening scene, while a caricatured understanding of the racial violence associated with the Black Power Movement, puts in motion a set of power dynamics between race, sex, and gender that speak to the potential he saw in the creation of a black power narrative. Tang's and T-Bone's interaction rests on the fears and excitement associated with real and imagined black organized violent rebellion against the white mainstream.

A masculine movement that often marginalized black women, black power and the threat of organized black violence are reimagined by Himes as central to the liberation of black womanhood. Tang's role as the narrative's premier black nationalist undermines traditional notions of black power that seek to fuse blackness and maleness.[27] Not only does she play the role of black nationalist, but Tang imagines that her embrace of black power will bring about the end of her sexual exploitation and commodification, something for which she is willing to kill both black and white men. Interestingly, Himes's narrative constructs the true potential of black liberation as its power to free the working-class black woman from sexual subjugation. As many black feminist scholars have argued, black sexual deviance has been historically and persistently constructed in the racist, sexist, heteronormative context of the United States. And from enslavement to the contemporary moment, black women have attempted to counter such deviance with narratives of their own autonomy. Previous generations of black women interested in countering widespread notions of black female sexual deviance had practiced what Evelyn Higginbotham has termed the "politics of respectability" or had harbored what Candice Jenkins terms the "salvific wish"[28]—both of which affirm bourgeois ideals of female propriety and heteronormativity at the expense of sexual autonomy. Alternatively, they became the sensual, savvy, working-class "blues women," of which Angela Davis and Hazel Carby have written, who could use music to articulate and achieve alternative life trajectories.[29]

Tang, unlike any of these predecessors, turns to black power. The Black Power Movement is framed within the text as offering Tang an opportunity to imagine the practice of something other than dissemblance[30] and/or the need to entertain middle-class aspirations as a way to rectify her racialized-sexual oppression. More concretely, as Tang draws "the gun tight to her chest as though it were a lover" and utters the words, "This is the only thing that made me feel alive since I met you," she makes clear to T-Bone (and the reader) that black power, as it is symbolically represented by the rifle, affords her a reason for living (*Plan B*, 10). Tang's erotic autonomy,[31] her capacity to assert her own vision of how her body and sexuality will be used (or remain unused), is the unwritten promise housed in the anonymous package. Rejecting her heterosexual partnering and her heteronormative sexual subjection, Tang's lack of "proper" politics serves as a potential model for new black womanhood under the auspices of black power.

It is too bad Tang is murdered before she can be fully realized. Instead of developing into a Black Power feminist, Tang is murdered: "She tried to protect herself with the rifle but shortly he [T-Bone] had cut it out of her grasp. She backed around the table trying to keep away from the slashing blade. But soon the blade began reaching her flesh, the floor became covered with blood; she crumpled and fell and died, as she had known she would after she first saw the enraged look on his face" (*Plan B*, 12). The anonymous rifle, the symbolic stand-in for black power politics, offers Tang no true protection from T-Bone's aggressive affirmation of a capitalist, exploitative system that presumes, relies on, and enforces her sexual deviance. T-Bone tells Grave

Digger and Coffin Ed that he killed her because he is "a law-abiding man," thereby solidifying his own respectability within the context of the United States' system of law and order (17). Interestingly, Grave Digger murders T-Bone after realizing Tang has been murdered because "she wanted to be free" (19). His act of black power solidarity is tempered, however, when one considers it within the framework of a black patriarchal impulse to protect a woman.

It might first appear that Grave Digger kills T-Bone for being an agent of the state—oddly, exactly the work Grave Digger and Coffin Ed are paid to do—but Grave Digger seeks to inscribe Tang's quest for erotic autonomy in his own narrative of patriarchal desire to protect his mother: "I killed this black mother myself, I busted his skull alone, and I'd do it again. I did it because that woman [Tang] looked something like my ma looked as I remember her, a poor black woman wanting freedom. And I'd kill any black mother on earth that's low enough to waste her for that. But I'm not going to let you [Coffin Ed] share this feeling, man, because this is for my mama" (20). What is telling about Grave Digger's rationale for his violence is that in killing for Tang's honor and ostensibly the freedom of black women throughout history, he fails to embrace the collective spirit of black power. Her murder serves as the catalyst for the major action of the novel's plot, but her death reinforces a sense of the impossibility of black female sexual autonomy promised by the short vignette we are offered of her life.

Just as the opening of the novel is marked by Tang's murder, the close of the novel features a "strange" and "sexy" black woman (199). In fact, this woman is so mysteriously sexy that Grave Digger and Coffin Ed confuse her with a "high-class hooker looking for a bodyguard" (199). Perhaps she is Tang's black power double, what Tang might have been if T-Bone had allowed her to live long enough to embrace her liberation. This beautiful version of Tang might be read as what women could become who embrace the "black is beautiful" mantra of the black power generation. But it is exactly her beauty that continues to shape her cultural significance within the framework of black sexual deviance. While we are unsure of her true occupation, even in death and reincarnation, the working-class woman cannot be redeemed from the initial reading of her status as prostitute. Moreover, although the unnamed beautiful woman utters the last words of the novel—"I hope you know what you're doing" (203)—she advances the plot of the novel in no meaningful way. Perhaps a character-vessel waiting to be filled with meaning that Himes did not have time to develop before his death, the beautiful black woman reinforces the very complicated nature of black power when yoked to questions of black womanhood.

To simultaneously overthrow white supremacy and the shackles of sexual exploitation seems beyond the scope of Himes's black power narrative. In some way, then, his narrative is directly in line with what Lisa Gail Collins has noted about both the Black Power and Women's Liberation Movements of the 1960s and 1970s: "The easy equation of fulfilled manhood, brotherhood, and liberation in the Black Power Movement, as well as the high premium placed on shared experiences and safe sisterhood in the Women's Liberation Movement made it a supreme challenge for African American women to assert the validity of their uniqueness to their resistant peers."[32] Tang's death coupled with the limited appearance of the beautiful black woman and her uncertainty at the novel's closing speak into the profound insecurity of black female autonomy, even as one begins to imagine the fight for black liberation.

In addition to beginning and ending with the unfulfilled potential for radical racial and gender reformation, *Plan B* also addresses the inevitable break with the production of black cultural knowledge— namely, the professions of sociology, anthropology, and even policing and criminal justice—that has been central to *Black Regions of the Imagination*. While the professions of sociology, anthropology, and urban policing have separate histories, methods, and intellectual trajectories, they share the colonial impulse to confine marginalized cultures through observation and analysis. In two instances in *Plan B*, Himes directly critiques these professions for the ways they conspire to manage, contain, and undermine black life and freedom. The first example takes place during a shootout between a black gunman and the all-white police force in Harlem, while Grave Digger and Coffin are absent from the scene because the former is suspended for murdering T-Bone and the latter is on desk duty due to an injury. Himes begins to imagine what an anthropologist might find most interesting about Harlem:

> An anthropologist might be more interested in the graffiti inside than in the gun battle outside, or even the sweating bodies of the black people squirming on the floors. Why do slum dwellers express themselves in graffiti depicting exaggerated genitals, he might ask himself. Why always the genitals? Why oversized genitals? Why are black slum dwellers obsessed with these enlarged genitals, penises as big, comparatively, as telephone poles, and heads as small as cocoanuts [sic]? What are they trying to tell themselves? That as humans their heads might be small in the white man's sight but their unseen genitals were as big as field artillery? (Plan B, 58)

Directly in line with a culture that expects the hypersexualization and sexual deviance of black women, Himes's imagined anthropologist is unconcerned with the reality of urban black life, which is filled with racially fueled violence that terrorizes black Harlem citizens and leaves them "moaning, frowning, praying, and muttering vile curses while the gun battle raged outside" (58). Himes's anthropologist is interested, instead, in the sexual graffiti that covers the walls of the apartment buildings in "sexually historic" Harlem.[33] The extrapolations of this imagined anthropologist seek to reinforce only those readings of black culture that confirm notions of black sexual deviance. The questions asked by this anthropologist leave no space for the graffiti to speak to some impulse of artistic protest, which might have been aimed at destroying the notion of white ownership and confinement within black neighborhoods. The anthropologist is unable to see the radical critique offered by the graffiti because he or she is too busy contemplating the deviance of black people.

Similarly, in a second example, Himes muddles the distinctions made among a variety of state-sanctioned service workers who are responsible for the creation and maintenance of black ghettos and a particular type of urban black experience:

> The cops heard this [the order to shoot any black man on sight] and remembered it. They were literal minded, and they did not see any extenuating circumstances, any kind of mitigating behavior. That was for judges and juries. They were cops, and cops were responsible for law and order, shoot them if they resisted or tried to escape. *A cop is a cop, not a welfare worker, a city planner, a sociologist.* If black people lived in slums that wasn't the cop's fault; the cop's duty was to see that they obeyed the law and kept the order, no matter where they lived. It was coincidental that rich and educated white people who lived in large, roomy, airy houses, in clean, fresh, well-kept neighborhoods were more likely to keep the law and the order, but cops didn't have so much to do in these neighborhoods. (*Plan B*, 61, my emphasis)

In the passage, we see cops, judges, juries, welfare workers, city planners, and, most importantly, sociologists linked as a systemic rank-and-file group that works to deny black Harlem residents their rights to citizenship, freedom, and a higher quality of life. It is most telling that sociologists, like anthropologists in the previous passage, are charged with the work of making sense of black life but do so poorly. Inasmuch as the police officers attempt to differentiate themselves from these other professionals and workers, we may read them as inextricably linked in a system of racialized oppression that is itself geographically tied to the space of black Harlem. And the connection between the novel's black residents and the policed space they inhabit is also associated with a systemic presumption that blackness, confined urban dwelling, and violence are rightfully subject to the regulation of state-sanctioned actors. Moreover, as Roderick Ferguson argues, canonical sociology presumes "morality as the subjective counterpart to the material and social conditions that originated in African American life in the twentieth century," and under such a presumption, "minority culture, thus, [stands] as that figure of unpredictability in need of moral regulation by Western bourgeois culture."[34] Himes's novel represents the police officer's musings on law and order in the black community that naturalize the pathology of the community, just as they naturalize the normality of the white middle-class community. All these professionals function as arms of a state that creates knowledge about black culture that is meant only to affirm the status of the nation's racial hierarchy and to normalize the violence needed to maintain the hierarchy.

If law-and-order and other government workers are central to the continued affirmation of black pathology carried out by the state, Himes's ending to his cycle of Harlem detective novels speaks volumes about his sense of the racial dilemma created by cultural crossovers such as Grave Digger and Coffin Ed. Nowhere is this more apparent than in the conclusion of *Plan B*. Pieced together from an outline and notes found after Himes's death, the novel ends with the murders of both Grave Digger and Coffin Ed. Still stinging from Tang's death and hot on the trail of proving that Tomsson Black is behind the chaotic nationwide black rebellion, Grave Digger shoots Coffin Ed when Coffin Ed threatens to kill Black because Black's "Plan B" makes too many black people collateral damage to achieve its goal. Unable to maintain control over the distribution and use of the firearms, Black's rebellion spirals downward, and all he can do is "complete the distribution of the guns and let maniacal, unorganized, and uncontrolled blacks massacre enough whites to make a dent in the white man's hypocrisy, before the entire black race [is] massacred in retaliation" (*Plan B*, 201). In short, the goal of "Plan B" becomes so outrageous that it can be achieved only at a high cost of black life, and that is a price Coffin Ed is not willing to pay. Grave Digger, on the other hand, is willing to pay any price for black liberation. Still, Black shoots Grave Digger in the head because he cannot risk Digger turning state's evidence against the movement. Black justifies his actions by saying, "Whitey would make him talk if they had to take him apart, nerve by nerve" (203).

The death of these black detectives coupled with the ambiguous words of the beautiful black woman speak ultimately to Himes's inability to reconcile both the gender component of black liberation and the utility of black cultural workers who have spent a lifetime translating black culture to the white establishment. Grave Digger and Coffin Ed die because they are too ideologically muddled and dangerous to a liberation movement that ceases to define itself within the framework of law, order, and the white establishment.

In the end, *Plan B* is as disappointing as it is violent and more fragmented than it is thrilling, but what is special about the novel is the fact that its existence forces us to think about black power's discursive significance for a previous generation of writers—providing them with new imaginative models for exploring the limits of black freedom. It is telling that Himes was not able to finish *Plan B* in his lifetime. While he understood the potential for the movement and for mass black rebellion against a system of racial inequity, Himes could not quite pull the trigger with the novel. Although I do not wish to psychoanalyze Himes, the novel's lack of completion tells a very interesting story of literary traditions and transitions. As I said earlier, I believe it is fruitful to think about *Plan B* as Himes's Black Power novel, but its failure to fully realize a way to integrate his detectives into the black power milieu, to kill them off but never to put it into print, speaks to an understanding of the incompatibility of Grave Digger and Coffin Ed with the literary and cultural age that set the attitudes of many young African American writers during the 1960s and 1970s. How does one reconcile and redeem black cop protagonists in a moment of black cultural nationalism? One does not; one kills them off in literary solidarity. But how does one kill off the very protagonists who revived your literary career? One never finishes the story in which these protagonists die. As Michael Denning describes, Coffin Ed and Grave Digger are "mediators, between black and white, life and death, law and crime," ambiguous figures, "at once enforcers of the law and figures of violence and death."[35] And this is why they cannot live in the Black Power and Black Arts moment.

In short, there is a disconnect between the black nationalist ideology and the generation of writers explored in *Black Regions of the Imagination*. While Wright used the phrase "black power" over a decade before Carmichael did, he died before he could witness the proliferation of the phrase as an ideological and aesthetic imperative. Moreover, as I have argued, Wright's *Black Power* exposes his own unease with what it might mean to embrace Africa as both an imagined "homeland" and a site of beauty. Likewise, Baldwin's embrace of black beauty does not undermine the emphasis placed on revolutionary heterosexual black manhood by many of the most vocal writers of the Black Power and Black Arts Movements. And Himes's embrace of a black power rhetoric in his Harlem domestic cycle not only remained unfinished in his lifetime, but even when he imagined its end, it meant the end of his beloved detectives. In all these instances, we should not lament the failures of foundational African American authors but instead acknowledge a literary transition from black cultural translation to black cultural affirmation.

Look Down! Creating a Nation within a Nation

I would like to end with the most striking dissonance between the Black Arts generation of writers and the those explored in *Black Regions of the Imagination*: their relationship to both nationalism and internationalism. Consistent in the thrust of this book has been the significance of mobility to writers such as Hurston, Wright, Baldwin, and Himes as they created works that were able to represent racial segregation. As I have argued throughout this book, all these writers used distance from the

United States to craft critical narratives in a variety of ways. Yet, as I consider the transition between literature produced under segregation and in the midst of desegregation versus literature produced in the midst of the Black Power Movement, I see a growing refusal to relinquish the United States. This is not to say that these Black Arts writers remained parochial or land locked in their perspectives. Indeed, they all found Third World politics central to their affirmations of black nationalism—as they watched the world decolonize and postcolonial states arise in Africa and Asia, these writer-activists found solidarity with a world community of color seeking to liberate itself from Western rule. Writers such as Addison Gayle, Hoyt Fuller, Larry Neal, Amiri Baraka, and others refused to cede the nation. As Amiri Baraka dictates, "What the Black Man must do now is look down at the ground upon which he stands, and claim it as his own."[36] Refusing to leave the United States, these writers who claim a nation within a nation go about the work of imagining a world of black liberation and self-determination that does not require them to flee the country. Rather, they plot—through imagination, artistic creation, and planned political infraction— the nation's destruction from the inside. Remember, "The Black Artist's role in America is to aid in the destruction of America as he knows it."[37] It is a different relationship than earlier writers had to the nation and to the work of black writing, but it would have been impossible without writers such as Hurston, Wright, Baldwin, and Himes, all of whom attempted the difficult work of imaginatively creating the destruction of the United States as they knew it.

Notes

Preface

1. Richard Wright, "I Bite the Hand That Feeds Me," *Atlantic Monthly* 165 (June 1940): 828.

2. Richard Wright, *American Hunger* (New York: HarperPerennial, 1993), 452–453.

Introduction

1. James Baldwin, *James Baldwin: From Another Place*, quoted in Magdalena Zaborowska, *James Baldwin's Turkish Decade: Erotics of Exile* (Durham, NC: Duke University Press, 2009), 1.

2. Richard Elman, review of *A Rap on Race*, by Margaret Mead and James Baldwin, *New York Times Book Review*, 27 June 1971.

3. David Leeming, *James Baldwin: A Biography* (New York: Penguin, 1994), 311.

4. James Baldwin and Margaret Mead, *A Rap on Race* (New York: Lippincott, 1971), 4–5.

5. James Clifford, *The Predicament of Culture: Twentieth-Century Ethnography, Literature, and Art* (Cambridge, MA: Harvard University Press, 1988), 13.

6. For more extensive analysis of these New Negro writers' use of ethnographic methods and forms, see Daphne Lamothe, *Inventing the New Negro: Narrative, Culture and Ethnography* (Philadelphia: University of Pennsylvania Press, 2008).

7. Ibid., 9.

8. W. E. B. Du Bois, *The Souls of Black Folk*, ed. Henry Louis Gates Jr. (1903; repr., New York: Oxford University Press, 2007), 1.

9. Mary Louis Pratt notes that Bronislaw Malinowski's *Argonauts of the Western Pacific* (1922) and Raymond Firth's *We, the Tikopia* (1936) both open with personal narratives about their own first encounters, each revealing that "ethnographic writing as a rule subordinates narrative to description but personal narrative is still conventionally founded." She goes on to contend that both these writers open their texts not with the self-effacement expected of scientific writing. See Mary Louis Pratt, "Fieldwork in Common Places," in *Writing Culture: The Poetics and Politics of Ethnography*, ed. James Clifford and George Marcus (Berkeley: University of California Press, 1986), 35.

10. By "participant-observation," I am referring to the traditional method in which social science researchers take part in the daily activities, rituals, interactions, and events of a group of people in order to learn something about their lives and culture. For more on this topic, see George McCall and J. L. Simmons, *Issues in Participant Observation: A Text and Reader* (Reading, PA: Addison-Wesley, 1969); James Spradley, *Participant Observation* (New York: Holt, Rinehart, and Winston, 1980); John Van Maanen, *Tales of the Field: On Writing Ethnography* (Chicago: University of Chicago Press, 1988); Michael Agar, *The Professional Stranger: An Informal Introduction to Ethnography* (San Diego: Academic Press, 1996); and Kathleen DeWalt and Billie DeWalt, *Participant Observation: A Guide for Fieldworkers* (New York: AltaMira, 2002).

11. I am making the deliberate choice to think of these black writers as native ethnographers rather than native informants. Edward Said has argued that "native informants" are natives who have so internalized the Western point of view regarding their own culture that they are "Orientalist on the inside." "Native informant" seems a divisive term and does not speak to the complicated relationship to nation, race, and discourse that the writers of this project cultivate throughout their careers. In my mind, to be called a "native informant" is akin to being called a "sellout" or "oreo" in the black vernacular tradition. In any case, it does not capture the multifaceted work done by Hurston, Wright, Himes, or Baldwin.

12. Lamothe, *Inventing the New Negro*, 11–12.

13. While many scholars use the Cold War (post–World War II to 1991) as a way to frame the writing of the mid-twentieth century, such a historical framing does not exactly speak to the literary conventions being explored and created during these decades. More recently, Brian Norman and Piper Kendrix Williams compiled an edited volume entitled *Representing Segregation: Toward an Aesthetics of Living Jim Crow, and Other Forms of Racial Division* (Albany: State University of New York Press, 2010), in which they argue that we might begin to group literature written between the *Plessy v. Ferguson* (1896) and *Brown v. Board of Education* (1954) Supreme Court

decisions as "segregation narrative tradition." Norman and Williams argue that there are both qualities and concerns that mark narratives written under American racial segregation that, once collected, begin to shape the aesthetic and political contours of black fiction written between 1896 and 1954. Similarly, Lawrence Jackson argues in his book *Indignant Generation: A Narrative History of African American Writers, 1934–1960* (Princeton, NJ: Princeton University Press, 2011) that the period might be marked by looking at the careers of midcentury writers and their shared stances toward American liberal ideals. From interactions with the mainstream publishing world to shared failures and accomplishments, Jackson considers the period through the creation of a set of generational experiences that he argues made it possible for racially militant writers of the 1960s to come into being. In short, while I find each mode of periodization intriguing, it is still unclear if this period will or should become codified into a black literary tradition.

14. Lamothe, *Inventing the New Negro*, 10–12.

15. James Clifford suggests that the twentieth-century crisis in ethnographic authority came about largely due to the breakup and redistribution of colonial power. See Clifford, *Predicament of Culture*, 22.

16. Robert Reid-Pharr, *Once You Go Black: Choice, Desire, and the Black American Intellectual* (New York: NYU Press, 2007), 104.

17. For more on African American "worldliness," see Nikhil Singh, *Black Is a Country: Race and the Unfinished Struggle for Democracy* (Cambridge, MA: Harvard University Press, 2004).

18. Edward Said, *Culture and Imperialism* (New York: Vintage Books, 1993), 32.

19. Paul Gilroy, *The Black Atlantic: Modernity and Double Consciousness* (Cambridge, MA: Harvard University Press, 1993), 4.

20. See Brent Edwards, *The Practice of Diaspora: Literature, Translation, and the Rise of Black Internationalism* (Cambridge, MA: Harvard University Press, 2003).

21. For more on how actual travel and metaphors of travel in cultural criticism exclude women and their points of view, see Janet Wolff, "On the Road Again: Metaphors of Travel in Cultural Criticism," in *Resident Alien: Feminist Cultural Criticism*, 115–134 (New Haven, CT: Yale University Press, 1995). Additionally, for more on black women's erasure from diasporic discourse, see T. Denean Sharpley-Whiting, "Erasures and the Practice of Diaspora Feminism," *Small Axe* 17 (March 2005): 129–133.

22. Jacqueline Nassy Brown, "Black Liverpool, Black America, and the Gendering of Diasporic Space," *Cultural Anthropology* 13:3 (1998): 301.

23. Leigh Anne Duck, *The Nation's Region: Southern Modernism, Segregation, and U.S. Nationalism* (Athens: University of Georgia Press, 2006), 8.

24. See Penny Von Eschen, *Satchmo Blows Up the World: Jazz Ambassadors Play the Cold War* (Cambridge, MA: Harvard University Press, 2004).

25. Imani Perry, *Prophets of the Hood: Politics and Poetics in Hip Hop* (Durham, NC: Duke University Press, 2004), 13.

26. Ibid., 20.

1 / Becoming American through Ethnographic Writing

1. Langston Hughes, *The Big Sea: An Autobiography* (New York: Thunder's Mouth, 1986), 239.

2. Hurston to Huie, 6 September 1954, in Carla Kaplan, *Zora Neale Hurston: A Life in Letters* (New York: Anchor Books, 2003), 719.

3. Wright abandoned the sentimentality of Jim Crow black rural life after publishing his novella collection *Uncle Tom's Children* (New York: Harper and Brothers, 1938). In "How Bigger Was Born" (in *Early Works: Lawd Today! Uncle Tom's Children, Native Son* [New York: Library of America, 1991], 874), Wright explains that in writing *Uncle Tom's Children* he had committed the grave mistake of writing a book that "even bankers daughters could read and weep over and feel good about." Wright links white sentimentality and representations of black rural life in a way that colored all his future writings. See chapter 2 for a more detailed discussion of Wright, white readership, and black identity.

4. Daphne Lamothe, *Inventing the New Negro: Narrative, Culture, and Ethnography* (Philadelphia: University of Pennsylvania Press, 2008), 2.

5. Alain Locke, "The New Negro," in *The New Negro*, ed. Alain Locke (New York: Simon and Schuster, 1992), 6.

6. Houston Baker Jr., *Modernism and the Harlem Renaissance* (Chicago: University of Chicago Press, 1987), xiv.

7. Lamothe, *Inventing the New Negro*, 143.

8. Zora Neale Hurston, *Mules and Men* (Bloomington: Indiana University Press, 1935), 200, 230.

9. At the urging and arranging of Hurston's adviser, Franz Boas, she had taken her first trip into the field during the last months of her final year at Barnard College and only a few months before her second trip. This first trip was funded by a fellowship arranged by Boaz in conjunction with Carter G. Woodson's Association for the Study of Negro Life and History.

10. Robert Hemenway, *Zora Neale Huston: A Literary Biography* (Urbana: University of Illinois Press, 1977), 105.

11. Zora Neale Hurston, "How It Feels to Be Colored Me," in *I Love Myself When I Am Laughing . . . and Then Again When I Am Looking Mean and Impressive: A Zora Neale Hurston Reader*, ed. Alice Walker (Old Westbury, NY: Feminist Press, 1979), 152.

12. Baker, *Modernism and the Harlem Renaissance*, 17.

13. Hurston to Hughes, 8 March 1928, in Kaplan, *Zora Neale Hurston*, 114.

14. Hurston wrote *Their Eyes Were Watching God* during her first eight weeks collecting in Haiti.

15. Zora Neale Hurston, *Dust Tracks on a Road* (New York: HarperPerennial, 2006), 144.

16. Hurston to Boas, 29 March 1927, in Kaplan, *Zora Neale Hurston*, 97.

17. Ibid.

18. For more on the history of liberal anthropology, see Kamala Visweswaran, *Fictions of Feminist Ethnography* (Minneapolis: University of Minnesota Press, 1994).

19. Hurston to Hughes, 12 April 1928, in Kaplan, *Zora Neale Hurston*, 116 (emphasis in original).

20. Hurston to Hughes, 21 September 1927, in ibid., 106.

21. Hurston to Hughes, 12 April 1928, in ibid., 116 (emphasis in original).

22. Elin Diamond, "Deploying/Destroying the Primitivist Body in Hurston and Brecht," in *Against Theatre: Creative Destructions of the Modernist Stage*, ed. Alan Ackerman and Martin Puchner (New York: Palgrave Macmillan, 2006), 112.

23. Baker, *Modernism and the Harlem Renaissance*, 79.

24. Richard Wright accuses her of this much in his review of *Their Eyes Were Watching God* (*New Masses*, 5 October 1937, 22–23).

25. J. Martin Favor, *Authentic Blackness: The Folk in the New Negro Renaissance* (Durham, NC: Duke University Press, 1999), 16.

26. Hazel Carby, "The Politics of Fiction, Anthropology, and the Folk," in *New Essays on "Their Eyes Were Watching God,"* ed. Michael Awkward (New York: Cambridge University Press, 1990), 74–75.

27. Ibid., 76.

28. For more on the role of migration in the African American literary tradition, see Farah Jasmine Griffin, *"Who Set You Flowin'?": The African-American Migration Narrative* (New York: Oxford University Press, 1995). Also, see the same text for Griffin's treatment of the figure of "the stranger" to explore similar concerns regarding insider/outsider status in African American narrative.

29. Carby, "Politics of Fiction," 77.

30. Ibid., 79.

31. Robin Kelley, "Notes on Deconstructing 'The Folk,'" *American History Review* 97:5 (1992): 1402.

32. Zora Neale Hurston, "Spirituals and Neo-Spirituals," in *Negro: An Anthology*, ed. Nancy Cunard, 223–225 (New York: Ungar, 1970).

33. Dickson Bruce, *Black American Writing from the Nadir: The Evolution of a Literary Tradition, 1877–1915* (Baton Rouge: Louisiana State University Press, 1989).

34. Langston Hughes notes that hundreds of copies of the first issue of *Fire!!* were destroyed, ironically, when a fire broke out in the basement in which they were being stored (see Hughes, *Big Sea*). The original contributors to the quarterly were never able to recoup the costs of producing the journal and were not able to fund another.

35. Hughes, *Big Sea*, 235.

36. For more on the role of the "impolite" in the creation of queer black identity in *Fire!!* and the Harlem Renaissance more generally, see Michael Cobb, "Insolent Racing, Rough Narrative: The Harlem Renaissance's Impolite Queers," *Callaloo* 23:1 (2000): 328–351.

37. Alain Locke, "Fire: A Negro Magazine," *Survey*, 15 August–15 September 1927, 563.

38. Jean Toomer, "The *Cane* Years," in *The Wayward and the Seeking: A Collection of Writings by Jean Toomer*, ed. Darwin T. Turner (Washington, DC: Howard University Press, 1980), 123.

39. While I find Jennifer Wilks's argument compelling, I disagree with her reading of *Cane*, in which she argues that Toomer used his "art as a means of rescuing African American culture, especially its rural variants, from the early-twentieth-century threats of primitivism, propaganda, and industrialization." Toomer's *Cane* is not a resurrection but a burial of black southern life. Jennifer Wilks, "Writing Home: Comparative Black Modernism and Form in Jean Toomer and Aimé Césaire," *Modern Fiction Studies* 51:4 (2005): 806–807.

40. Cheryl Wall, *Women of the Harlem Renaissance* (Bloomington: Indiana University Press, 1995), 163.

41. Hurston to Hughes, 10 July 1928, in Kaplan, *Zora Neale Hurston*, 121.

42. Zora Neale Hurston, "Characteristics of Negro Expression," in Cunard, *Negro*, 27.

43. Hurston, *Mules and Men*, 10.

44. Victor Turner, *The Anthropology of Performance* (New York: PAJ, 1986), 22.

45. Visweswaran, *Fictions of Feminist Ethnography*, 77.

46. Wall, *Women of the Harlem Renaissance*, 151.

47. The success of *Mules and Men* was facilitated by a number of things. The ethnography came on the heels of a successful run of Hurston's first novel, *Jonah's Gourd Vine* (Philadelphia: Lippincott, 1934), which her publishers J. B. Lippincott & Company took as a sign of the public's interest in "authentic" black folk material. *Mules* used nonscientific language, making it one of the first black-authored folklore collections that provided an ethnographer's analysis of black culture without subscribing to the scientific language that had historically distanced the general reader.

48. Franz Boas, preface to Hurston, *Mules and Men*, x.

49. Hurston, *Mules and Men*, 4.

50. Hemenway, *Zora Neale Huston*, 165. See also Deborah Gordon, "The Politics of Ethnographic Authority: Race and Writing in the Ethnography of Margaret Mead and Zora Neale Hurston," in *Modernist Anthropology: From Fieldwork to Text*, ed. Marc Manganaro, 146–162 (Princeton, NJ: Princeton University Press, 1990); Amy Fass Emery, "The Zombie in/as the Text: Zora Neale Hurston's *Tell My Horse*," *African American Review* 39:3 (2005): 327–336.

51. Emery, "Zombie in/as the Text," 327.

52. Hurston, *Mules and Men*, 9.

53. When I suggest that Hurston is interested in the performance of ethnography, I do not suggest that she is simply an overwilling participant in order to get her "informants" to "act." For more on this sort of performance, see James Clifford's discussion of Marcel Griaule in *Predicament of Culture: Twentieth-Century Ethnography, Literature, and Art* (Cambridge, MA: Harvard University Press, 1988), 79.

54. From Richard Wright to Hazel Carby, as I have previously detailed.

55. For more on the role of time in anthropology's construction of "savage" and "primitive" cultures, see Johannes Fabian, *Time and the Other: How Anthropology Makes Its Object* (New York: Columbia University Press, 1983).

56. Kelley, "Notes on Deconstructing 'The Folk,'" 1402.

57. Clifford, *Predicament of Culture*; see chapter titled "On Ethnographic Authority."

58. Hurston, *Mules and Men*, 11.

59. Ibid., 71.

60. Ibid., 74.

61. Saidiya Hartman, *Scenes of Subjection: Terror, Slavery, and Self-Making in Nineteenth-Century America* (New York: Oxford University Press, 1997), 116.

62. Carby, "Politics of Fiction."

63. Paul Gilroy, *The Black Atlantic: Modernity and Double Consciousness* (Cambridge, MA: Harvard University Press, 1993), 45.

64. Harold Courlander, "Witchcraft in the Caribbean Islands," review of *Tell My Horse*, by Zora Neale Hurston, *Saturday Review of Literature*, 15 October 1938, 6.

65. Hemenway, *Zora Neale Huston*, 248.

66. For more on the text's generic ambivalence, see Gordon, "Politics of Ethnographic Authority."

67. Ibid., 154.

68. Lamothe, *Inventing the New Negro*, 143.

69. Ifeoma Nwankwo, "Insider and Outsider, Black and American: Rethinking Zora Neale Hurston's Caribbean Ethnography," *Radical History Review* 87 (Fall 2003): 74.

70. Zora Neale Hurston, *Tell My Horse: Voodoo and Life in Haiti and Jamaica* (1938; repr., New York: Harper and Row, 1990), 3.

71. Ibid., 4 (my emphasis).

72. Hurston, *Mules and Men*, 195.

73. Hurston, *Tell My Horse*, 7.

74. Ibid., 9.

75. Sibylle Fischer, *Modernity Disavowed: Haiti and the Cultures of Slavery in the Age of Revolution* (Durham, NC: Duke University Press, 2004), 38.

76. Hurston, *Tell My Horse*, 17. I find Hurston's use of the phrase "continental America" most interesting, as it makes reference to the realities of the imperial relations, holdings, and occupations of the United States in the mid-twentieth century but also places "noncontinental American" locations, for example, Jamaica and Haiti, in subordinate conversation.

77. My argument reads Hurston's *Tell My Horse* through a fairly literal lens. However, critics such as Daphne Lamothe and Amy Fass Emery both encourage a less literal and more ironic reading. While I find value in a focus on Hurston's use of literary indirection in her writing, I also believe the literal meanings that present themselves within the text provide another set of valuable lenses for thinking through the racial, national, and gender work Hurston does in *Tell My Horse*. That is to say, rather than redeeming her from what appear to be very nonprogressive nationalist arguments that complicate our notions of race and gender within the United States and the Caribbean, I find thinking through her impulse toward nationalism a very important project for that very same reason.

78. Accompong is one of the historical maroon villages settled by blacks that escaped enslavement throughout the late seventeenth and eighteenth centuries. Accompong, then, is one of many historical emblems of slave and black resistance on the island of Jamaica.

79. Hurston, *Tell My Horse*, 22.

80. Ibid., 22.

81. Ibid., 22–23.

82. Ibid., 23.

83. Ibid., 376.

84. Shameem Black, "Fertile Cosmofeminism: Ruth L. Ozeki and Transnational Reproduction," *Meridians: Feminism, Race, Transnationalism* 5:1 (2004): 228.

85. Houston Baker Jr., "Workings of the Spirit: Conjure and the Space of Black Women's Creativity," in *Zora Neale Hurston: Critical Perspectives Past and Present*, ed. Henry Louis Gates Jr. and Kwame Anthony Appiah, 280–308 (New York: Amistad, 1993).

86. Hurston, *Tell My Horse*, 57.

87. Zora Neale Hurston, *Their Eyes Were Watching God* (1937; repr., New York: Negro Universities Press, 1969).

88. Lamothe, *Inventing the New Negro*, 151.

2 / Escaping through Ethnography

1. Wright to his agent, Paul Reynolds, 7 November 1953, quoted in Michel Fabre, *The Unfinished Quest of Richard Wright* (New York: Morrow, 1973), 468.

2. Travel Journal, Box 22, Folder 340, JWJ MSS 3, Richard Wright Papers, The Beinecke Rare Book and Manuscript Library, Yale University.

3. Richard Wright, *White Man, Listen!* (New York: Greenwood, 1978), 17.

4. Paul Gilroy, *The Black Atlantic: Modernity and Double Consciousness* (Cambridge, MA: Harvard University Press, 1993), 5.

5. Diana Fuss, *Essentially Speaking: Feminism, Nature and Difference* (New York: Routledge, 1989), xi.

6. Gilroy, *Black Atlantic*, 148.

7. Richard Wright, *Black Boy* (New York: World, 1945), 228.

8. Richard Wright, *American Hunger* (New York: HarperPerennial, 1993), 452–453.

9. Jeff Karem, "'I Could Never Really Leave the South': Regionalism and the Transformation of Richard Wright's *American Hunger,*" *American Literary History* 13:4 (2001): 701.

10. Ibid.

11. Ibid., 704.

12. Ibid., 708.

13. The division between American literary realism and literary regionalism is blurry, as often the two resist easy separating. American literary realism, of which American regionalism is traditionally considered a subgenre (with all the connotations of "sub-" being played on), has its roots in the late nineteenth century and coincides with the rise of technology. Realism, according to William Dean Howell, depicted "the simple, natural, and the honest" and resisted romantic representations of humanity. William Dean Howell, *Criticism and Fiction* (New York: Harper and Brothers, 1891), 14.

14. Ann Kaplan, "Nation, Region, and Empire," in *The Columbia History of the American Novel*, ed. Emory Elliott (New York: Columbia University Press, 1991), 251.

15. Eric Sundquist, "Realism and Regionalism," in *The Columbia Literary History of the United States*, ed. Emory Elliott (New York: Columbia University Press, 1988), 508.

16. For instance, revisionists Judith Fetterley and Marjorie Pryse redefine the power of regional writing in their book *Writing Out of Place* (Urbana: University of Illinois Press, 2003). Likewise, Fetterley has also argued that regionalism, which for her is synonymous with nineteenth-century women's writing, is inherently an "unAmerican" genre that allows "persons made silent or vacant through terror to tell stories which the dominant culture labels trivial," to "change our perspective and thus to destabilize the meaning of margin and center." Judith Fetterley, "'Not in the Least American': Nineteenth-Century Literary Regionalism," *College English* 56:8 (1994): 887.

17. Richard Brodhead, *Cultures of Letters: Scenes of Reading and Writing in Nineteenth-Century America* (Chicago: University of Chicago Press, 1993), 117.

18. William Andrews argues in his introduction to Johnson's *The Autobiography of an Ex-Colored Man* that Johnson was able to overcome this burden by employing the literary genre of autobiography because whites were more receptive to that genre than the novel—although it is not without

comment that *The Autobiography of an Ex-Colored Man* is a travel narrative featuring the narrator's traversal through many remote and marginal locales. William Andrews, introduction to *The Autobiography of an Ex-Colored Man*, by James Weldon Johnson, vii–xxvii (New York: Penguin Books, 1990).

19. Ibid., xvi.

20. Brodhead, *Cultures of Letters*, 116.

21. Albert Murray, "Regional Particulars and Universal Statement in Southern Writing," *Callaloo* 38 (Winter 1989): 3.

22. Ibid., 4.

23. Ibid.

24. Houston Baker Jr., *Turning South Again: Re-thinking Modernism/Rereading Booker T.* (Durham, NC: Duke University Press, 2001), 26.

25. Flannery O'Connor, "The Regional Writer," in *Mystery and Manners: Occasional Prose*, ed. Sally Fitzgerald and Robert Fitzgerald (New York: Farrar, Straus, and Giroux, 1961), 54.

26. Lori Robison, "Region and Race: National Identity and the Southern Past," in *A Companion to the Regional Literatures of America*, ed. Charles Crow, 57–73 (Malden, MA: Blackwell, 2003). Robison argues that the South vacillates in meaning and importance to the United States. Sometimes the site of what America is not, sometimes the nostalgic site of what it wishes it could be again. According to Robison, the American South is often treated as the symbolic register of the nation's relationship to race. But even Robison's analysis of how race affects the national importance of the South fails to consider how African Americans in the South register their own national longings and belonging.

27. Toni Morrison has noted that the tension between the particular and the universal is a constant concern for African American writers: she argues that many black writers believe they are burdened with the task of making the particular experience of blackness readable to white people. Morrison renounces this sentiment and activity in black writing because she sees little value in universalism and, instead, relishes the local/regional. In this sense, Morrison's understanding conforms to the vision that I offer in this chapter. See Thomas LeClair, "The Language Must Not Sweat: A Conversation with Toni Morrison," in *Conversations with Toni Morrison*, ed. Danille Taylor-Guthrie, 119–128 (Jackson: University Press of Mississippi, 1994).

28. For more on the black counterpublic, see Michael Dawson, *Black Visions: The Contemporary Roots of African-American Political Ideologies* (Chicago: University of Chicago Press, 2001).

29. Richard Wright, "Blueprint for Negro Writing," in *Richard Wright Reader*, ed. Ellen Wright and Michel Fabre, 36–49 (New York: Harper and Row, 1978),

30. Ibid., 42.

31. Ibid., 41.

32. Ibid., 42.

33. Ibid.

34. Fabre, *Unfinished Quest*, 320.

35. Ibid., 319.

36. Virginia Whatley Smith, introduction to *Richard Wright's Travel Writings: New Reflections*, ed. Virginia Whatley Smith (Jackson: University of Mississippi Press, 2001), xi.

37. John Reilly, "Richard Wright and the Art of Non-fiction: Stepping Out on the Stage of the World," *Callaloo* 28 (Summer 1986): 512.

38. Lori Robison contends in "Region and Race" that ethnography, like regional writing, serves the cultural function of providing mainstream readers an authoritative introduction to new cultures. Ethnography and regionalism both, through the creation of an outside observer, "enact through their very form, a hierarchical relationship between observer and observed that assumes the superiority of the voice that 'looks down upon what the other is'" (64).

39. James Clifford describes ethnographic participant-observation as a method that places the ethnographer between "inside" and "outside" the events he or she is recording. The value of this particular type of ethnography is that it allows the impression of dialectical interaction between author and subjects but still privileges the voice of the ethnographer and his or her ability to make sense of the culture being described. James Clifford, *Predicament of Culture: Twentieth-Century Ethnography, Literature, and Art* (Cambridge, MA: Harvard University Press, 1988).

40. Ibid., 34.

41. Richard Wright, *The Color Curtain: A Report on the Bandung Conference* (1956; repr., Jackson: University of Mississippi Press, 1995), 25.

42. S. Shankar, "Richard Wright's *Black Power*: Colonial Politics and the Travel Narrative," in *Richard Wright's Travel Writings: New Reflections*, ed. Virginia Smith (Jackson: University of Mississippi Press, 2001), 6.

43. Wright, *Color Curtain*, 176.

44. Ibid., 177.

45. Ibid., 178.

46. Ibid.

47. *Color Curtain* Developmental Draft, Box 29, Folder 420, JWJ MSS 3, Richard Wright Papers, The Beinecke Rare Book and Manuscript Library, Yale University, 94–95 (emphasis in second paragraph mine; emphasis in third paragraph in original).

48. Wright, *Color Curtain*, 184 (my emphasis).

49. Ibid., 187.

50. Ibid., 188.

51. Shankar, "Richard Wright's *Black Power*," 5.

52. Ibid., 18.

53. Richard Wright, *Black Power: A Record of Reactions in a Land of Pathos* (1954; repr., New York: HarperPerennial, 1995), xxxvii.

54. Ibid., xxxvii.

55. Ibid., 6.

56. Ibid., 4.

57. Ibid., 7.

58. Manthia Diawara, *In Search of Africa* (Cambridge, MA: Harvard University Press, 1998), 75.

59. Wright, *Black Power*, 73.

60. Kevin Gains, "Revisiting Richard Wright in Ghana: Black Radicalism and the Dialectics of Diaspora," *Social Text* 19:2 (2001): 77.

61. Brent Edwards, *The Practice of Diaspora: Literature, Translation, and the Rise of Black Internationalism* (Cambridge, MA: Harvard University Press, 2003), 14.

62. Ibid., 13.

63. James Baldwin, "Alas, Poor Richard," in *James Baldwin: Collected Essays* (New York: Library of America, 1998), 226.

64. Earl Lewis, "To Turn as on a Pivot: Writing African Americans into a History of Overlapping Diasporas," *American Historical Review* 100:3 (1995): 772.

65. Edwards, *Practice of Diaspora*, 138.

66. Wright, *Black Power*, dust jacket.

67. Susan Sontag, *On Photography* (New York: Delta, 1973), 3–4.

68. Photograph, Box 24, Folder 367, JWJ MSS 3, Richard Wright Papers, The Beinecke Rare Book and Manuscript Library, Yale University.

69. Photograph, Box 24, Folder 365, JWJ MSS 3, Richard Wright Papers, The Beinecke Rare Book and Manuscript Library, Yale University.

70. Sontag, *On Photography*, 163.

71. Ibid., 167 (my emphasis).

72. Phyllis Palmer, *Domesticity and Dirt: Housewives and Domestic Servants in the United States* (Philadelphia: Temple University Press, 1998), 138.

73. Wright, *Black Power*, 393.

74. For more detailed description of this failed writing project, see Fabre, *Unfinished Quest*.

75. Wright to Reynolds, 7 November 1953, quoted in ibid., 468.

76. Reynolds to Wright, 24 January 1956, quoted in ibid., 432 (my emphasis).

3 / Deconstructing the Romance of Ethnography

1. James Baldwin, "My Dungeon Shook: Letter to My Nephew," in *James Baldwin: Collected Essays*, 291–295 (New York: Library of America, 1998).

2. James Baldwin and Margaret Mead, *A Rap on Race* (New York: Lippincott, 1971), 72.

3. James Baldwin, "The Price of the Ticket," in *James Baldwin: Collected Essays* (New York: Library of America, 1998), 836–837 (emphasis in original).

4. For more on how arrival scenes function to frame relationships between "natives" and "travelers"/ethnographers, see Mary Louise Pratt, "Fieldwork in Common Places," in *Writing Culture: The Poetics and Politics of Ethnography*, ed. James Clifford and George Marcus, 27–50 (Berkeley: University of California Press, 1986).

5. Ibid., 73 (my emphasis).

6. James Clifford, "Introduction: Partial Truths," in *Writing Culture: The Poetics and Politics of Ethnography*, ed. James Clifford and George Marcus (Berkeley: University of California Press, 1986), 3.

7. Baldwin, "Price of the Ticket," 841.

8. Ibid., 842.

9. Kamala Visweswaran, *Fictions of Feminist Ethnography* (Minneapolis: University of Minnesota Press, 1994), 4.

10. Sociological texts such as Gunnar Myrdal's *An American Dilemma: The Negro Problem and Modern Democracy* (1944) or Daniel Patrick Moynihan's 1965 Labor Department study, *The Negro Family: The Case for National Action* (a.k.a. The Moynihan report) are representative texts produced by a liberal state wishing to address racial inequality, only to turn the cause of racial inequity back on African Americans. Although these are not ethnographic texts, they are more quantitative than qualitative, and they do signify a national focus on black pathology during the mid-twentieth century. For more detailed exploration of canonical sociology's measure of African American unfitness for national inclusion, see Roderick Ferguson, *Aberrations in Black: Toward a Queer of Color Critique* (Minneapolis: University of Minnesota Press, 2004).

11. Lee Baker, *From Savage to Negro: Anthropology and the Construction of Race, 1896–1954* (Berkeley: University of California Press, 1998), 3.

12. Bronislaw Malinowski, *Argonauts of the Western Pacific: An Account of Native Enterprise and Adventure in the Archipelagoes of Melanesian New Guinea* (1922; repr., Prospect Heights, IL: Waveland, 1961), xvi.

13. Ibid., 7.

14. Pratt, "Fieldwork in Common Places," 27.

15. Malinowski, *Argonauts*, 9–10.

16. Malinowski argues that the trained ethnographer understands the cultures of "natives" to be far from childish or quaint. Such falsehoods have been "killed by Science." For more on this, see ibid., 11.

17. Ibid., 7.

18. Pratt contends that Malinowski employs the image and language of being "cast away" in "Fieldwork in Common Places," 38.

19. Mary Louise Pratt, *Imperial Eyes: Travel Writing and Transculturation* (New York: Routledge, 1992), 64.

20. Andrew P. Killick, "The Penetrating Intellect: On Being White, Straight, and Male in Korea," in *Taboo: Sex, Identity and Erotic Subjectivity in Anthropological Fieldwork*, ed. Don Kulick and Margaret Willson (New York: Routledge, 1995), 82.

21. Ibid., 76.

22. For two collections of essays on the subject of sex and sexuality in the field, see Kulick and Willson's *Taboo* and Tony Whitehead and Mary Conaway's *Self, Sex, and Gender in Cross-Cultural Fieldwork* (Chicago: University of Illinois Press, 1986).

23. Killick, "Penetrating Intellect," 85.

24. Ibid., 76.

25. James Baldwin, *Another Country* (1962; repr., New York: Vintage Books, 1993), 28.

26. For more on early critical reception, see William Cohen, "Liberalism, Libido, Liberation: Baldwin's *Another Country*," *Genders* 12 (Winter 1991): 1–21.

27. Baldwin, *Another Country*, 347.

28. Cohen, "Liberalism, Libido, Liberation," 16.

29. Baldwin, "My Dungeon Shook," 294.

30. Kevin Ohi, "'I'm Not the Boy You Want': Sexuality, 'Race,' and Thwarted Revelation in Baldwin's *Another Country*," *African American Review* 33:2 (1999): 261–281.

31. Ernesto Javier Martinez, "Dying to Know: Identity and Self-Knowledge in Baldwin's *Another Country*," *PMLA* 124:3 (2009): 786.

32. Ibid., 794.

33. I am focusing on the white characters and knowledge because Baldwin actually leaves little space for self-doubt in his characterization of Ida, the only African American character in the novel once Rufus dies. While Rufus was, in fact, very confused, Ida seems less so. I do not believe Baldwin does black women a service by depicting Ida as such a "wise" character, but I think he does so in order to focus his critique on the type of knowing of which liberals are capable.

34. Baldwin, *Another Country*, 7. Subsequent references to this source appear parenthetically in the text.

35. Cohen, "Liberalism, Libido, Liberation," 3, 5.

36. Ibid., 3.

37. Killick, "Penetrating Intellect," 85.

38. *Another Country* was published only three years after Norman Mailer's *Dissent* article, "The White Negro" (Fall 1957), in which Mailer articulates postwar white masculinity's reliance on "black cool" to formulate itself as antiestablishment. Baldwin went on to explore his friendship with Mailer and critique Mailer's essay in his own essay, "The Black Boy Looks at the White Body," which was part of his *Nobody Knows My Name* (1961; in *James Baldwin: Collected Essays*, 269–290 [New York: Library of America, 1998]).

Vivaldo seemingly displays some of the relationship to blackness that Mailer articulates in his essay, and my critique of Vivaldo should be read in relation to a critique of Mailer's liberal-minded primitivization of black masculinity.

39. Killick, "Penetrating Intellect," 102 (emphasis in original).

40. Ibid., 102.

41. Cohen, "Liberalism, Libido, Liberation," 5.

42. Killick, "Penetrating Intellect," 85.

43. Ibid.

44. Martinez, "Dying to Know," 784.

45. Ohi, "I'm Not the Boy You Want," 275.

46. For more on Vivaldo's sexual desire for Rufus, see Martinez, "Dying to Know"; and Ohi, "I'm Not the Boy You Want."

47. Martinez, "Dying to Know," 789.

48. Leo Bersani, "Is the Rectum a Grave?," *October* 43 (Winter 1987): 212.

49. Ibid., 222.

50. For critiques of Baldwin's erasure of black queer sensibility, see Martinez, "Dying to Know"; and Ohi, "I'm Not the Boy You Want."

51. For more projects linking "queer" and "black," see also Lee Edelman, "The Part for the (W)hole: Baldwin, Homophobia, and the Fantasmatics of 'Race,'" in *Homographesis: Essays in Gay Literary and Cultural Theory*, 42–76 (New York: Routledge, 1994); Ferguson, *Aberrations in Black*; Robert Reid-Pharr, *Black Gay Man: Essays* (New York: NYU Press, 2001); and Darieck Scott, *Extravagant Abjection: Blackness, Power, and Sexuality in the African American Literary Imagination* (New York: NYU Press, 2010).

52. Kathryn Bond Stockton, *Beautiful Bottom, Beautiful Shame: Where "Black" Meets "Queer"* (Durham, NC: Duke University Press, 2006), 27.

53. For more on Baldwin's life in Turkey, see Magdalena Zaborowska, *James Baldwin's Turkish Decade: Erotics of Exile* (Durham, NC: Duke University Press, 2009).

54. Baldwin, "My Dungeon Shook," 294.

4 / Ethnography of the Absurd

1. "Impressions of Europe" Draft, Box 7, Folder 82, JWJ MSS 42, Chester Himes Papers, The Beinecke Rare Book and Manuscript Library, Yale University.

2. Marcel Duhamel was the editor of the *Série noir* and had previously translated Himes's *If He Hollers Let Him Go* (New York: Doubleday, Doran, 1945).

3. Until Himes, the *Série noir* consisted mainly of translations of American hard-boiled detective fiction. Himes was the first author to write original fiction for the series.

4. Himes often cites Richard Wright, James Baldwin, and Melvin Van Peebles among his peers while living in Paris and Europe.

5. In a 1970 interview, Himes told his interviewer that he wrote the first novel only because he was "very broke and desperate for some money," and "the *Série noir* was the best-paid series in France. So they starting off paying [him] a thousand-dollar advance, which was the same as the Americans were paying, and they went up to fifteen hundred dollars, which was more." John Williams, "My Man Himes: An Interview with Chester Himes," in *Conversations with Chester Himes*, ed. Michel Fabre and Robert E. Skinner (Jackson: University Press of Mississippi, 1995), 34.

6. The novel (trans.: "The Queen of Apples") is translated and published under the titles *For the Love of Imabelle* and *A Rage in Harlem* when released in the United States.

7. Williams, "My Man Himes," 48.

8. Jonathan Eburne, *Surrealism and the Art of Crime* (Ithaca, NY: Cornell University Press, 2008), 247.

9. See Stephen Soitos, *The Blues Detective: A Study of African American Detective Fiction* (Amherst: University of Massachusetts Press, 1996). Soitos argues that black detectives have figured in black writing in the late nineteenth and early twentieth centuries by Pauline Hopkins.

10. Michel Fabre, "Chester Himes Direct," in *Conversations with Chester Himes*, ed. Michel Fabre and Robert E. Skinner (Jackson: University Press of Mississippi, 1995), 129.

11. The Harlem cycle usually refers to *A Rage in Harlem* (1957), *The Real Cool Killers* (1959), *The Crazy Kill* (1959), *All Shot Up* (1960), *The Big Gold Dream* (1960), *Cotton Comes to Harlem* (1965), *The Heat's On* (1966), and *Blind Man with a Pistol* (1969). However, Himes's *Run Man Run* (1966) should be added to this list because it is also a detective novel set predominantly in Harlem, although it lacks Grave Digger and Coffin Ed. Likewise, in 1993, Himes's incomplete manuscript titled *Plan B* was published—he had been working on it at the same time he wrote *Blind Man with a Pistol* but failed to ever complete it. Grave Digger and Coffin Ed meet their demises in *Plan B*, thus marking the end of the Harlem cycle.

12. Manthia Diawara, "Noir by Noirs: Towards a New Realism in Black Cinema," *African American Review* 27:4 (1993): 526.

13. Wendy Walters, "Limited Options: Strategic Maneuverings in Himes's Harlem," *African American Review* 28:4 (1994): 615.

14. Megan Abbott, *The Street Was Mine: White Masculinity in Hardboiled Fiction and Film Noir* (New York: Palgrave Macmillan, 2002), 162.

15. It should be noted that in *Blind Man with a Pistol* Grave Digger and Coffin Ed are unable to solve the novel's mystery because of the white power structure.

16. Christopher Breu, *Hard-Boiled Masculinities* (Minneapolis: University of Minnesota Press, 2005), 11.

17. Chester Himes, *A Rage in Harlem* (1957; repr., New York: Vintage Books, 1989), 6.

18. In an interview for the Sunday *New York Times Magazine*, Himes is quoted as saying, "When most people write about the American Negro he is either a functional character, or a vehicle for sociological comment. In my case the two are indivisible." Philip Oakes, "The Man Who Goes Too Fast," in *Conversations with Chester Himes*, ed. Michel Fabre and Robert E. Skinner (Jackson: University Press of Mississippi, 1995), 18. Additionally, Himes titles the second volume of his autobiography *My Life of Absurdity*, making apparent his awareness of French existentialism. However, his awareness is merely that and not engagement—Himes never defines exactly what he means by "absurdity" in his autobiography. In fact, he notes in a 1983 interview with Michel Fabre that he did not become acquainted with surrealism (the absurd) "until the fifties, and French friends had to explain it. I have no literary relationship with what is called the surrealist school. It just so happens that in the lives of black people, there are so many absurd situations, made that way by racism, that black life could sometimes be described as surrealistic. The best expression of surrealism by black people, themselves, is probably achieved through blues musicians." Fabre, "Chester Himes Direct," 140.

19. Oakes, "Man Who Goes Too Fast," 18.

20. Kevin Bell, *Ashes Taken for Fire: Aesthetic Modernism and the Critique of Identity* (Minneapolis: University of Minnesota Press, 2007), 212–213.

21. Himes was sentenced to a twenty-year prison term in 1928 for robbery. He served almost eight years of the term and was paroled for good behavior. It was during his prison sentence that Himes began writing. He also read the detective fiction of Dashiell Hammett and Raymond Chandler while incarcerated. Himes claims that these two writers, along with Faulkner, influenced his writing the most.

22. Fabre, "Chester Himes Direct," 126.

23. Raymond Nelson, "Domestic Harlem: The Detective Fiction of Chester Himes," in *The Critical Response to Chester Himes*, ed. Charles L. P. Silet (Westport, CT: Greenwood, 1999), 54.

24. Chester Himes, *Blind Man with a Pistol* (1969; repr., New York: Vintage Books, 1989), 19–20.

25. Michel de Certeau, *The Practice of Everyday Life* (Berkeley: University of California Press, 1984), 93.

26. Chester Himes, *My Life of Absurdity: The Autobiography*, vol. 2 (New York: Doubleday, 1976), 126.

27. Michael Mok, "Chester Himes," in *Conversations with Chester Himes*, ed. Michel Fabre and Robert E. Skinner (Jackson: University Press of Mississippi, 1995), 105.

28. Michael Denning, "Topographies of Violence: Chester Himes's Harlem Domestic Novels," in *The Critical Response to Chester Himes*, ed. Charles L. P. Silet (Westport, CT: Greenwood, 1999), 157, 167.

29. John Cawelti, *Adventure, Mystery, and Romance: Formula Stories as Art and Popular Culture* (Chicago: University of Chicago Press, 1976), 141, 155.

30. Himes, *Rage in Harlem*, 67.

31. Ibid., 93.

32. Ibid., 28.

33. Himes, *Blind Man with a Pistol*, 7.

34. Ibid., 8.

35. Ibid., 36–37.

36. I am going out on a limb here by designating the readers of Himes's novels as white. I feel justified in taking this step, however, because all these texts were published and released in France first. Himes often commented that his readership was predominantly a white, French audience, who do not get him. Likewise, his U.S. readership was not established until the 1980s, when Vintage began to republish his detective fiction.

37. Himes, *Blind Man with a Pistol*, 21.

38. Walters, "Limited Options," 618.

39. Soitos, *Blues Detective*, 150.

40. Michel Fabre, "Interview with Chester Himes," in *Conversations with Chester Himes*, ed. Michel Fabre and Robert E. Skinner (Jackson: University Press of Mississippi, 1995), 85.

41. Chester Himes, *The Real Cool Killers* (1959; repr., New York: Vintage Books, 1988), 41.

42. In "Limited Options," Wendy Walters notes that Himes's description of the black faces as "strange purple fruit" resonates with the blues song "Strange Fruit," which alludes to lynching (620). Walters thus suggests that the scene has the potential to become a lynching.

43. Throughout this section on Himes are references to Middle Eastern and Arab culture. I do not believe it is merely a coincidence that Himes is playing with the connections between African Americans and Arab culture. Writing in the midst of the rise of a black Muslim identity association in the United States, Himes was aware of the African American relationship to Islam. Moreover, the connection between a history of profiling and discrimination against blacks in the United States helps to us to elucidate the patterns in the United States' contemporary relationship to the Arab world and its profiling of Arab Americans.

44. Denning, "Topographies of Violence," 160.

45. Himes, *Real Cool Killers*, 43.

46. Himes, *Blind Man with a Pistol*, 158–159.

47. Himes, *Rage in Harlem*, 37.

48. Goldy is ultimately killed by the grifters, but not before he has totally figured out the mystery concerning what is in Imabelle's trunk. Himes seems to realize that free agents such as Goldy have their place within the Harlem community and the policing system, but because they are so close to the community, there is a higher risk involved in their type of investigation.

49. Chester Himes, *Run Man Run* (New York: G. P. Putnam's Sons, 1966), 152. This quote is also interesting because it links black arts to black space. Jimmy feels safe in Harlem because he is reminded of its history of literary production.

50. Ibid., 162.

51. Ibid., 188–189.

52. Ibid., 189.

53. Breu, *Hard-Boiled Masculinities*, 144.

Conclusion

1. LeRoi Jones (Amiri Baraka), "The Legacy of Malcolm X, and the Coming of the Black Nation," in *Home: Social Essays* (1966; repr., Hopewell, NJ: Ecco, 1998), 244.

2. *Report of the National Advisory Commission on Civil Disorders*, 1 March 1967 (Washington, DC: U.S. Government Printing Office, 1968).

3. Ibid., 19.

4. Ibid., 95.

5. Ibid., 113.

6. Lisa Gail Collins and Margo Natalie Crawford, introduction to *New Thoughts on the Black Arts Movement*, ed. Lisa Gail Collins and Margo Crawford (New Brunswick, NJ: Rutgers University Press, 2006), 7.

7. *Report of the National Advisory Commission*, 111.

8. *Report of the National Advisory Commission*, 1.

9. Jones, "Legacy of Malcolm X," 239.

10. Ibid., 247–248.

11. James Edward Smethurst, *The Black Arts Movement: Literary Nationalism in the 1960s and 1970s* (Chapel Hill: University of North Carolina Press, 2005), 14–15.

12. LeRoi Jones (Amiri Baraka), "state/meant," in *Home: Social Essays* (1966; repr., Hopewell, NJ: Ecco, 1998), 251.

13. Addison Gayle, introduction to *The Black Aesthetic*, ed. Addison Gayle (Garden City, NY: Anchor Books, 1971), xx.

14. Ibid., xxii.

15. Ibid.

16. Smethurst, *Black Arts Movement*, 3.

17. Eldridge Cleaver, "Notes on a Native Son," in *Soul on Ice* (New York: Ramparts Books, 1968), 99.

18. Margo Natalie Crawford, "Natural Black Beauty and Black Drag," in *New Thoughts on the Black Arts Movement*, ed. Lisa Gail Collins and Margo Natalie Crawford (New Brunswick, NJ: Rutgers University Press, 2006), 167.

19. Ibid., 170.

20. Smethurst, *Black Arts Movement*, 56.

21. Michel Fabre and Robert Skinner, introduction to *Plan B*, by Chester Himes, ed. Michel Fabre and Robert Skinner (Jackson: University of Mississippi Press, 1993), ix.

22. Ibid.

23. John Williams, "Review of *Plan B*," *African American Review* 30:3 (1996): 492.

24. Ibid.

25. Fabre and Skinner, introduction to *Plan B*, xxvi.

26. Chester Himes, *Plan B* (Jackson: University of Mississippi Press, 1993), 8. Subsequent references to this source appear parenthetically in the text.

27. Stephen Ward argues that during the mid- to late-1960s, black women were encouraged to "recede into the background in deference to male leadership," a demand that was tied to the "ostensibly revolutionary objective of reclaiming 'black manhood.'" Stephen Ward, "The Third World Women's Alliance: Black Feminist Radicalism and Black Power Politics," in *The Black Power Movement: Rethinking the Civil Rights–Black Power Era*, ed. Peniel E. Joseph (New York: Routledge, 2006), 124. Ward, however, goes on to explore the role both the Civil Rights and Black Power Movements played in fostering an intellectual and political space for black women to reimagine themselves as agents of their own liberation.

28. Evelyn Brooks Higginbotham, *Righteous Discontent: The Women's Movement in the Black Baptist Church* (Cambridge, MA: Harvard University Press, 1993), 186–187; Candice Jenkins, *Private Lives, Proper Relations: Regulating Black Intimacy* (Minneapolis: University of Minnesota Press, 2007), 13.

29. Hazel Carby, "Policing the Black Woman's Body in an Urban Context," *Critical Inquiry* 18:4 (1992): 754–755; Angela Davis, *Blues Legacies and Black Feminism: Gertrude "Ma" Rainey, Bessie Smith, and Billie Holiday* (New York: Vintage Books, 1999).

30. Darlene Clark Hine, "Rape and the Inner Lives of Black Women in the Middle West: Preliminary Thoughts on the Culture of Dissemblance," *Signs* 14:4 (1989): 915.

31. Jacqui M. Alexander, *Pedagogies of Crossing: Meditations on Feminism, Sexual Politics, Memory, and the Sacred* (Durham, NC: Duke University Press, 2005), 22.

32. Lisa Gail Collins, "The Art of Transformation: Parallels in the Black Arts and Feminist Art Movement," in *New Thoughts on the Black Arts Movement*, ed. Lisa Gail Collins and Margo Natalie Crawford (New Brunswick, NJ: Rutgers University Press, 2006), 292.

33. Kevin Mumford, "Homosex Changes: Race, Cultural Geography, and the Emergence of the Gay," *American Quarterly* 48:3 (1996): 402.

34. Roderick Ferguson, *Aberrations in Black: Toward a Queer of Color Critique* (Minneapolis: University of Minnesota Press, 2004), 74.

35. Michael Denning, "Topographies of Violence: Chester Himes's Harlem Detective Novels," in *The Critical Response to Chester Himes*, ed. Charles L. P. Silet (Westport, CT: Greenwood, 1999), 160.

36. Jones, "Legacy of Malcolm X," 244.

37. Jones, "state/meant," 251.

BIBLIOGRAPHY

Abbott, Megan. *The Street Was Mine: White Masculinity in Hardboiled Fiction and Film Noir*. New York: Palgrave Macmillan, 2002.

Agar, Michael. *The Professional Stranger: An Informal Introduction to Ethnography*. San Diego: Academic Press, 1996.

Alexander, M. Jacqui. *Pedagogies of Crossing: Meditations on Feminism, Sexual Politics, Memory, and the Sacred*. Durham, NC: Duke University Press, 2005.

Andrews, William. Introduction to *The Autobiography of an Ex-Colored Man*, by James Weldon Johnson, vii–xxvii. New York: Penguin Books, 1990.

Baker, Houston, Jr. *Modernism and the Harlem Renaissance*. Chicago: University of Chicago Press, 1987.

———. *Turning South Again: Re-thinking Modernism/Re-reading Booker T.* Durham, NC: Duke University Press, 2001.

———. "Workings of the Spirit: Conjure and the Space of Black Women's Creativity." In *Zora Neale Hurston: Critical Perspectives Past and Present*, ed. Henry Louis Gates Jr. and Kwame Anthony Appiah, 280–308. New York: Amistad, 1993.

Baker, Lee. *From Savage to Negro: Anthropology and the Construction of Race, 1896–1954*. Berkeley: University of California Press, 1998.

Baldwin, James. "Alas, Poor Richard." In *James Baldwin: Collected Essays*, 247–268. New York: Library of America, 1998.

———. *Another Country*. 1962. Reprint, New York: Vintage International, 1993.

———. "The Black Boy Looks at the White Body." In *Nobody Knows My Name* (1961), in *James Baldwin: Collected Essays*, 269–290. New York: Library of America, 1998.

———. *Giovanni's Room*. New York: Dell, 1956.

———. "My Dungeon Shook: Letter to My Nephew." In *James Baldwin: Collected Essays*, 291–295. New York: Library of America, 1998.

———. "The Price of the Ticket." In *James Baldwin: Collected Essays*, 830–844. New York: Library of America, 1998.

Baldwin, James, and Margaret Mead. *A Rap on Race*. New York: Lippincott, 1971.

Bell, Kevin. *Ashes Taken for Fire: Aesthetic Modernism and the Critique of Identity*. Minneapolis: University of Minnesota Press, 2007.

Bersani, Leo. "Is the Rectum a Grave?" *October* 43 (Winter 1987): 197–222.

Black, Shameem. "Fertile Cosmofeminism: Ruth L. Ozeki and Transnational Reproduction." *Meridians: Feminism, Race, Transnationalism* 5:1 (2004): 226–256.

Boas, Franz. Preface to *Mules and Men*, by Zora Neale Hurston, xiii–xiv. Bloomington: Indiana University Press, 1935.

Breu, Christopher. *Hard-Boiled Masculinities*. Minneapolis: University of Minnesota Press, 2005.

Brodhead, Richard. *Cultures of Letters: Scenes of Reading and Writing in Nineteenth-Century America*. Chicago: University of Chicago Press, 1993.

Brown, Jacqueline Nassy. "Black Liverpool, Black America, and the Gendering of Diasporic Space." *Cultural Anthropology* 13:3 (1998): 291–325.

Bruce, Dickson. *Black American Writing from the Nadir: The Evolution of a Literary Tradition, 1877–1915*. Baton Rouge: Louisiana State University Press, 1989.

Carby, Hazel. "Policing the Black Woman's Body in an Urban Context." *Critical Inquiry* 18:4 (1992): 738–755.

———. "The Politics of Fiction, Anthropology, and the Folk." In *New Essays on "Their Eyes Were Watching God,"* ed. Michael Awkward, 71–94. New York: Cambridge University Press, 1990.

Cawelti, John. *Adventure, Mystery, and Romance: Formula Stories as Art and Popular Culture*. Chicago: University of Chicago Press, 1976.

Certeau, Michel de. *The Practice of Everyday Life*. Berkeley: University of California Press, 1984.

Cleaver, Eldridge. "Notes on a Native Son." In *Soul on Ice*, 97–111. New York: Ramparts Books, 1968.

Clifford, James. "Introduction: Partial Truths." In *Writing Culture: The Poetics and Politics of Ethnography*, ed. James Clifford and George Marcus, 1–26. Berkeley: University of California Press, 1986.

———. *The Predicament of Culture: Twentieth-Century Ethnography, Literature, and Art*. Cambridge, MA: Harvard University Press, 1988.

Cobb, Michael. "Insolent Racing, Rough Narrative: The Harlem Renaissance's Impolite Queers." *Callaloo* 23:1 (2000): 328–351.

Cohen, William. "Liberalism, Libido, Liberation: Baldwin's *Another Country*." *Genders* 12 (Winter 1991): 1–21.

Collins, Lisa Gail. "The Art of Transformation: Parallels in the Black Arts and Feminist Art Movement." In *New Thoughts on the Black Arts Movement*, ed. Lisa Gail Collins and Margo Natalie Crawford, 273–296. New Brunswick, NJ: Rutgers University Press, 2006.

Collins, Lisa Gail, and Margo Natalie Crawford. Introduction to *New Thoughts on the Black Arts Movement*, ed. Lisa Collins and Margo Crawford, 1–20. New Brunswick, NJ: Rutgers University Press, 2006.

Courlander, Harold. "Witchcraft in the Caribbean Islands." Review of *Tell My Horse*, by Zora Neale Hurston. *Saturday Review of Literature*, 15 October 1938, 6–7.

Crawford, Margo Natalie. "Natural Black Beauty and Black Drag." In *New Thoughts on the Black Arts Movement*, ed. Lisa Collins and Margo Crawford, 154–172. New Brunswick, NJ: Rutgers University Press, 2006.

Davis, Angela. *Blues Legacies and Black Feminism: Gertrude "Ma" Rainey, Bessie Smith, and Billie Holiday*. New York: Vintage Books, 1999.

Dawson, Michael C. Dawson. *Black Visions: The Contemporary Roots of African-American Political Ideologies*. Chicago: University of Chicago Press, 2001.

Denning, Michael. "Topographies of Violence: Chester Himes's Harlem Domestic Novels." In *The Critical Response to Chester Himes*, ed. Charles L. P. Silet, 155–168. Westport, CT: Greenwood, 1999.

DeWalt, Kathleen, and Billie DeWalt. *Participant Observation: A Guide for Fieldworkers*. New York: AltaMira, 2002.

Diamond, Elin. "Deploying/Destroying the Primitivist Body in Hurston and Brecht." In *Against Theatre: Creative Destructions of the Modernist Stage*, ed. Alan Ackerman and Martin Puchner, 112–132. New York: Palgrave Macmillan, 2006.

Diawara, Manthia. *In Search of Africa*. Cambridge, MA: Harvard University Press, 1998.

———. "Noir by Noirs: Towards a New Realism in Black Cinema." *African American Review* 27:4 (1993): 525–537.

Du Bois, W. E. B. *The Souls of Black Folk*. 1903. Edited by Henry Louis Gates Jr. New York: Oxford University Press, 2007.

Duck, Leigh Anne. *The Nation's Region: Southern Modernism, Segregation, and U.S. Nationalism*. Athens: University of Georgia Press, 2006.

Eburne, Jonathan. *Surrealism and the Art of Crime*. Ithaca, NY: Cornell University Press, 2008.

Edelman, Lee. "The Part for the (W)hole: Baldwin, Homophobia, and the Fantasmatics of 'Race.'" In *Homographesis: Essays in Gay Literary and Cultural Theory*, 42–76. New York, Routledge, 1994.

Edwards, Brent. *The Practice of Diaspora: Literature, Translation, and the Rise of Black Internationalism*. Cambridge, MA: Harvard University Press, 2003.

Elman, Richard. Review of *A Rap on Race*, by Margaret Mead and James Baldwin. *New York Times Book Review*, 27 June 1971.

Emery, Amy Fass. "The Zombie in/as the Text: Zora Neale Hurston's *Tell My Horse*." *African American Review* 39:3 (2005): 327–336.

Fabian, Johannes. *Time and the Other: How Anthropology Makes Its Object*. New York: Columbia University Press, 1983.

Fabre, Michel. "Chester Himes Direct." In *Conversation with Chester Himes*, ed. Michel Fabre and Robert E. Skinner, 125–142. Jackson: University Press of Mississippi, 1995.

———. "Interview with Chester Himes." In *Conversations with Chester Himes*, ed. Michel Fabre and Robert E. Skinner, 83–94. Jackson: University Press of Mississippi, 1995.

———. *The Unfinished Quest of Richard Wright*. New York: Morrow, 1973.

Fabre, Michel, and Robert Skinner. Introduction to *Plan B*, by Chester Himes, edited by Michel Fabre and Robert Skinner, v–xxx. Jackson: University of Mississippi Press, 1993.

Favor, J. Martin. *Authentic Blackness: The Folk in the New Negro Renaissance*. Durham, NC: Duke University Press, 1999.

Ferguson, Roderick. *Aberrations in Black: Toward a Queer of Color Critique*. Minneapolis: University of Minnesota Press, 2004.

Fetterley, Judith. "'Not in the Least American': Nineteenth-Century Literary Regionalism." *College English* 56:8 (1994): 877–895.

Fetterley, Judith, and Marjorie Pryse. *Writing Out of Place: Regionalism, Women, and American Literary Culture*. Urbana: University of Illinois Press, 2003.

Firth, Raymond. *We, the Tikopia: A Sociological Study of Kinship in Primitive Polynesia*. London: Allen and Unwin, 1936.

Fischer, Sibylle. *Modernity Disavowed: Haiti and the Cultures of Slavery in the Age of Revolution*. Durham, NC: Duke University Press, 2004.

Fuss, Diana. *Essentially Speaking: Feminism, Nature and Difference*. New York: Routledge, 1989.

Gains, Kevin. "Revisiting Richard Wright in Ghana: Black Radicalism and the Dialectics of Diaspora." *Social Text* 19:2 (2001): 75–101.

Gayle, Addison. Introduction to *The Black Aesthetic*, ed. Addison Gayle, xv–xxiv. Garden City, NY: Anchor Books, 1971.

Gilroy, Paul. *The Black Atlantic: Modernity and Double Consciousness*. Cambridge, MA: Harvard University Press, 1993.

Gordon, Deborah. "The Politics of Ethnographic Authority: Race and Writing in the Ethnography of Margaret Mead and Zora Neale Hurston." In *Modernist Anthropology: From Fieldwork to Text*, ed. Marc Manganaro, 146–162. Princeton, NJ: Princeton University Press, 1990.

Griffin, Farah Jasmine Griffin. *"Who Set You Flowin'?": The African-American Migration Narrative*. New York: Oxford University Press, 1995.

Hartman, Saidiya. *Scene of Subjection: Terror, Slavery, and Self-Making in Nineteenth-Century America*. New York: Oxford University Press, 1997.

Hemenway, Robert. *Zora Neale Huston: A Literary Biography*. Urbana: University of Illinois Press, 1977.

Higginbotham, Evelyn Brooks. *Righteous Discontent: The Women's Movement in the Black Baptist Church*. Cambridge, MA: Harvard University Press, 1993.

Himes, Chester. *All Shot Up*. 1960. Reprint, Chatham, NJ: Chatham Bookseller, 1973.

———. *The Big Gold Dream*. 1960. Reprint, Chatham, NJ: Chatham Bookseller, 1973.

———. *Blind Man with a Pistol*. 1969. Reprint, New York: Vintage Books, 1989.

———. *Cotton Comes to Harlem*.1965. Reprint, New York: Vintage Books, 1988.

———. *The Crazy Kill*. 1959. Reprint, New York: Vintage Books, 1989.

———. *The Heat's On*. 1966. Reprint, New York: Vintage Books, 1988.

———. *If He Hollers Let Him Go*. New York: Doubleday, Doran, 1945.

———. *My Life of Absurdity: The Autobiography*. Vol. 2. New York: Doubleday, 1976.

———. *Plan B*. Jackson: University of Mississippi Press, 1993.

———. *A Rage in Harlem*. 1957. Reprint, New York: Vintage Books, 1989.

———. *The Real Cool Killers*. 1959. Reprint, New York: Vintage Books, 1988.

———. *Run Man Run*. New York: G. P. Putnam's Sons, 1966.

Hine, Darlene Clark. "Rape and the Inner Lives of Black Women in the Middle West: Preliminary Thoughts on the Culture of Dissemblance." *Signs* 14:4 (1989): 912–920.

Howell, William Dean. *Criticism and Fiction*. New York: Harper and Brothers, 1891.

Hughes, Langston. *The Big Sea: An Autobiography*. New York: Thunder's Mouth, 1986.

Hurston, Zora Neale. "Characteristics of Negro Expression." In *Negro: An Anthology*, ed. Nancy Cunard, 24–46. New York: Ungar, 1970.

———. *Dust Tracks on a Road*. New York: HarperPerennial, 2006.

———. "How It Feels to Be Colored Me." In *I Love Myself When I Am Laughing . . . and Then Again When I Am Looking Mean and Impressive: A Zora Neale Hurston Reader*, ed. Alice Walker, 152–155. Old Westbury, NY: Feminist Press, 1979.

———. *Jonah's Gourd Vine*. Philadelphia: Lippincott, 1934.

———. *Mules and Men*. Bloomington: Indiana University Press, 1935.

———. "Spirituals and Neo-Spirituals." In *Negro: An Anthology*, ed. Nancy Cunard, 223–225. New York: Ungar, 1970.

———. *Tell My Horse: Voodoo and Life in Haiti and Jamaica*. 1938. Reprint, New York: Harper and Row, 1990.

———. *Their Eyes Were Watching God*. 1937. Reprint, New York: Negro Universities Press, 1969.

Jackson, Lawrence. *Indignant Generation: A Narrative History of African American Writers, 1934–1960*. Princeton, NJ: Princeton University Press, 2011.

Jenkins, Candice. *Private Lives, Proper Relations: Regulating Black Intimacy*. Minneapolis: University of Minnesota Press, 2007.

Jones, LeRoi. "The Legacy of Malcolm X, and the Coming of the Black Nation." In *Home: Social Essays*, 238–250. 1966. Reprint, Hopewell, NJ: Ecco, 1998.

———. "state/meant." In *Home: Social Essays*, 251–252. 1966. Reprint, Hopewell, NJ: Ecco, 1998.

Kaplan, Ann. "Nation, Region, and Empire." In *The Columbia History of the American Novel*, ed. Emory Elliott, 240–266. New York: Columbia University Press, 1991.

Kaplan, Carla. *Zora Neale Hurston: A Life in Letters*. New York: Anchor Books, 2003.

Karem, Jeff. "'I Could Never Really Leave the South': Regionalism and the Transformation of Richard Wright's American Hunger." *American Literary History* 13:4 (2001): 694–715.

Kelley, Robin. "Notes on Deconstructing 'The Folk.'" *American Historical Review* 97:5 (1992): 1400–1408.

Killick, Andrew P. "The Penetrating Intellect: On Being White, Straight, and Male in Korea." In *Taboo: Sex, Identity and Erotic Subjectivity in Anthropological Fieldwork*, ed. Don Kulick and Margaret Willson, 76–106. New York: Routledge, 1995.

Lamothe, Daphne. *Inventing the New Negro: Narrative, Culture, and Ethnography*. Philadelphia: University of Pennsylvania Press, 2008.

LeClair, Thomas. "The Language Must Not Sweat: A Conversation with Toni Morrison." In *Conversations with Toni Morrison*, ed. Danille Taylor-Guthrie, 119–128. Jackson: University Press of Mississippi, 1994.

Leeming, David. *James Baldwin: A Biography*. New York: Penguin, 1994.

Lewis, Earl. "To Turn as on a Pivot: Writing African Americans into a History of Overlapping Diasporas." *American Historical Review* 100:3 (1995): 765–787.

Locke, Alain. "Fire: A Negro Magazine." *Survey*, 15 August–15 September 1927, 563.

———. "The New Negro." In *The New Negro*, ed. Alain Locke, 3–18. New York: Simon and Schuster, 1992.

Mailer, Norman. "The White Negro: Superficial Reflections on the Hipster" (1957). In *Advertisements for Myself*, 337–358. 1959. Reprint, Cambridge, MA: Harvard University Press, 1992.

Malinowski, Bronislaw. *Argonauts of the Western Pacific: An Account of Native Enterprise and Adventure in the Archipelagoes of Melanesian New Guinea*. 1922. Reprint, Prospect Heights, IL: Waveland, 1961.

———. *A Diary in the Strict Sense of the Term*. 1967. Reprint, Stanford, CA: Stanford University Press, 1989.

Martinez, Ernesto Javier. "Dying to Know: Identity and Self-Knowledge in Baldwin's *Another Country*." *PMLA* 124:3 (2009): 782–797.

McCall, George, and J. L. Simmons. *Issues in Participant Observation: A Text and Reader*. Reading, PA: Addison-Wesley, 1969.

Mok, Michael. "Chester Himes." In *Conversations with Chester Himes*, ed. Michel Fabre and Robert E. Skinner, 105–107. Jackson: University Press of Mississippi, 1995.

Moynihan, Daniel Patrick. *The Negro Family: The Case for National Action*. Washington, DC: Office of Policy Planning and Research, U.S. Department of Labor, 1965.

Mumford, Kevin. "Homosex Changes: Race, Cultural Geography, and the Emergence of the Gay." *American Quarterly* 48:3 (1996): 395–414.

Murray, Albert. "Regional Particulars and Universal Statement in Southern Writing." *Callaloo* 38 (Winter 1989): 3–6.

Myrdal, Gunnar. *An American Dilemma: The Negro Problem and Modern Democracy*. New York: Harper and Row, 1944.

Nelson, Raymond. "Domestic Harlem: The Detective Fiction of Chester Himes." In *The Critical Response to Chester Himes*, ed. Charles L. P. Silet, 53–63. Westport, CT: Greenwood, 1999.

Norman, Brian, and Piper Kendrix Williams. *Representing Segregation: Toward an Aesthetics of Living Jim Crow, and Other Forms of Racial Division*. Albany: State University of New York Press, 2010.

Nwankwo, Ifeoma. "Insider and Outsider, Black and American: Rethinking Zora Neale Hurston's Caribbean Ethnography." *Radical History Review* 87 (Fall 2003): 49–77.

Oakes, Philip. "The Man Who Goes Too Fast." In *Conversations with Chester Himes*, ed. Michel Fabre and Robert E. Skinner, 17–22. Jackson: University Press of Mississippi, 1995.

O'Connor, Flannery. "The Regional Writer." In *Mystery and Manners: Occasional Prose*, ed. Sally Fitzgerald and Robert Fitzgerald, 51–59. New York: Farrar, Straus, and Giroux, 1961.

Ohi, Kevin. "'I'm Not the Boy You Want': Sexuality, 'Race,' and Thwarted Revelation in Baldwin's *Another Country*." *African American Review* 33:2 (1999): 261–281.

Palmer, Phyllis. *Domesticity and Dirt: Housewives and Domestic Servants in the United States.* Philadelphia: Temple University Press, 1998.

Perry, Imani. *Prophets of the Hood: Politics and Poetics in Hip Hop.* Durham, NC: Duke University Press, 2004.

Pratt, Mary Louise. "Fieldwork in Common Places." In *Writing Culture: The Poetics and Politics of Ethnography*, ed. James Clifford and George Marcus, 27–50. Berkeley: University of California Press, 1986.

———. *Imperial Eyes: Travel Writing and Transculturation.* New York: Routledge, 1992.

Reid-Pharr, Robert. *Black Gay Man: Essays.* New York: NYU Press, 2001.

———. *Once You Go Black: Choice, Desire, and the Black American Intellectual.* New York: NYU Press, 2007.

Reilly, John. "Richard Wright and the Art of Non-fiction: Stepping Out on the Stage of the World." *Callaloo* 28 (Summer 1986): 507–520.

Report of the National Advisory Commission on Civil Disorders. Washington, DC: U.S. Government Printing Office, 1 March 1968.

Robison, Lori. "Region and Race: National Identity and the Southern Past." In *A Companion to the Regional Literatures of America*, ed. Charles Crow, 57–73. Malden, MA: Blackwell, 2003.

Said, Edward. *Culture and Imperialism.* New York: Vintage Books, 1993.

Scott, Darieck. *Extravagant Abjection: Blackness, Power, and Sexuality in the African American Literary Imagination.* New York: NYU Press, 2010.

Shankar, S. "Richard Wright's *Black Power*: Colonial Politics and the Travel Narrative." In *Richard Wright's Travel Writings: New Reflections*, ed. Virginia Smith, 3–19. Jackson: University of Mississippi Press, 2001.

Sharpley-Whiting, T. Denean. "Erasures and the Practice of Diaspora Feminism." *Small Axe* 17 (March 2005): 129–133.

Singh, Nikhil. *Black Is a Country: Race and the Unfinished Struggle for Democracy.* Cambridge, MA: Harvard University Press, 2004.

Smethurst, James. *The Black Arts Movement: Literary Nationalism in the 1960s and 1970s.* Chapel Hill: University of North Carolina Press, 2005.

Smith, Virginia Whatley. Introduction to *Richard Wright's Travel Writings: New Reflections*, ed. Virginia Whatley Smith, xi–xv. Jackson: University of Mississippi Press, 2001.

Soitos, Stephen. *The Blues Detective: A Study of African American Detective Fiction.* Amherst: University of Massachusetts Press, 1996.

Sontag, Susan. *On Photography.* New York: Delta, 1973.

Spradley, James. *Participant Observation.* New York: Holt, Rinehart, and Winston, 1980.

Stockton, Kathryn Bond. *Beautiful Bottom, Beautiful Shame: Where "Black" Meets "Queer."* Durham, NC: Duke University Press, 2006.

Sundquist, Eric. "Realism and Regionalism." In *The Columbia Literary History of the United States,* ed. Emory Elliott, 501–525. New York: Columbia University Press, 1988.

Toomer, Jean. "The *Cane* Years." In *The Wayward and the Seeking: A Collection of Writings by Jean Toomer,* ed. Darwin T. Turner, 116–127. Washington, DC: Howard University Press, 1980.

Turner, Victor. *The Anthropology of Performance.* New York: PAJ, 1986.

Van Maanen, John. *Tales of the Field: On Writing Ethnography.* Chicago: University of Chicago Press, 1988.

Visweswaran, Kamala. *Fictions of Feminist Ethnography.* Minneapolis: University of Minnesota Press, 1994.

Von Eschen, Penny. *Satchmo Blows Up the World: Jazz Ambassadors Play the Cold War.* Cambridge, MA: Harvard University Press, 2004.

Wall, Cheryl. *Women of the Harlem Renaissance.* Bloomington: Indiana University Press, 1995.

Walters, Wendy. "Limited Options: Strategic Maneuverings in Himes's Harlem." *African American Review* 28:4 (1994): 615–631.

Ward, Stephen. "The Third World Women's Alliance: Black Feminist Radicalism and Black Power Politics." In *The Black Power Movement: Rethinking the Civil Rights–Black Power Era,* ed. Peniel E. Joseph, 119–144. New York: Routledge, 2006.

Whitehead, Tony and Mary Conaway. *Self, Sex, and Gender in Cross-Cultural Fieldwork.* Chicago: University of Illinois Press, 1986.

Wilks, Jennifer. "Writing Home: Comparative Black Modernism and Form in Jean Toomer and Aimé Césaire." *Modern Fiction Studies* 51:4 (2005): 801–823.

Williams, John. "My Man Himes: An Interview with Chester Himes." In *Conversations with Chester Himes,* ed. Michel Fabre and Robert E. Skinner, 29–82. Jackson: University Press of Mississippi, 1995.

———. "Review of *Plan B.*" *African American Review* 30:3 (1996): 492–494.

Wolff, Janet. "On the Road Again: Metaphors of Travel in Cultural Criticism." In *Resident Alien: Feminist Cultural Criticism*, 115–134. New Haven, CT: Yale University Press, 1995.

Wright, Richard. *American Hunger*. New York: HarperPerennial, 1993.

———. *Black Boy*. New York: World, 1945.

———. *Black Power: A Record of Reactions in a Land of Pathos*. 1954. Reprint, New York: HarperPerennial, 1995.

———. "Blueprint for Negro Writing." In *Richard Wright Reader*, ed. Ellen Wright and Michel Fabre, 36–49. New York: Harper and Row, 1978.

———. *The Color Curtain: A Report on the Bandung Conference*. 1956. Reprint, Jackson: University of Mississippi Press, 1995.

———. "How Bigger Was Born." In *Early Works: Lawd Today! Uncle Tom's Children, Native Son*, 851–881. New York: Library of America, 1991.

———. "I Bite the Hand That Feeds Me." *Atlantic Monthly* 165 (June 1940): 828.

———. *Native Son*. New York: Harper and Brothers, 1940.

———. *Pagan Spain*. 1957. Reprint, New York: HarperPerennial, 2008.

———. Review of *Their Eyes Were Watching God*, by Zora Neale Hurston. *New Masses*, 5 October 1937, 22–23.

———. *Uncle Tom's Children*. New York: Harper and Brothers, 1938.

———. *White Man, Listen!*. 1957. Reprint, New York: Greenwood, 1978.

Zaborowska, Magdalena. *James Baldwin's Turkish Decade: Erotics of Exile*. Durham, NC: Duke University Press, 2009.

Index

and *A Rap on Race*, 1–3; on Wright, xi. *See also specific works by title*
Bandung Asian-African Conference (1955), 69–78
Baraka, Amiri, 153, 155, 156, 171
Barnard College, 23–24, 176*n*9
Beautiful Bottom, Beautiful Shame (Stockton), 124
Bell, Kevin, 133
Bersani, Leo, 120
Black, Shameem, 53
The Black Aesthetic (Gayle), 68, 156
Black Arts Movement, 5, 14, 129, 157–158
The Black Atlantic (Gilroy), 58
Black Boy (Wright), 58, 60–61, 62–63
"The Black Boy Looks at the White Body" (Baldwin), 186*n*38
black determinism, 155–156
black diaspora: narrative space for, 7–8, 9; overlapping of, 82; Wright's framing of, 78–90
black folk culture: adaptability of, 35; dynamic nature of, 26–27, 43–44; and modernity, 17; and performance, 34–43; and primitivism, 20, 21
"black is beautiful" mantra, 164–165
black modernity: and Caribbean communities, 47–57; Great Migration as flight to, 17, 19, 44; in Hurston's works, 25; intraracial view of, 79–90; and performance, 36–43; and regionalism, 66; and slavery, 46. *See also* black rural modernity
black nationalism: and Black Power Movement, 170; and Caribbean communities, 51; and cultural translation, 129; and freedom, 61, 161, 164; and gender, 54; national unease over, 95; and Third World solidarity, 171
Black Power (Wright), 12–13, 60, 70–71, 78–90, 158
Black Power Movement: and black nationalism, 170; Kerner Report

on, 154–155; literary and social importance of, 14, 157–158; masculinization of, 162, 165, 169, 192*n*27
black radical consciousness, 109
black rural modernity: duality of, 30, 42; ethnography of, 17; and migration, 19, 21, 29; and racial violence, 29; and regionalism, 43–47. *See also* black modernity
black separatism, 68, 155–156
black sexuality: and *Fire!!* magazine, 32–33; and heteronormativity, 32, 162–163; hypersexualization, 166–167. *See also* sexuality
black writers: as cultural translators, 4, 5, 129; and ethnography, 2; mobility of, 5–6. *See also specific writers*
Blind Man with a Pistol (Himes), 13–14, 130, 134, 141–142, 146–147
"Blueprint for Negro Writing" (Wright), 67, 69
Boas, Franz, 17, 21, 24–25, 38–39, 176*n*9
Book-of-the-Month Club, 62
Breu, Christopher, 131, 151
Brodhead, Richard, 65
Brown, Sterling, 3
Brown v. Board of Education (1954), 133, 153

Cane (Toomer), 33, 178*n*39
Carby, Hazel, 29, 163
Caribbean, 17, 47–57
Carmichael, Stokely, 158
"Celebration" (Wright), 89
celibacy in ethnography, 102
Certeau, Michel de, 137
Césaire, Aimé, 70
Chandler, Raymond, 189*n*21
Chesnutt, Charles, 65
Civil Rights Act of 1964, 153
Civil Rights Movement, 6, 89, 95, 192*n*27
Cleaver, Eldridge, 158
Clifford, James, 175*n*15, 183*n*39
Cohen, William, 105–106

ABOUT THE AUTHOR

Eve Dunbar is Associate Professor of English at Vassar College.